TRANSLATING TAGORE'S *STRAY BIRDS* INTO CHINESE

Translating Tagore's Stray Birds *into Chinese* explores the choices in poetry translation in light of Systemic Functional Linguistics (SFL) and illustrates the ways in which readers can achieve a deeper understanding of translated works in English and Chinese.

Focusing on Rabindranath Tagore's *Stray Birds*, a collection of elegant and philosophical poems, as a source text, Ma and Wang analyse four Chinese target texts by Zheng Zhenduo, Yao Hua, Lu Jinde and Feng Tang and consider their linguistic complexities through SFL. This book analyses the source text and the target texts from the perspectives of the four strata of language, including graphology, phonology, lexicogrammar and context.

Ideal for researchers and academics of SFL, Translation Studies, Linguistics, and Discourse Analysis, *Translating Tagore's* Stray Birds *into Chinese* provides an in-depth exploration of SFL and its emerging prominence in the field of Translation Studies.

Yuanyi Ma and **Bo Wang** received their doctoral degrees from the Hong Kong Polytechnic University. Their research interests include Systemic Functional Linguistics, translation studies, discourse analysis and language description. They are co-authors of *Lao She's Teahouse and Its Two English Translations: Exploring Chinese Drama Translation with Systemic Functional Linguistics* (Routledge), *Systemic Functional Translation Studies: Theoretical Insights and New Directions* (Equinox) and *Systemic Functional Insights on Language and Linguistics* (Springer). Bo Wang is currently Associate Research Fellow from School of International Studies, Sun Yat-sen University, China. Yuanyi Ma is Lecturer from Guangdong Polytechnic of Science and Technology, China.

Routledge Studies in Chinese Translation

Series Editor: Chris Shei, Swansea University, UK

This series encompasses scholarly works on every possible translation activity and theory involving the use of Chinese language. Putting together an important knowledge base for Chinese and Westerner researchers on translation studies, the series draws on multiple disciplines for essential information and further research that is based on or relevant to Chinese translation.

A Discourse Analysis of News Translation in China
Liang Xia

Translating Chinese Art and Modern Literature
Edited by Yifeng Sun and Chris Song

An Overview of Chinese Translation Studies at the Beginning of the 21st Century
Past, Present, Future
Weixiao Wei

Lao She's Teahouse and its Two English Translations
Exploring Chinese Drama Translation with Systemic Functional Linguistics
Bo Wang and Yuanyi Ma

Legal Translation and Bilingual Law Drafting in Hong Kong
Challenges and Interactions in Chinese Regions
Clara Ho-yan Chan

Translating Tagore's *Stray Birds* into Chinese
Applying Systemic Functional Linguistics to Chinese Poetry Translation
Yuanyi Ma and Bo Wang

The Role of Henri Borel in Chinese Translation History
Audrey Heijns

Translation of Contemporary Taiwan Literature in a Cross-Cultural Context
A Translation Studies Perspective
Szu-Wen Kung

Terminology Translation in Chinese Contexts
Theory and Practice
Edited by Saihong Li and William Hope

For more information about this series, please visit: https://www.routledge.com/Routledge-Studies-in-Chinese-Translation/book-series/RSCT

TRANSLATING TAGORE'S *STRAY BIRDS* INTO CHINESE

Applying Systemic Functional Linguistics to Chinese Poetry Translation

Yuanyi Ma and Bo Wang

LONDON AND NEW YORK

First published 2021
by Routledge
2 Park Square, Milton Park, Abingdon, Oxon OX14 4RN

and by Routledge
52 Vanderbilt Avenue, New York, NY 10017

Routledge is an imprint of the Taylor & Francis Group, an informa business

British Library Cataloguing-in-Publication Data
A catalogue record for this book is available from the British Library

Library of Congress Cataloging-in-Publication Data
Names: Ma, Yuanyi, author. | Wang, Bo, (Professor of translation studies), author.
Title: Translating Tagore's Stray birds into Chinese : applying systemic functional linguistics to Chinese poetry translation / Yuanyi Ma, Bo Wang.
Identifiers: LCCN 2020028034 (print) | LCCN 2020028035 (ebook) | ISBN 9780367415457 (hardback) | ISBN 9780367415464 (paperback) | ISBN 9780367815141 (ebook)
Subjects: LCSH: Poetry--Translating. | Translating and interpreting--China. | Tagore, Rabindranath, 1861-1941. Stray birds. | Tagore, Rabindranath, 1861-1941--Translations into Chinese--History and criticism. | Systemic grammar. | Functionalism (Linguistics)
Classification: LCC PN1059.T7 M33 2020 (print) | LCC PN1059.T7 (ebook) | DDC 495.18/041--dc23
LC record available at https://lccn.loc.gov/2020028034
LC ebook record available at https://lccn.loc.gov/2020028035

ISBN: 978-0-367-41545-7 (hbk)
ISBN: 978-0-367-41546-4 (pbk)
ISBN: 978-0-367-81514-1 (ebk)

Typeset in Times New Roman
by SPi Global, India

献给我们的老头儿 Christian M.I.M. Matthiessen

CONTENTS

FOREWORD

The translation of poetry has frequently been considered the most difficult – and many believe an impossible – challenge for the translator. It has sometimes been claimed that the only voices with any kind of authority on the issue are those of poets who engage in translating, or re-creating, a poetic piece of art. Unsurprisingly, then, when the translation of poetry is theorized and taught, it often happens in contexts of comparative literature, rather than of linguistics or translation studies, or outside of academia altogether. However, semiotics as the discipline of signs, and semiotically-inspired schools of linguistics and translation have over the past decades made significant, creative and novel contributions to the analysis and trans-creation of literary texts, including poetry. It is such a contribution that is offered to us here in Yuanyi Ma's and Bo Wang's *Translating Tagore's* Stray Birds *into Chinese*. The authors apply their in-depth familiarity with a semiotically-grounded theory of language to a text that is trans-cultural in several respects, showing traces of Indian, English and Chinese contexts, and all of those across a significant time-span embodied in the four translations under consideration. What is offered to the reader in Yuanyi Ma's and Bo Wang's book is the joy fostered by and admiration for a significant trans-cultural work, yet combined with the realization that such works can be approached and enjoyed not only through empathy and intuition, but also through a theoretically-motivated methodology for reading and re-creating poetry. I feel privileged and happy to extend an invitation to prospective readers to embark on the exciting adventure promised by the poems offered here, by their translations and above all by the methodology provided for analyzing and enjoying them.

Erich Steiner
Saarland University, Saarbrücken

FIGURES

TABLES

ABBREVIATIONS AND SYMBOLS

BT	back translation
IG	interlinear glossing
PY	pinyin
RST	Rhetorical Structure Theory
SFL	Systemic Functional Linguistics
ST	source text
TT	target text
TT1	target text 1 – Zheng Zhenduo's translation (Tagore 2010)
TT2	target text 2 – Yao Hua's translation (Tagore 1921)
TT3	target text 3 – Lu Jinde's translation (Tagore 2008)
TT4	target text 4 – Feng Tang's translation (Tagore 2015, 2019)
WoS	Web of Science
^	ordering (followed by)
< >	enclosed group/phrase
<< >>	enclosed clause
<<< >>>	enclosed clause complex
ø	ellipsis
|||	clause complex, boundary markers
||	clause (not rankshifted), boundary markers
		phrase or group, boundary markers
[[[ ]]]	rankshifted (embedded) clause complex, boundary markers

[[ ]]	rankshifted (embedded) clause, boundary markers
[]	rankshifted group/phrase, boundary markers
α and other small Greek letters	elements of hypotactic interdependency structure
1 and other Arabic numerals	elements of paratactic interdependency structure
+	logico-semantic relation of extension
=	logico-semantic relation of elaboration
×	logico-semantic relation of enhancement
'	projection of idea
"	projection of locution
//	line break

ABBREVIATIONS FOR INTERLINEAR GLOSSING

ASP	clause particle: aspectual
CPART	clause particle
CV	coverb
DISP	voice coverb: dispositive
EMPH	emphatic
MADV	modal adverb
MEAS	measurer
MOD	verbal particle: modal
NEG	verbal particle: negative
PASS	voice coverb: passive
PV	postverb
SUB	subordinating
VADV	verbal adverb
VPART	verbal particle

ACKNOWLEDGEMENTS

We would like to express our heartfelt thanks to Dr. Chris Shei – the editor of the book series and to Andrea Hartill and Ellie Auton from Routledge for their generous help and continued support. Also, we are grateful to Professor Christian M.I.M. Matthiessen for his guidance and familial support all along. We thank Professor Erich Steiner for his insightful comments and for writing a foreword for this book. We also wish to thank Professor Juliane House, Professor Chu Chi-yu, Professor Huang Guowen, Professor Wendy Lee Bowcher, Professor Chang Chenguang, Mr. Zhang Haipeng (Feng Tang), Dr. Marvin Lam, Dr. Constance Wang, Dr. Elaine Espindola, Dr. Jorge Arús-Hita, Dr. Isaac Mwinlaaru, Ms. Zhang Yanshuo, Ms. Li Nannan, Ms. Zhao Wei from Yilin Press, Saritha Srinivasan and Natalie Hamil from SPi Global for their help during the process of writing this book. Our special thanks go to Dr. Mark Nartey for proofreading the draft of this book.

PREFACE

Written for researchers and students who apply Systemic Functional Linguistics (SFL) to poetry translation, this book provides a framework suitable for the investigation, discusses the choices that poetry translators face when they translate and proves the value of linguistic analysis in the studies on poetry translation.

The data of this book include fifty poems from Rabindranath Tagore's *Stray Birds* in English and its four Chinese translations (飞鸟集 *Fei Niao Ji*). The selected poems serve as very interesting data for research, as they were rendered in different historical periods by translators from different backgrounds and translated with different purposes. Moreover, there involved two different kinds of Chinese, viz. the classical (ancient) Chinese in classical Chinese poetry and the modern (contemporary) Chinese in prose poetry. For the convenience of readers who do not read Chinese, we provide pinyin, interlinear glossing, and back translation for the examples throughout the book.

Six chapters are included in this book.

Chapter 1 serves as a background of the book by briefly introducing the notion of poetry and poetry translation. We first define poetry and associate poetic style to the notion of foregrounding in linguistic analysis. Then we discuss some translators' opinions on poetry translation, including both translators in the East and those in the West in the last century. In addition, we report on some findings from a survey of papers on poetry translation published between 2002 and 2019 in journals indexed by the Web of Science database, involving issues such as the number of publications, the journals that publish research on poetry translation, and the research topics of poetry translation.

Chapter 2 offers an introduction to the application of SFL to translation studies, highlighting Matthiessen's (2001, 2014b) environments of translation and conceptualization of translation as recreation of meaning in context through choice. We then introduce the data of the present study, i.e. *Stray Birds* by Rabindranath Tagore (the source text, ST) and its four Chinese translations (target texts, TTs) by Zheng Zhenduo (TT1), Yao Hua (TT2), Lu Jinde (TT3), and Feng Tang (TT4). Further, based on a pilot study, we propose an analytical framework, which models on stratification of language and involves analyses from graphological, phonological, lexicogrammatical, and contextual perspectives.

Chapter 3 discusses the choices made on the expression plane of language in the ST and the TTs in terms of graphology and phonology. On the one hand, the graphological analysis deals with the layout patterns and describes the line breaks according to the experiential structures of clauses. On the other hand, the phonological analysis focuses on the choices of rhyme.

Chapter 4 examines the choices made from the perspective of lexicogrammar in systems of THEME and TRANSITIVITY. In Theme analysis, we discuss the different kinds of Theme choices, including textual, interpersonal, unmarked topical, marked topical, and predicated Themes. In transitivity analysis, we focus on the different process types. Also, we point out the different Theme shifts and process type shifts.

Chapter 5 approaches the data from the perspective of the three contextual parameters, i.e. field, tenor, and mode. We first point out the field of activity in the data and compare the fields in the ST with those in the TTs. Then, we analyze the data in terms of tenor to evaluate the ST and the TTs in terms of institutional roles and familiarity. In terms of mode, we analyze the data by investigating the medium and channel. Finally, we relate the contextual analysis to the analyses on the content plane and expression plane of language and summarize some patterns of translation shift in the data.

Chapter 6 summarizes the contributions of the book in terms of the significance of studying Tagore's *Stray Birds* and its translations, the framework proposed, the further development of "the environments of translation" and "metafunctional translation shift," and the implications of the study on translation practice and translation universals. Further, we suggest some directions for future research.

1

DELINEATING THE SPECIFICITY OF POETRY TRANSLATION

This chapter serves as a background for the book by briefly introducing poetry and poetry translation. We first define poetry and relate the concept of poetic style to the notion of foregrounding in linguistics. We then highlight some translators' opinions on poetry translation, including both translators in the East and the West in the last century. Further, we conduct a survey on poetry translation to investigate the current status and the research topics in papers published between 2002 and 2019 in journals indexed by the Web of Science database.

1.1 Understanding poetry

This book deals with poetry translation, specifically the translation of a collection of poems titled *Stray Birds* by Rabindranath Tagore in the Chinese context. In history, poetry translation has often been regarded as "a difficult job" (Jones 2011: 1; cf. Bassnett 1980; Boase-Beier 2006, 2009). Robert Frost (1997: 856), one of the most famous American poets known for his depictions of rural life, has made the following remark on poetry translation: "I like to say, guardedly, that I could define poetry this way: It is that which is lost out of both prose and verse in translation." Similarly, Roman Jakobson (1959: 238), a Russian-born American linguist and the founder of Prague School, has admitted that "poetry is by definition untranslatable."

In general, poetry has been found to be difficult to translate because of poetry's "resistance to facile communication" (Shepherd 2007: 71). The concept of poetry varies according to culture and evolves with time. Literary critics, since Aristotle's time, have come up with a number of varied accounts of poetry. Various notable poets, such as Philip Sidney, William Wordsworth,

Samuel Taylor Coleridge, Percy Bysshe Shelley, Matthew Arnold, and T.S. Eliot, have proposed a number of definitions of poetry (see Strachan & Terry 2000; Wainwright 2011).

In the *Oxford English Dictionary* (OED), poetry is defined as "[t]he art or work of the poet," with the creativity of the user of language, (i.e. the poet), being highlighted (see Strachan & Terry 2000: 10). In addition, the OED interprets poetry as "[c]omposition in verse or metrical language, or in some equivalent patterned arrangement of language, usually also with choice of elevated words and figurative uses, and option of a syntactical order, differing more or less from those of ordinary speech or prose writing" (ibid.). From these definitions, it is deducible that poetry is regarded as a form of elevated language that is different from everyday usage or ordinary language. According to Strachan and Terry (2000), the above-mentioned characteristics of poetry are rather patterns that are realized by sound in English poetry, with free verse being an exception.

One of the key features that distinguishes poetry from prose and common language is meter or the regularity of rhythm identified within the recurring sound patterns (Wainwright 2011). Example 1.1, selected from the first stanza of "I Wandered Lonely as a Cloud" by William Wordsworth, illustrates the language of poetry. Written in a stanza that is composed of six lines, the poem rhymes with the end words in each line, following a regular pattern of "a b a b c c". Also, it can be observed that the poem is written in iambic tetrameter. Each line of the poem consists of four metrical feet and each metrical foot consists of two syllables – a short one followed by a long one.

EXAMPLE 1.1

I wandered lonely as a cloud
That floats on high o'er vales and hills,
When all at once I saw a crowd,
A host, of golden daffodils;
Beside the lake, beneath the trees,
Fluttering and dancing in the breeze.

(Wordsworth 2010: 265)

However, in Example 1.2, which is selected from the first paragraph in the preface of Michael Halliday's (1985a) monograph titled *Spoken and Written Language*, there is the absence of rhyme and the regular rhythmic patterns, and the passage has not been arranged in the style of a poem like Example 1.1. Although the language is simple and reads fluently, as Halliday (1985a: 1) intends to do so during his process of writing, it is not regarded as poetry.

EXAMPLE 1.2

We live in what is called a "literate society", which means that a reasonably large proportion of older children and adults in the community use language in a written as well as in a spoken form. They have learnt to read and write. Speaking and listening come naturally, unless one is born deaf; they also have to be learnt, of course, but – like walking and running – they are learnt young and without benefit of instruction. To get to read and write, however, one is usually taught; this is one step, perhaps the most important step, in the process of education. Reading and writing are associated with educated practice from the start.

Although the choices of sound pattern are essential to poetry, there are poems that do not conform to this tradition – for example, poems written in free verse (also called nonmetrical verse or *vers libre*). As a rebellious offspring of the conventional meter, free verse does not conform to the regular meter and the choices of rhyme and fixed patterns of line length are also optional (cf. Wesling & Bollobaś 1993; Strachan & Terry 2000).

Besides the sound patterns, poetry is characterized by the meaning and feeling expressed. As seen in *The New Princeton Encyclopedia of Poetry and Poetics*, poetry is defined in the following manner: "A poem is an instance of verbal art, a text set in verse, bound speech. More generally, a poem conveys heightened forms of perception, experience, meaning, or consciousness in heightened language, i.e. a heightened mode of discourse" (Brogan 1993: 938).

The heightened language discussed in the previous definition coincides with what William Wordsworth suggested in his preface to the *Lyrical Ballads* in 1800: "all good poetry is the spontaneous overflow of powerful feelings..." (Wordsworth 1991: 237). In 1816, Wordsworth further made the following remark, emphasizing the importance of meaning in poetry: "Poetry proceeds ... from the soul of man, communicating its creative energies to the images of the external world" (Strachan & Terry 2000: 13).

The data of the present study (i.e. *Stray Birds* written by Rabindranath Tagore) belongs to the category of poems that evoke powerful feelings. As shown in Example 1.3, even though the poem neither rhymes nor conforms to a traditional format, it reveals an optimistic state of mind, informing readers to face their sufferings positively instead of making complaints.

EXAMPLE 1.3

The world has kissed my soul with its pain, asking for its return in songs.

(Tagore 2010: 85)

Poetry, as one form of verbal art, is made of language and can thus be accessed by analyzing language from the perspective of linguistics with reference to descriptions of linguistic systems in the context of culture. There have been various engagements of literature in general and poetry in particular with the help of linguistic theories. For instance, Jan Mukařovský (e.g. 1964, 1977), one of the leading figures among Prague School scholars, engaged with literature from a linguistic point of view by developing the formalist concept of "defamiliarization" into a more systematic "foregrounding" and examined the "aesthetic function" of language (see Halliday 1982 for investigations of de-automatization based on insights from the Prague School; cf. Selden et al. 1997; Verdonk 2002). In addition, Jakobson (1959: 238; cf. Jakobson & Jones 1970 for an overall inquiry of one sonnet by William Shakespeare) has summarized the uniqueness of poetic language as follows:

> In poetry, verbal equations become a constructive principle of the text. Syntactic and morphological categories, roots, and affixes, phonemes and their components (distinctive features) – in short, any constituents of the verbal code – are confronted, juxtaposed, brought into contiguous relation according to the principle of similarity and contrast and carry their own autonomous signification. Phonemic similarity is sensed as semantic relationship. The pun, or to use a more erudite, and perhaps more precise term – paronomasia, reigns over poetic art…

Systemic Functional Linguistics (SFL), as one kind of appliable linguistics (see e.g. Halliday 2008; Matthiessen 2014a for discussions on appliable linguistics), is suitable to be employed in the analysis of poetry (e.g. Butt 1984a, 1984b, 1988; Halliday 1988; Hasan 1985, 1988; Lukin 2003; Webster 2015). Such linguistic studies of poems or literature in general are based on the description of language as a whole rather than on the personal or arbitrary statements. Also, the SFL perspective allows for the comparison of these texts with other texts, whether written by same or different authors and whether in the same or different genres (Halliday 1964).

Following this approach, linguistic analysis has been applied to the investigation of poetry. For instance, Halliday (1987) approaches the central passages in Tennyson's *In Memoriam* from the perspectives of logical structure, transitivity, and mood, and identifies the scientific and poetic forces of meaning in the poem. As suggested by Halliday (1987: 40), the stanzas analyzed "fall within the tradition of the scientific imagination: the works of the great poet-scientists from Lucretius onwards whose poetic text displays in a unique form the grammatical construction of reality." The grammar creates an intricate semiotic helix, which moves by way of the following steps: "the concept of evolution rehumanizes science," "the knowledge is made accessible (through poetic discourse)," "this understanding raises man still

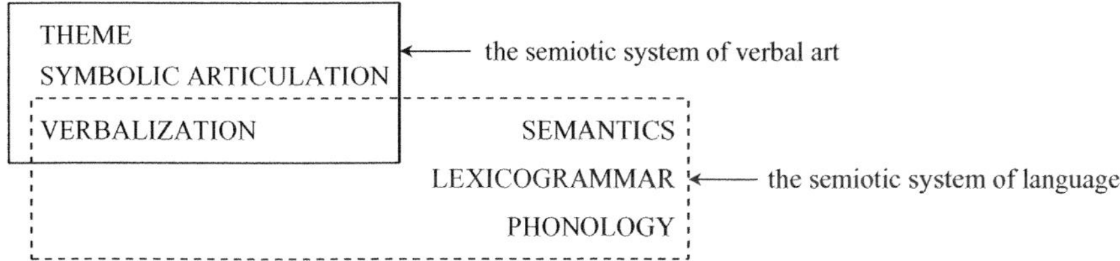

FIGURE 1.1   Verbal art and language (Adapted from Hasan 1985: 99)

higher," "man's place in nature is restored," "man has lost his 'soul'," "nature destroys species – including man," "nature destroys individuals – including humans," and finally "my loved friend has perished" (Halliday 1987: 43). In this way, Halliday (1987: 44) reveals the lexicogrammatical choices made by Tennyson, who constructs "a semiotic universe at the intersection of science and poetry."

Based on Halliday's SFL, Hasan (e.g. 1971, 1975, 1985) develops a methodology for analyzing literary texts (verbal art). As shown in Figure 1.1, Hasan (1985) identifies three strata in the functional operation of language in literature, including the strata of theme,[1] symbolic articulation, and verbalization. Among the three, verbalization is where the semiotic system of verbal art gets in touch with the semiotic system of language. The semiotic system of language, modeling on the stratification model in SFL, covers the different strata of language, including semantics, lexicogrammar, and phonology (or graphology in the written mode of language).

In addition, Hasan (1985: 99) makes the following observations of the two levels of meanings in verbal art, which echo our previous discussions on the complexity of poetic language:

> …there exist two levels of semiosis: one that is the product of the use of natural language, itself a semiotic system; and the other which is the product of the artistic system through foregrounding and repatternings of the first order meanings. This is why paraphrase is never sufficient to describe the meanings of a literature text. The art of verbal art consists of the use of language in such a way that this second order semiosis becomes possible.

Therefore, when we analyze the poetry data in this book, we first engage with the semiotic system of language and gradually move to the semiotic system of verbal art (see Section 2.3). We start from the stratum of verbalization and move to the stratum of theme, i.e. the deepest level of meaning in verbal art. Before building an analytical framework in Chapter 2, we first explore the multifaceted views on poetry translation in the remaining sections of this chapter.

1.2 Translators' perspectives on poetry translation

According to Lefevere (1995), problems in poetry translation, on the one hand, can be listed but cannot be solved once and for all. On the other hand, the solution to the problems always depends on the strategies adopted by the translators. In this section, we approach poetry translation from the perspective of translators whose aim is to explore ways of producing accurate and effective translation (cf. Halliday 2001).[2]

Famous translators may have their own understandings of translation, but some of them tend to undervalue translation theories and highlight the importance of translation in teaching and learning Chinese culture, as well as the value of comprehending Chinese literary texts and translating classic Chinese poems (see Minford 1987). Arthur Waley is one example of this kind. As a famous sinologist and translator who created a style both suitable to the Chinese verse and the taste of his day, Waley (1958) was strongly against translation theory and rarely touched on formal translation theories, not even in the area of Chinese poetry, where his authority mainly lay. As noted by Hawkes (1989: 257–258), Waley's articles "were often the jottings of a translator: explanations of the meaning of obsolete expressions or rare words and phrases suggested and supported by his voluminous reading and passed on to assist other toilers in the same vineyard."

Many poets in the English culture held various opinions on translation. In the seventeenth century, while translating *Ars Poetica*, one of the most significant works by Horace, Ben Johnson indicated his preference of literal or word-to-word translation. Though his translation proved to be problematic and were occasionally criticized (Moul 2007), Johnson's line-to-line method was supported by other translators of his time. Another poet named George Sandys also followed this practice when producing a translation of *Metamorphoses* (see Fan 1986).

During the mid-seventeenth century, a new strategy that was fundamentally different from word-to-word or line-to-line translation appeared when a famous poet named Abraham Cowley rendered the odes written by Pindar. In the translation, Cowley adapted the content of the odes to the form and revised the content to a large extent so that readers would never know in what style Pindar had written the odes. Thus, by "distilling Pindar to his 'manner of speaking' rather than 'precisely what he spoke,' Cowley self-consciously creates an epistemology that obscures its origins and undermines its ability to construct and convey knowledge" (Stogdill 2012: 489).

In comparison with Cowley, John Dryden adopted an approach that focused less on his own will in his translation and opted for the method of "paraphrase" ("translation with latitude") – an eclectic choice between the two extremes of "metaphrase" ("to translate word by word and line by line") and "imitation." As a result, the translator had the liberty to deal with both word and sense (Davis 2001). In a similar vein, John Denham from the same period emphasized the need to translate the "spirit" of poetry in addition to translating one language to another (see Fan 1986), claiming that without the spirit, the translation of the poem would be of no value.

In the eighteenth century, Alexander Pope, who was also a great translator, highly praised Dryden's translation of *Aeneid* (Pope 1711; cf. Warton 2004). In Pope's own translation, he tended to adopt a free style by extending or abridging the original, or making changes to the original context. In Pope's view, the essence of translation was in the spirit of the poem.

In the nineteenth century, an English poet named Edward Fitzgerald translated *Rubayat* from Persian into English, eventually making *Rubayat* a world classic. Fitzgerald adopted a freer way of translation by omitting the original content he disliked, combining various parts according to his own will, rewriting some important poems, and even adding works by other Persian poets. According to Dryden's standard, Fitzgerald's translation should be classified as imitation. However, the popularity of his translation suggested that readers were not totally against this method of translation.

By the nineteenth century, when Dante Gabriel Rossetti translated Cavalcanti's Italian poems, he "forced the originals to serve as the object of his representation, since his own sensibility served as the determining field in which these poems could be reshaped into specific rhetorical and ideological moulds" (Preda 2001: 220). Rossetti aimed at fidelity rather than literalism and opted for the paraphrase strategy. As a result, the Italian style of the thirteenth century was fully erased in favor of his readers at modern Victorian time, leading to translations that not only read like modern Victorian poems, but were also regarded as "the translations natural and transparent for Rossetti's contemporaries" (Preda 2001: 221).

A century later, while translating Guido Cavalcanti, Ezra Pound chose a literal way of translation by retaining the original word order. Attempting to build a connection between himself and Cavalcanti, Pound included the source text along with his translation. He named his translation "translations of accompaniment," which signaled a rejection of the invisibility and unavailability of the original. Pound explained his motivation as follows:

> It is conceivable the poetry of a far-off time or place requires a translation not only of word and of spirit, but of "accompaniment," that is that the modern audience must in some measure be made aware of the mental content of the old audience, and of what these others drew from certain fashions of thought and speech. Six centuries of derivative convention and loose usage have obscured the exact significances of such phrases as: "The death of the heart," and the "The departure of the soul"
>
> *(Cavalcanti 1991; cited from Preda 2001: 222).*

In Pound's translation, meaning was shifted back and forth between the original and the translation. Readers were invited to explore the Italian original and to enjoy the rhythm of Italian language. In this way, Pound regarded his own work as "a type of translation that would 'deny' itself in order to give the impression of the authenticity of material presence, without delegation and without appropriation by the translator as subject" (Preda 2001: 222).

As our book deals with poetry translation from English to Chinese, we have included some ideas on poetry translation from Chinese translators. Three translators' views on translation that are relevant to our discussion in this book have been presented, including those by Zheng Zhenduo (郑振铎), Bian Zhilin (卞之琳), and Sun Dayu (孙大雨), who were all influential in the Chinese context during the twentieth century.

Zheng Zhenduo, whose translation of Tagore's *Stray Birds* became a classic in China, was an important poet, writer, and translator at the beginning of the twentieth century (for an introduction to Zheng's translation of *Stray Birds*, see Section 2.2). Zheng (1921) opposed the notion that poetry was untranslatable and suggested a literal translation strategy to express the style of the original. Further, when translating prose poetry, Zheng (1921, 2004a) did not regard prosody as the key element and chose to focus on the reproduction of the adequate skills, essence, beauty, and art in the original.

Bian Zhilin, a Chinese poet and translator, was not too optimistic about poetry translation, in comparison with Zheng's (1921) views mentioned above. Bian (1987, 2004) held that the essence of poetry was in its consistency of content and expression, which then led to the untranslatability of poems. Although he stressed the importance of meter and rhyme arrangements in foreign-regulated poetry, Bian believed that Chinese "new poems" or "free verse" should not include such elements as meter or rhymes, and some addition or deletion of words would not harm the flavor of the translation, but may even add some harmony to it.

Sun Dayu (2014), a Chinese scholar and translator from the same era as Bian, regarded meter as one of the most important factors in a poem. Sun (2014) defined meter as regular units equal or almost equal in time, and rhythm as the effect of such units. He also defined verse as text with meters. These ideas on meter were significant in the development of new poetry, which overturned the popularity of traditional poems.

Taking a step back, we can interpret the comments by the translators from the perspective of the architecture of language in SFL. For instance, the translators' contrasting views can be characterized by their different priorities in translation poetry: whether they are approaching lexicogrammar "from below" (i.e. from rhyme, alliteration, and meter) or "from above" (i.e. from "sense" and "spirit") (cf. Halliday 1978, 1979, 1996). With the help of the trinocular vision provided by SFL, it is possible to incorporate all these considerations in our analytical framework, which includes the phonological, graphological, and lexicogrammatical perspectives of poetry translation (see Section 2.3).

1.3 A survey of recent studies on poetry translation

The critical question that studies on poetry translation has to answer, according to Boase-Beier (2009), is the translatability of poetry, i.e. whether poetry can be translated or not (cf. Jakobson 1959; Hermans 2009). On the one hand, poetry can be (and has been) translated in several cultures around the world for a long time. On the other hand, poetry is difficult or even impossible to be translated. Boase-Beier (2009: 194) provides two assumptions that lead to the impossibility of poetry translation: "(i) translated poetry should be poetry in its own right" (e.g. Coleridge 1990) and "(ii) poetry is difficult, cryptic, ambiguous and exhibits a special relationship between form and meaning" (e.g. Furniss & Bath 1996).

To handle the difficulty of poetry translation, various proposals have been made, such as (i) poetry translators should have special writing and critical abilities (e.g. Raffel 1988; Weissbort 1989) and (ii) poetry translation should preserve the style, poetic effects, spirit, and energy of the original (e.g. Lefevere 1992, 1995; Gutt 1991). Boase-Beier (2009: 195) suggests that the abstract notions mentioned above be made concrete by summarizing the distinctive properties of poetic style:

- its physical shape (Furniss & Bath 1996: 13), including the use of lines and spaces on a page
- its use of inventive language (Eagleton 2007: 46) and, in particular, patterns of sound and structure (Jakobson 1960: 358)
- its openness to different interpretations (Furniss & Bath 1996: 225)
- its demand to be read non-pragmatically (Eagleton 2007: 38).

Due to its uniqueness, poetry translation has engaged the attention of scholars in recent decades. In this section, we report on the findings of a meta-analysis of research papers on poetry translation, pointing out various features on the current status and research themes, as well as development of the area. Our database for meta-analysis and research synthesis was constructed by following the methods developed by Norris and Ortega (2000, 2006) as well as those applied in Dong and Chen (2015). The research included were collected from the online Web of Science (WoS) databases, i.e. the Science Citation Index Expanded (SCI-E), the Social Sciences Citation Index (SSCI), and the Arts and Humanities Citation Index (A&HCI). We chose the WoS databases for analysis because they include the most important journals in the world and are appropriate for a meta-study of this kind (e.g. Boyack et al. 2005; Dong & Chen 2015).

We first searched for "poetry translation" as a keyword in the WoS databases. We then refined the records by selecting the Web of Science Category as "Language Linguistics or Linguistics" and Document Type as "Article." We also excluded the research areas of "Psychology," "Audiology Speech Language Pathology," and "Philosophy" and found 147 records published between 2002 and 2019. We then read the abstracts of the publications and manually excluded the studies that were not focused on poetry translation from the database, including those on novel translation (e.g. Li et al. 2011) and language teaching (e.g. Dever 2008).

Following this approach, we built our database that consisted of 82 publications written by 92 authors in 23 different journals. The authors were affiliated with various institutions located in 29 countries. Table 1.1 tabulates the information of the countries and provides the percentage of their occurrence in the database. Countries with only one record were not listed.

It is observed from the table that authors from the UK have contributed the largest number (i.e. 16) of publications from 2002 to 2019. The other active countries that contributed more than ten publications include the USA (14), China (12), and Spain (10). It can also be noted that 56.5% of the total publications were contributed by these four countries, with the scholars in these countries playing a leading role in poetry translation. Moreover, except for China, Jordan, India, Columbia, Argentina, and Saudi Arabia, the other ten countries in Table 1.1 are all characterized as countries of the "Western World," indicating that there is still potential for countries like China to increase their research output in this area.

Figure 1.2 sketches the amount of the publications on poetry translation from 2002 to 2009. Unlike Dong and Chen's (2015) survey of publications on translation studies in general, in which a sharp increase is found from 2007 onwards, our meta-analysis reveals a significant increase in 2011 and 2013,

TABLE 1.1 Publications on poetry translation according to different countries

Country	Freq.	% of 92
UK	16	17.391
USA	14	15.217
China	12	13.043
Spain	10	10.870
France	3	3.2609
Italy	3	3.2609
Jordan	3	3.2609
Germany	3	3.2609
Ireland	2	2.1739
Australia	2	2.1739
India	2	2.1739
Columbia	2	2.1739
Argentina	2	2.1739
Finland	2	2.1739
Saudi Arabia	2	2.1739
Portugal	2	2.1739

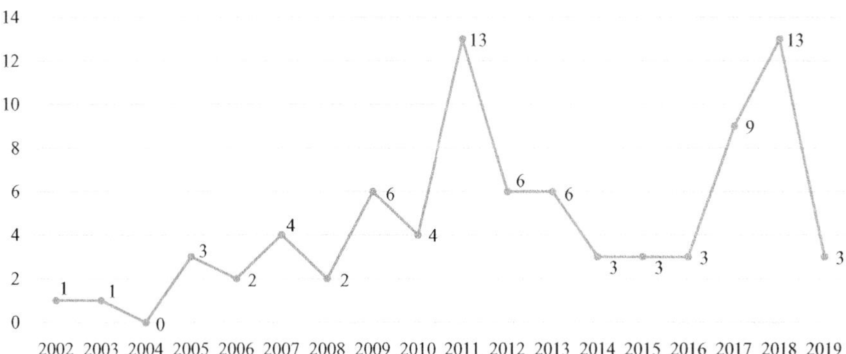

FIGURE 1.2   Number of publications on poetry translation from 2002 to 2009

where 13 publications are found. From 2005 onwards, more than two publications are found each year. The numbers fluctuate throughout the years and both increases and decreases are frequently seen. After 2004, an average amount of five papers on poetry translation were published annually, which reflects scholars' increased interest in the area.

The 82 publications in the database have been published in 23 journals and nine of them are journals specifically focused on translation studies (see Table 1.2). All the top six journals (in which more than 66% of the 82 papers have been published) specialize in translation studies. These journals include *Translation Studies* (15), *Babel* (10), *Translator* (9), *Target* (8), *Meta* (8), and *Translation and Interpreting Studies* (4). Journals focusing on linguistics or literature can also be seen in the list, but their numbers of publications are not huge, e.g. *Journal of Pragmatics* (1), *Language and Literature* (1), and *Modern Philology* (1). Different from Dong and Chen's (2015) research, where academic articles on translation are scattered in various journals, our analysis shows that papers on poetry translation tend to be concentrated in the six journals mentioned above.

Among the 82 studies in the database, 12 of them approached poetry translation from a linguistic perspective, involving aspects such as pragmatics (Dahlgren 2005; Pallavi & Mojibur 2018), multimodal analysis (Torres-Martínez 2019), stylistics (e.g. Cheng & Li 2019), intertextuality (Bassnett 2007), syntactic indeterminacy (Jiang 2010), and corpus-based empirical analysis (Pan et al. 2018). For instance, Pallavi and Mojibur (2018) construct a model to assess the quality of poetry translation by drawing on pragmatic theories of speech acts and conversational maxims. Their model is based on previous frameworks proposed by House (e.g. 1997) and Dastjerdi et al. (2008, 2011) and incorporates analysis of coherence and implicature. The model is expected to reveal the pragmatic features in poetry translation. Further, Nida's (e.g. 1964; Nida & Taber 1969) dynamic equivalence is adopted to investigate whether the pragmatic force has been translated or not.

TABLE 1.2 Publications on poetry translation in journals from the WoS databases

Journal	Freq.	% of 82
Translation Studies	15	18.2926
Babel	10	12.1951
Translator	9	10.9756
Target	8	9.7560
Meta	8	9.7560
Translation and Interpreting Studies	4	4.8780
Forum for Modern Language Studies	4	4.8780
Translation Review	4	4.8780
Perspectives	3	3.6585
Modern Language Review	3	3.6585
Estudios Filológicos	2	2.4390
Círculo de Lingüística Aplicada a la Comunicación	1	1.2195
Digital Scholarship in the Humanities	1	1.2195
Journal of Literary Semantics	1	1.2195
Journal of Pragmatics	1	1.2195
Journal of Specialised Translation	1	1.2195
Language and Literature	1	1.2195
Lingua e Stile	1	1.2195
Modern Philology	1	1.2195
Neophilologus	1	1.2195
Revista de Filología Española	1	1.2195
Semiotica	1	1.2195
Style	1	1.2195

In their quantitative study, Pan et al. (2018) examine 20 randomly-selected sonnets by William Shakespeare and their four Chinese translations. The corpus-based empirical investigation involves various perspectives such as vocabulary, word frequency distribution, and part-of-speech (POS) frequency distribution. Both similarities and differences between the source text and the target texts are found. For example, based on analytical methods such as vocabulary-related "a-index"[3] and word-frequency-related "Zipf's law,"[4] they find that the source text and the target texts are similar in terms of the vocabulary richness and the styles of text management, whereas the analysis of ALSCAL (Alternative Least Square Scaling) suggests that the target texts are different from the source text in terms of POS arrangements. From an SFL perspective, we argue that the corpus-based automated method is suitable for conducting analyses at the ranks of group/phrase and word to bring out the similarities and differences syntagmatically. However, if we want to explore the paradigmatic choices at the clause rank, we still need manual analysis that is labor-intensive (cf. Matthiessen 2014a).

Studies from the perspectives of literary criticism or comparative literature were also found in our database. For instance, Bergam (2013) discusses the global reception of Vasko Popa, one of the foremost Yugoslav poets. She borrows the notion of "translationscape" to examine (i) how Popa's works are translated globally and (ii) the personal experiences of the translators. It is found that both British and American translators have not only focused on the stylistic features of the source text and the target texts, but also strived to preserve the overall aesthetic effect and literary value of Popa. Bergam's (2013) study highlights the role that translators play in the reception of target texts. In this book, similar descriptions of the translators' motivation and the sociocultural background are carried out based on the contextual analysis in SFL, which has a traceable history to Malinowski's (e.g. 1923, 1944) work on anthropology (see Chapter 5).

Moreover, we found various applications of the theoretical approaches in translation studies. As seen in Milani's (2017) paper, Bourdieu's (e.g. 1984) sociological theories are applied to analyze the role played by Einaudi, a local publishing house in Italy, during the 1960s. Milani (2017) selects the unpublished archives of the publishing house as her data and reassesses the role that Einaudi played in the publication of poetry translation during the various political and poetic movements of the time. The analysis shows that the poetry translations have modified the publishing, literary, and political fields.[5] In addition, the Einaudi editors' intellectual identities are redefined by publishing the poetry translations.

Among the 82 studies in the database, Paul Celan's poems and their translations have been examined in various researches (e.g. Boase-Beier 2011a; Beals 2014; Torres-Martínez 2019). As an influential poet from a Jewish family, Celan suffered various hardships right from his childhood. He wrote in German and criticized the atrocity of the Nazis. In Boase-Beier's (2011a, cf. 2015) study, she analyzes Celan's "Espenbaum," a Holocaust poem, and points out how silence is translated. The difficulty in translating this poem, as discussed by Boase-Beier (2011a: 168), lies in view that it "demands translation in order to be understood beyond the language it was first written in, and its poetics demands that its silences be recognized and recreated by the translator, in order that the translation's new reader can participate in the cognitive acts necessary to fill them." By analyzing the poem, Boase-Beier (2011a) identifies the various stylistic features, such as how concepts of absence, loss, and grief blend in the poem, with reference to cognitive studies (e.g. Fauconnier & Turner 2002). In this way, Boase-Beier (2011a: 175) points out the significance of poetry translation, which allows readers to realize "the voice of the poetry", i.e. to speak in place of the poet, and further conceptualizes translation as "a proxy" (cf. Boase-Beier 2011b).

We also found several frameworks on poetry translation in the database (e.g. Dahlgren 2005; García 2008). In Dahlgren's (2005) paper, for instance, a framework is proposed, which incorporates analysis at the levels of phonology, syntax, semantics, and pragmatics. Modeling on pragmatic theories, Dahlgren's (2005) framework takes both the form and content of poetry into consideration and is more comprehensive than Pallavi & Mojibur's (2018) pragmatic framework for assessing the quality of poetry translation previously discussed. Her framework is complex in that various layers of analysis are involved to point out the difficulty in poetry translation and the trade-offs made by translators. To illustrate how the model works, Dahlgren (2005) analyzes one poem by Emily Dickinson and its three translations in Spanish, pointing out the translators' failures in preserving prosodic elements, lexical mistranslations, and syntactic oddity. She further demonstrates how linguistic theory can offer a powerful tool for analyzing poetry translation and comments on the effects of overt and covert translation (cf. House 1997, 2015).

Our analytical framework is similar to Dahlgren's (2005) in its comprehensiveness, i.e. taking various levels into consideration and incorporating analyses at the strata of phonology, graphology, lexicogrammar, and context. The survey in this chapter provides a background for the analysis and discussion later presented in this book. In the next chapter, we introduce our SFL-inspired linguistic framework for the analysis of poetry translation.

Notes

1 Hasan (e.g. 1985) uses the term "theme" as the deepest level of meaning in the semiotic system of verbal art. It is different from the lexicogrammatical system of THEME in the analysis of textual meaning (see Sections 2.3 and 4.1). The stratum of theme in verbal art, which is similar to the literary concept of generalization, has been interpreted in different schools of literary criticism.
2 Halliday (2001) associates translation theories with the lexicogrammatical system of MOOD, and categorizes translation studies into two categories: descriptive (indicative) theories and prescriptive (imperative) theories. For translators, they aim to achieve a better or more effective product of translation, and their theory is the study of how things ought to be. In contrast, a linguist's theory of translation is the study of how things are, with the purpose of investigating the nature of the translation process and the relation between the source text and target text.
3 The "a-index" is used to quantitatively describe the features of texts from different genres.
4 Zipf's law represents one way of quantitatively describing the word frequency in text.
5 The term "field" here means something different compared to the contextual parameter of field in SFL. In Bourdieu's (e.g. 1984, 1996) work, "field" refers to an autonomous sphere of interaction, in which the agents share a common set of rules and agenda.

2

DEMYSTIFYING TRANSLATION AS RECREATION OF MEANING THROUGH CHOICE

In this chapter, we first offer an introduction to the application of SFL to translation studies, with a focus on Christian Matthiessen's work in the area. We then introduce the data of the present study, i.e. *Stray Birds* written by Rabindranath Tagore and its four Chinese translations. Finally, we propose an analytical framework for analyzing poetry translation from the SFL perspective.

2.1 Matthiessen's conceptualization of translation

As previously discussed, SFL is a kind of appliable linguistics, which is designed to be applied to different domains (Matthiessen 2014a). Translation has been on the agenda of SFL scholars since the inception of the theory, marked by Halliday's (e.g. 1956, 1962) research on machine translation. Halliday (2009) holds that translation is a specialized area, as few scholars in formal and functional linguistics have paid attention to this field of inquiry. He further regards translation as a testing ground for his theory and submits that his theory would be inadequate if it cannot account for translation.

The first overall application of SFL to translation was carried out by Catford (1965), who applied scale and category grammar (i.e. an early version of SFL [see Halliday 1961]) to the description and analysis of translation (see Steiner 2015, 2019; Wang & Ma 2020, in press for overviews of the area). In Catford's (1965) study, translation equivalence and translation shift were theorized in terms of rank and stratification (level), and the search for translation equivalence was recognized as the central problem of translation practice.

Over the years, there have been a significant number of studies on translation from the SFL perspective. In Table 2.1, we point out the different aspects of SFL theory applied to translation. Some studies focus on the overall application of all dimensions in SFL, such as Catford (1965) and

TABLE 2.1 Aspects of SFL applied to translation (Adapted from Matthiessen 2021: 525)

Aspects of SFL			*Studies that apply SFL*
all dimensions:	SFL as resource in translation studies		Catford (1965); Wang & Ma (in press)
	nature of translated vs. original texts		Teich (2003)
	contextualism		Matthiessen (2001); Steiner (2005, 2015)
stratification:	context in translation evaluation		House (1977, 1997, 2001, 2015)
instantiation:	register variation (functional variation in context)		Teich (1999), Lavid (2000), Steiner (2004); Hansen-Schirra, Neumann & Steiner (2012)
	particular registers, e.g.	poetry	Huang (2006)
		drama	Wang & Ma (2020)
		novel	Munday (2002); Wang (2007)
		film subtitle	Espindola (2016)
		legal document	Espindola & Wang (2015)
		advertisement	Steiner (2004)
		public notice	Zhang (2009)
	process and product		Alves et al. (2010)
metafunction:	all metafunctions		Matthiessen (2014b)
	textual		Kim & Matthiessen (2015); Kunz et al. (2017); Wang & Ma (2018)
	interpersonal		Lavid (2000); Munday (2012, 2018); Yu & Wu (2016); Wang & Ma (2019)
	experiential		Mason (2012); Huang (2013)
	logical		Li & Wu (2017); Wang & Ma (2018)
axis	systemic (paradigmatic) organization: choice		Halliday (2010); Matthiessen (2014b)
	probabilistic choice		Toury (2004)
rank	"level" of translation		Halliday (1962, 1966, 2009); Halliday, McIntosh & Strevens (1964)

Wang and Ma (in press). Other studies focus on one or several dimensions in SFL, such as House's (e.g. 1977, 1997, 2015) model of translation quality assessment that applies the notion of context to translation evaluation. Matthiessen (2001) has characterized these dimensions as the environments of translation, locating translation within an overall architecture of language in text. We will introduce these dimensions in detail in this section, as they serve as the foundation for the analytical framework in this book (see Section 2.3; for Matthiessen's ideas on translation, see Matthiessen, Wang & Ma 2017a, 2017b, 2018, 2020, Wang & Ma forthcoming).

The environments of translation represent an attempt to update Catford's (1965) and Halliday's (1966) exploration on translation equivalence and shift from the perspectives of rank and stratification. Matthiessen (2001) applies the theoretical developments of SFL after the 1960s to translation, such as the spectrum of metafunction, the cline of instantiation, and the hierarchy of axis, locating translation within a typology of systems. There are six semiotic dimensions, including three global semiotic dimensions and three local ones, which together define the environments of translation (see Figure 2.1). The global semiotic dimensions determine the overall organization of language, and they include the hierarchy of stratification, the cline of instantiation, and the spectrum of metafunction. One of these global dimensions, namely the hierarchy of stratification, organizes language in context into various systems. These systems are organized in terms of the local semiotic dimensions, including the hierarchies of rank and axis as well as the cline of delicacy.

The environments of translation that the translators have access to will determine the amount of information available to them when they make choices in translation. In literal translation, translators would have access to a fairly narrow grammatical environment of the text within this context of situation. Conversely, in free translation, translators would have access to a wide environment. As summarized by Matthiessen (2001: 74–75), the general principle of the environments of translation is that "the wider the environment of translation, the higher the degree of translation equivalence." The principle is a matter of contextualization, and "the 'widest' environment is that in which the text is 'maximally contextualized,' and is thus likely to be 'maximally effective'" (Halliday 2010: 16). The principle can also be formulated in an ecological way: "the higher the unit that you translate in terms of (i) stratification and (ii) within a given stratum, the more information you will have access to in order to make an informed choice." (Matthiessen 2021: 526).

Stratification refers to the way language in context is organized into a hierarchy of strata. Along the hierarchy of stratification, the strata include context and language. Within language, there are the strata of the content plane (semantics and lexicogrammar) and the expression plane (phonology and phonetics in spoken language or graphology and graphetics in written language). The strata are related to each other by way of realization, with context being the widest environment and phonetics the narrowest environment.

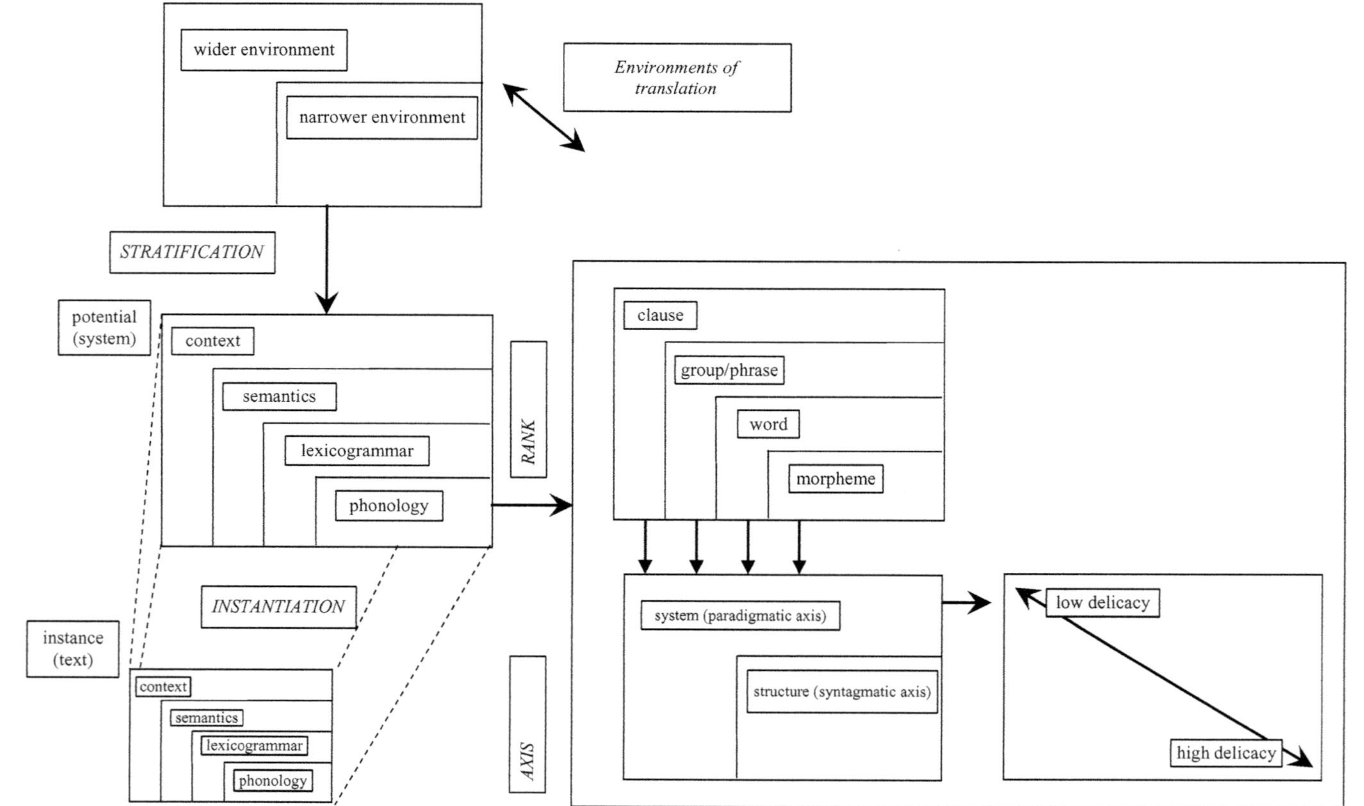

FIGURE 2.1 The environments of translation (Adapted from Matthiessen 2001: 77)

Instantiation is a cline that associates the instance (the text) with the potential (the system of language). When we examine translation as product, we observe the source text and the target text located at the instance pole of the cline. When doing translation, translators move up and down the scale along the cline, making generalizations about language based on the instances they have observed and looking for instances that meet the requirements of the source text to be translated. Between the two poles of the cline, there are intermediate patterns, viz. the instance types seen from the instance pole (text types operating in situation types) or subpotentials from the potential pole (registers operating in institutional domains). Further, it is noted that stratification and instantiation are two global dimensions that have to be maintained in translation, along which translation shifts will not be measured.

Metafunction is organized as a spectrum of different modes of meaning, including ideational, interpersonal, and textual. The ideational meaning provides resources for construing our experience of the world both around us and inside us as meaning. There are two modes of construing experience: the experiential mode that models experience configurationally and the logical mode that models experience serially. The interpersonal metafunction provides resources for interacting with others and introducing our judgements and perspectives. The textual metafunction provides resources for organizing ideational and interpersonal meanings as a flow of information in the context.

Rank refers to a hierarchy of units based on composition and is most clearly defined at the inner strata of lexicogrammar and phonology. According to the description of the grammar of English (e.g. Halliday 1985b; Halliday & Matthiessen 2014), the rank scale within lexicogrammar includes clause – group/phrase – word – morpheme, and the rank scale within phonology includes tone group – foot – syllable – phoneme. The relationship between the different units in the rank scale is composition and realization, e.g. clause rank is composed of and realized by group/phrase rank. Following Halliday's (e.g. 1962, 1966) ecological principle in the environment of rank in translation, if we move to a higher rank along the rank scale when we translate, we will have access to more information and the translation is more likely be effective and acceptable.

Axis is a hierarchy that distinguishes between the paradigmatic (systemic) organization and the syntagmatic (structural) organization. The paradigmatic axis, realized by the syntagmatic axis, is a wider environment while syntagmatic axis is a narrow environment. The paradigmatic axis is crucial to the notion of making choices in translation and defines the "translation potential", as it involves relations with the choices in the system that are not present.

Delicacy is a cline from general to specific or a scale from the most gross to the most delicate. In a system network, choices to the left have relatively low delicacy and choices towards the right have higher delicacy. Delicacy is seldom explored in translation studies, while in machine translation, it is examined under the heading of "granularity". Further, delicacy is difficult for translators to handle. If the scale of delicacy cannot be maintained, translators would have to shift at one place or at other places.

Moreover, given the complex nature of the process of translation, we can locate translation within an ordered typology of systems operating in different phenomenal realms (see Matthiessen 2001, 2021; cf. Halliday 2005). The four systems are ordered with an increasing complexity, including physical systems, biological systems (physical systems + "life"), social systems (biological systems + "value"), and semiotic systems (social systems + "meaning"). Translators can be aware of or trained to be sensitive to the following systems (see original version of Matthiessen 2021: 518–520, original emphasis):

- The physical environment plays a role, both enabling and constraining us; for example, enabling us by providing a physical **workspace** including a workbench providing electronic translation resources and tools (e.g. to support example-based translation and to provide technical glossaries) and constraining us through limitations imposed by these features.
- We inhabit this physical workspace as human **organisms**, drawing on certain key organ systems to carry out the process of translation as a biological activity. As we continue to translate texts over a period of time, we may become increasingly aware of our own bodies growing tired, failing to remember or making more mistakes so needing cups of tea or coffee, fresh air.
- At the same time, we are not just biological organisms; we are **persons** actively involved in different social networks, in each network in a different role, e.g. as professional translator in relation to colleagues in a team, possibly including editors, as translation service provider in relation to clients.
- But our primary experience is, naturally, as **multi-lingual meaners** who have mastered multilingual meaning potentials ranging over two or more languages, and who draw on these potentials to recreate meanings in context as we interpret the meanings of source texts instantiated in the meaning potential of one language and recreate them by instantiating the meaning potential of another language.

By following this approach, Matthiessen (2001, 2014b, 2021) adopts the semiotic interpretation of fourth-order systems and conceptualizes translation as the **recreation of meaning in context through choice**. The choice not only lies in the interpretation of the source text, but is also seen in the recreation of the target text. A translator needs to make all choices in the systems (meaning potentials) of the source language and the target language involved. Besides the choice made by the translator, there exist various alternative choices in the meaning potential of the languages (Matthiessen 2018). If we view text

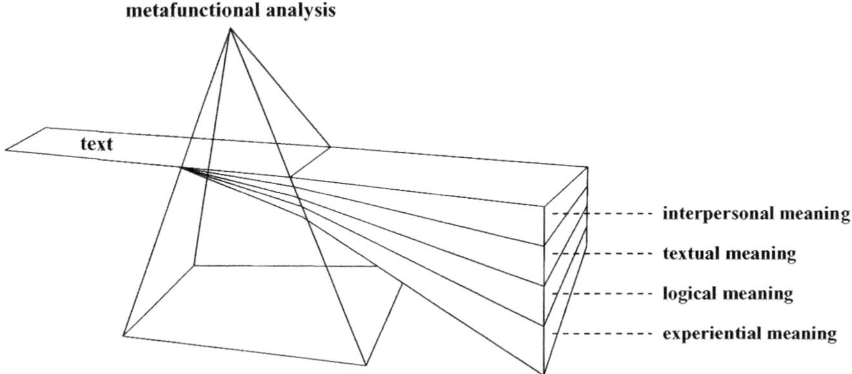

FIGURE 2.2 Modes of meaning in text revealed by the metafunctional part of discourse analysis (Adapted from Matthiessen 2014b: 277)

in terms of the metafunctional organization of language (e.g. Halliday 1978), we can identify the choices available to the translators and the ones they made with respect to the different modes of meaning (see Figure 2.2):

- In terms of **logical** meaning, translators choose how to interpret logico-semantic relations used in forming "coherent" source texts, and they choose among the options in the target language to **reconstrue** them in the translation they are producing.
- In terms of **experiential** meaning, translators choose how to interpret events as configurations of elements (processes, participants and circumstances) and larger "chunks" of experience made up of events such as episodes and procedures, and they choose among the options in the target language to **reconstrue** the experiential meanings in the translation they are producing.
- In terms of **interpersonal** meaning, translators choose how to interpret propositions, proposals and the assessments associated with them in the exchange of meaning embodied in the source text, and they choose among the options in the target language to **re-enact** the interpersonal meanings in the translation they are producing.
- In terms of **textual** meaning, translators choose how to interpret messages and the sequences of messages that create the flow of information in the source text, and they choose among the options in the target language to **re-present** the textual meanings in the translation they are producing. (Matthiessen 2014b: 277, original emphasis)

As previously discussed, translation equivalence and translation shift are important notions in the linguistic-oriented approach to translation studies (cf. Catford 1965; House 2018). Matthiessen (2014b) locates translation

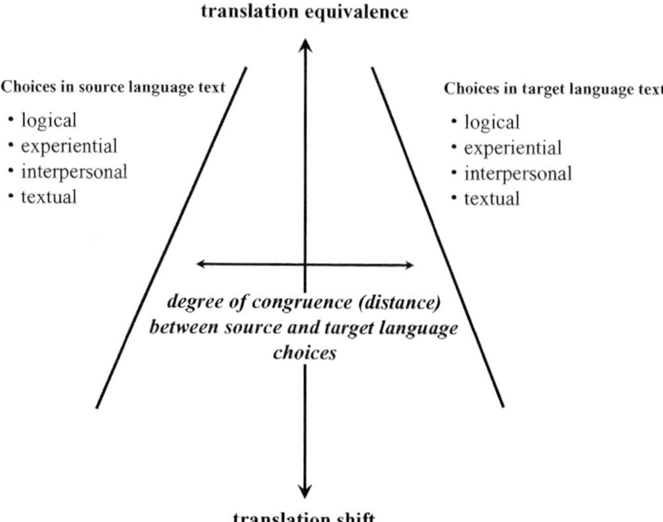

FIGURE 2.3 The cline from "translation equivalence" to "translation shift" as degree of congruence between source and target texts in terms of all four metafunctional modes of meaning (Adapted from Matthiessen 2014b: 280)

equivalence and shift as the two poles of a cline between languages.[1] In Figure 2.3, we point out the degree of congruence (distance) between the choices made in the source text and the target text. It can be observed that choices in one metafunction may be closer to the equivalence pole of the cline, and choices in another metafunction may be closer to the shift pole of the cline. Therefore, translation often involves **trade-offs** in terms of the choices made in different metafunctional modes of meaning.

Matthiessen (2014b) provides one way of examining translation shifts from the perspective of metafunction. As shown in Figure 2.4, shifts of different kinds are located in the matrix. The diagonal from top left to bottom right represents choices within the same metafunction, such as choices within textual metafunction taken place in the system of THEME as well as choices of MOOD or MODALITY within the interpersonal metafunction. Outside the diagonal, there are shifts from one metafunction to the other, such as shifts from textual to logical and vice versa. It can be observed that some boxes in the matrix are left empty because such shifts are less likely to be found. By carrying out more analyses and comparisons of originals and translations between different languages in the long-term, we can finally decide which boxes can be filled in and which boxes are more likely to remain empty (see Matthiessen, Wang & Ma 2017a).

In Chapter 4, we will introduce the delicate subtypes of two kinds of shift in the matrix, namely Theme shift (from textual to textual) and process type shift (from experiential to experiential).

TRANSLATION SHIFTS

From [source text]:

		textual	ideational: logical	ideational: experiential	interpersonal
To [target text]:	textual	textual > textual: e.g. theme shift	logical > textual: e.g. complex to cohesive sequence		
	ideational: logical	textual > logical: e.g. cohesive to complex sequence	logical > logical: e.g. tactic shift		interpersonal > logical: e.g. mood or modality represented by verbal or mental clause in clause complex of projection
	ideational: experiential		logical > experiential: e.g. clause (in clause complex) > phrase (as circumstance)	experiential > experiential: e.g. process type shift	
	interpersonal				interpersonal > interpersonal: e.g. mood type shift

FIGURE 2.4   Matrix of metafunctional translation shifts (Adapted from Matthiessen 2014b: 284)

2.2 *Stray Birds* and its four Chinese translations

The data in the present study include the English original of Rabindranath Tagore's *Stray Birds* (source text in this study, hereafter ST) and four of its Chinese translations (target text, hereafter TT) translated in different periods since the 1920s (see Table 2.2). Three translations, including TT1, TT3, and TT4, are in modern Mandarin Chinese – Putonghua (普通话) in China, Guoyu (国语) in Taiwan, or Hanyu (汉语) used worldwide. One translation, TT2, is in ancient Chinese in the form of classical poetry.

The ST, a collection of 325 short poems, was written by Rabindranath Tagore first in Bengali and translated by himself into English. As praised by Ezra Pound (1912: 40), the appearance of these poems that were translated from Bengali into

TABLE 2.2 Four Chinese translations of *Stray Birds*

	First Published	*Translator*
TT1	1922	Zheng Zhenduo (郑振铎)
TT2	1931	Yao Hua (姚华)
TT3	2008	Lu Jinde (陆晋德)
TT4	2015	Feng Tang (冯唐)

English was "an event in the history of English poetry and of world poetry." Tagore's poems were characterized by the Indian culture and philosophy, encompassing his meditation on life, the harmonious relationship between body and soul, and the ultimate concern of mankind (Xu 2018; cf. Liu 1984). Besides the Indian philosophy, his poems absorb the characteristics of Western civilization and reflect cross-cultural encounters between the East and the West (cf. Sen 2010). Example 2.1, which is written in the form of a motto, illustrates Tagore's thoughts on life and death with the purpose of inspiring and enlightening the readers.

EXAMPLE 2.1

I shall die again and again to know that life is inexhaustible.

(Tagore 2010: 142)

According to the Nobel Committee of the Swedish Academy, Tagore's poems are "the finest poems of an idealistic tendency."[2] Through these poems, Tagore praises natural beauty and expresses his love for nature (see Example 2.2).

EXAMPLE 2.2

Is not the mountain like a flower, with its petals of hills, drinking the sunlight?

(Tagore 2010: 128)

Also, Tagore expresses his optimism in *Stray Birds*. In Example 2.3, he voices his longing for the beautiful world and his yearning for an ideal society. However, when writing about the good and the evil, Tagore, on the one hand, sympathizes with the people who are marginalized and looks forward to their victory (see Example 2.4); on the other hand, he despises the people in power and indicates his hatred towards them (see Example 2.5). As commented by Pound (1912: 40–41), Tagore's poems, coming from Bengali culture, brought to us "the pledge of a calm which we need overmuch in an age of steel and mechanics. It brings a quiet proclamation of the fellowship between man and the gods; between man and nature."

EXAMPLE 2.3

My heart, with its lapping waves of song, longs to caress this green world of the sunny day.

(Tagore 2010: 131)

> **EXAMPLE 2.4**
>
> Man's history is waiting in patience for the triumph of the insulted man.
>
> (Tagore 2010: 160)

> **EXAMPLE 2.5**
>
> Power takes as ingratitude the writhings of its victims.
>
> (Tagore 2010: 80)

Target text 1 (TT1) was translated by Zheng Zhenduo (郑振铎) and was first published in 1922. Zheng was a famous Chinese writer and poet, a forerunner of new-vernacular literature thought during the May 4th Movement, and was one of the first people to introduce Tagore's poems to the Chinese readers. Zheng's translation was an attempt to pursue ideological emancipation and independence. His work influenced several famous writers in China, including Lu Xun, Qu Qiubai, Liu Bannong, Xu Zhimo, Bing Xin, and Guo Moruo (Xu 2018; cf. Guo 2005). Since its first publication in the 1920s, Zheng's translation has been reprinted many times and is now regarded as a classic.

Following TT1 in time, TT2 was published in 1931 and was translated by Yao Hua (姚华), a famous poet and painter. Yao selected 257 poems among the total 325 and translated them into the form of Chinese classical five-character poems based on Zheng Zhenduo's translation (TT1), as Yao did not speak English. In the preface by Xu Zhimo (1931), a famous concurrent poet in China, Yao's translation was praised as fluent and fresh. Xu (1931: 1, our translation) further regarded the relationship between Yao and Tagore as a "marriage": "In that year, Mr. Tagore and Mr. Yao Hua met each other, the two poets smiled at each other and took the admiration into their hearts."

Yao's translation is also preferred in the contemporary era. According to Xu Jun (2018), Yao translated the poems as a poet and presented a Sinicized and localized version of Tagore's *Stray Birds*. As a blend of Tagore's natural description and Yao's understanding of the topics in the poems, TT2 is a brief, simple, sensible, and aesthetic translation, like Tagore's original (cf. Jiang 1980/1986).

TT3 and TT4 were both translated in the new millennium. The translator of TT3, Lu Jinde, is a Taiwanese businessman and an amateur writer. His translation of *Stray Birds* was published by one of the famous publishing houses, Yilin Press in mainland China, and is widely known among readers.

TT4, the latest version among the four TTs, was translated by Feng Tang, a doctor, businessman, and writer of a dozen novels and essays, and was published in 2015. Its publication generated heated discussion and was accused of transforming "Tagore's tranquil verse into a vulgar selfie of hormone saturated innuendo" (Zhou 2016). Consequently, Feng was criticized for being unfaithful and showing disrespect to Tagore's works.[3] Due to the huge controversy caused by Feng's translation and the various tip-offs received, the publishing house removed all of Feng's published books of *Stray Birds* from the shelves.[4]

In 2019, Feng Tang's translation was republished in Hong Kong by Cosmo Books, with no omission being made compared to the mainland version. At the beginning of the book, Feng (2019a) claimed that the publishing house in mainland China was under enormous pressure from various senior translators who could not "stand" his translation and repeatedly complained to the superior. Feng (2019b) summarized the criticism to his translation into three aspects, namely (i) distortion of Tagore's original meaning, (ii) contamination of Tagore's purity, and (iii) hype in the name of Tagore.

Despite the acclaims and criticisms, we treat all the TTs in the analysis in this book equally. The SFL-based analysis will provide linguistic evidences to the literary criticism or comments and help us understand poetry translation instead of merely concentrating on being loyal or faithful to the original. To attain these objectives, two steps will be taken: (i) to study the nature of the ST and translations of the four TTs by analyzing them linguistically and trying to bring out the trade-offs in the TTs and (ii) to raise the issue of whether TT4 breaks the "norms" and/or is a good or bad translation (cf. Halliday 2001).

According to functional text typology (see e.g. Matthiessen 2014c, 2015a, 2015b; Matthiessen, Wang & Ma 2019; see Section 5.1), poetry in general falls into the category of recreating, which is a semiotic process that recreates "various aspects of life … through narration and/or dramatization" (Matthiessen 2014c: 32).[5] While translating different types of texts, translators tend to adopt different strategies of translation (cf. Reiss 1971; Newmark 1988; Snell-Hornby 1995; Trosborg 1997a, 1997b). The discussions of context or register would also contribute to the analysis in this study (see Chapter 5).

2.3 Analytical framework and data size

As a specific literary form, poetry occupies a central position among all the literary genres (cf. Culler 1975). In literary creation and translation, the content and the form of poetry have both played their parts (see e.g. Bassnett 1980; Strand & Boland 2000; Landers 2001). Therefore, an analytical framework for analyzing poems and their translations should take both the content and the form of poetry into consideration.

In terms of stratification (e.g. Firth 1957, 1968; Halliday 1978; Halliday & Matthiessen 2014; see Section 2.1), poetry "means" in terms of both the content plane (i.e. semantics and lexicogrammar) as well as the expression plane (i.e. phonology and phonetics or graphology and graphetics), which can be related to previous studies by SFL scholars on poetry or verbal art (cf. Lukin & Webster 2004; Lukin 2015; see Section 1.1) and their references to Russian Formalism or the Prague School (e.g. Mukařovský 1964, 1977; Garvin 1964).

Modeled in terms of stratification in SFL, the following analytical framework (which draws on the expression plane, the content plane, and context) is constructed. The analysis covers four strata both inside language and outside language, including graphology, phonology, lexicogrammar, and context (see Figure 2.5). The four strata are located along the hierarchy of stratification by way of realization, e.g. lexicogrammar is realized by phonology (graphology). Such relation can be represented as follows: context ↘ (semantics ↘ (lexicogrammar ↘ (phonology ↘ phonetics))).

Graphologically, we examine our data in terms of the layout of the poems. Phonologically, we investigate the rhyme scheme of the ST and the TTs. Lexicogrammatically, when comparing the ST and the TTs based on a pilot study, we find similar choices in the systems of POLARITY, MOOD, and MODALITY and different choices in the systems of THEME and TRANSITIVITY. Therefore, we consider the analysis of Theme and transitivity in the framework (cf. Ma & Wang forthcoming for a framework involving analysis of four different modes of meaning and targeting the description and quality assessment of poetry translation).

Theme is the point of departure of the message and it serves to locate and orient the clause (see e.g. Halliday 1967a, 1967b; Halliday & Matthiessen 2014; Wang & Ma 2020: Chapter 3). By making one part of the clause prominent, the speaker guides the listener in processing the message. The Rheme is what follows the Theme in a clause. Thus, a clause is composed of Theme and Rheme.

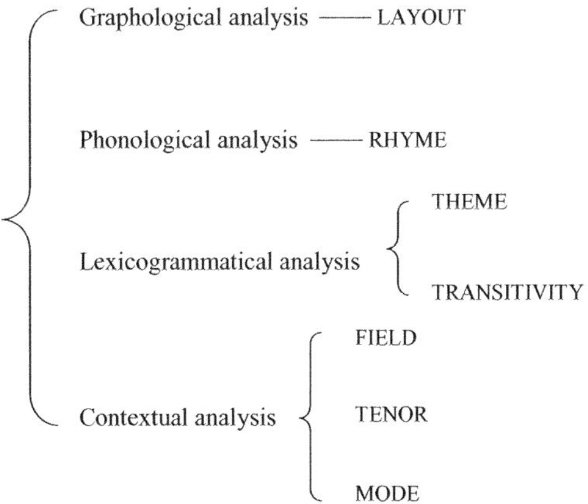

FIGURE 2.5 Analytical framework of the present study

TRANSITIVITY offers grammatical resources for construing experiences as quanta of change in the flow of events (Matthiessen & Halliday 1999, 2014). Within the structure of transitivity, there are elements of process, participants, and circumstance, while process metaphorically occupies the central position, similar to how the sun is located within the solar system. As one of the most significant systems in the system network of TRANSITIVITY, the system of PROCESS TYPE construes human experience into six types: material, mental, relational, behavioral, verbal, and existential (see Matthiessen 1999).

After the analysis of Theme and transitivity, translation shifts of different kinds are expected to be identified and quantified. We will further discuss the reasons that led to the shifts. For instance, some shifts are due to the differences between languages, some are related to the poetic form, and some are a result of the translator's personal choice or habitus (cf. Simeoni 1998; Sela-Sheffy 2005). Hansen and Hansen-Schirra (2012) have summarized these factors as typological variations between languages, registerial characteristics, as well as the translators' cognitive factors.

Contextually, since the translations are produced during different periods of Chinese history and the four translators have different backgrounds, the field, tenor, and mode of the ST and TTs are not the same. Analysis of the contextual parameters will further help us to identify the norms that are followed when translating poetry from English to Chinese in different times and explain why the translator of TT4 has been criticized.

The lexicogrammatical analysis of the English ST is based on the descriptions provided in Matthiessen (1995) and Halliday and Matthiessen (2014). In most cases, the clause boundaries are straightforward. Hypotactic clauses with no Subjects are analyzed as separate clauses. As seen in Example 2.6 and Example 2.7 (see Table 2.3 and Table 2.4), the clause complex is divided into three ranking clauses: two free clauses and one bound clause. For each clause, analysis is made in the major systems of the clause, most centrally in systems of THEME, MOOD, and TRANSITIVITY. Also, while analyzing the second and the third clauses, the omitted Themes – "*Stray birds* of summer" are reinstated.

According to previous descriptions of Mandarin Chinese, the functional demesne of Chinese is similar to that of English (e.g. Halliday & McDonald 2004; Li 2007). Clause complexes are segmented into clauses in accordance with previous SFL descriptions. Compared to the English ST, Subjects in

TABLE 2.3 Example 2.6 (Adapted from Tagore 2010: 2)

Stray birds of summer come to my window	*[ø: stray birds] to sing*	*and [ø: stray birds] fly away.*
1α	1×β	×2
clause: free	clause: bound	clause: free

TABLE 2.4 Example 2.7 (Adapted from Tagore 2010: 2)

Stray birds of summer	come		to my window
Theme	Rheme		
Subject	Finite	Predicator	Adjunct
Mood		Residue	
Actor	Process		Place
nominal group	verbal group		prepositional phrase

TABLE 2.5 Example 2.8 (Adapted from Tagore 2010: 2)

	夏天 的 飞 鸟，飞 到 我 窗 前	[ø: 夏天 的 飞 鸟] 唱 歌，	[ø 夏天 的 飞 鸟] 又 飞 去 了。
PY	xià tiān de fēi niǎo, fēi dào wǒ chuāng qián	xià tiān de fēi niǎo chàng gē,	xià tiān de fēi niǎo yòu fēi qù le.
IG	summer SUB flying bird fly to my window front	summer SUB flying bird sing song	summer SUB flying bird then fly away ASP
	1	×2	×3
	clause: free	clause: free	clause: free

the Chinese TTs are more often omitted, as they are not involved in marking Mood structures (Halliday & McDonald 2004). Example 2.8 (see Table 2.5), which is taken from TT1, shows how one clause complex is divided into three clauses and how the omitted Themes are reinstated in the analysis.

In the present study, we will analyze the first 50 poems out of the 325 poems in *Stray Birds* (excluding Poem 5, 22, and 31, as they are not translated in TT2). In the poems selected, there are 111 clauses in the ST, while the number of clauses in the four TTs are 141, 306, 144, and 146 respectively. Trade-offs are made here between comprehensiveness of analysis and volume of text involved (cf. Matthiessen 2014a). On the one hand, we try to make our analysis comprehensive by involving a selective number of systems. On the other hand, we try to include a relatively large volume of text in the manual analysis. We hope our selected systemic analyses are capable of offering a revealing account of how *Stray Birds* and its translations are organized to effectively function in their contexts of situation and contexts of culture. From Chapter 3 to Chapter 5, we carry out our analyses based on the theoretical framework proposed by proceeding from the expression plane, moving to the content plane, and finally providing a descriptive account of the contextual stratum.

Notes

1 A translation shift is different from an error in translation. In translation practice, there will always be shifts in some dimension, as total equivalence can seldom be achieved. Hence, translators may need to shift at certain places in order to gain equivalence elsewhere.

2 See http://www.nobelprize.org/nobel_prizes/literature/laureates/1913/press.html/ for the award ceremony speech by Harald Hjärne, Chairman of the Nobel Committee of the Swedish Academy, on December 10, 1913.

3 See http://www.telegraphindia.com/1151222/jsp/nation/story_59755.jsp#.VnoE7fnhuI4 and http://europe.chinadaily.com.cn/epaper/2016-01/01/content_22894013.htm for news, criticism and discussions on TT4.

4 See http://www.china.org.cn/arts/2015-12/29/content_37415858.htm for a news report on why Feng Tang's *Stray Birds* were taken off shelves.

5 But in principle, other fields of activity could also be pursued in the form of poetry, which really depends on how we define poetry from the trinocular terms: from below, from above, and from roundabout (cf. Matthiessen 2013).

3

TRANSLATING ON THE EXPRESSION PLANE OF LANGUAGE

Graphological and phonological choices

In this chapter, we point out and compare the choices on the expression plane of language in the ST and the TTs. According to Halliday (e.g. 1992, 1996), graphology and phonology are both treated as the strata of the expression plane of language, with graphology being a stratum of written mode and phonology of spoken mode. The poems (and their translations) we analyze in this book are special in that they are not only printed in books, but are also written to be read aloud by readers. Therefore, both graphological and phonological choices are considered in this study.

3.1 Analysis of graphological choices

The graphological analysis is based on the layout in the ST and the TTs (see Bateman 2008 for descriptions of base units in terms of page layout) and is expected to reveal how lower units of organization compose larger units. According to Figure 3.1, the clause, subsentence, tone group, and line are analogic in that they serve respectively as grammatical unit, graphological unit, phonological unit, and unit of verse. The lower units of organization can constitute higher units, i.e. clauses can form clause complexes, subsentences form sentences, tone groups form tone group complexes, and line form metrical stanzas. In this way, it is possible to identify the pattern of organization in poetry.

3.1.1 Analysis of graphological choices in the ST

As shown in Figure 3.2, which characterizes the layout of the first poem (Poem 1) in *Stray Birds*, the layout of the ST follows the style of prose and prose poem. Following the rank scale of the lexicogrammar of English

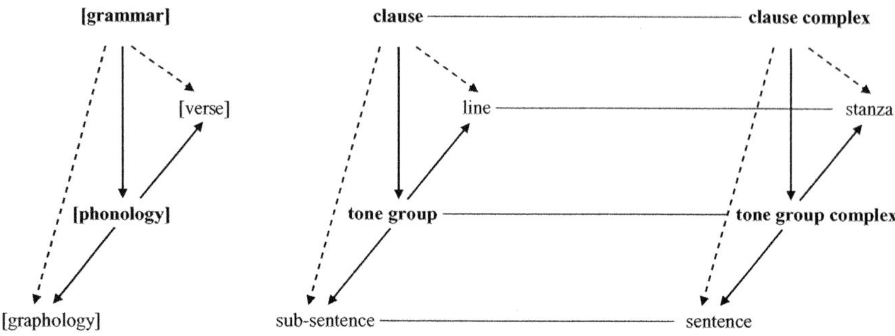

FIGURE 3.1   Analogic patterning of units across content (lexicogrammar) and expression (phonology, graphology) (Adapted from Halliday & Matthiessen 2014: 16)

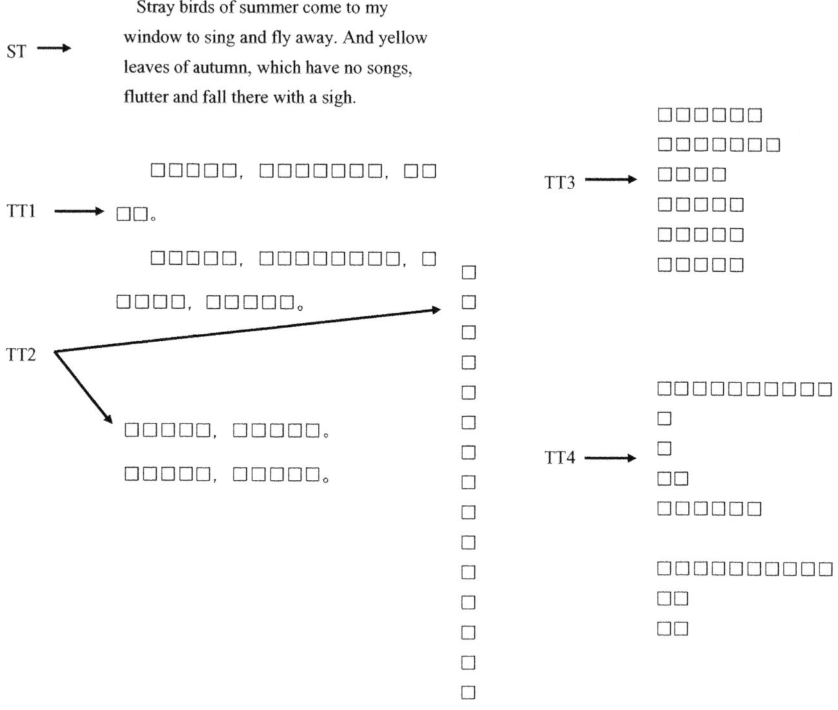

FIGURE 3.2   Example of graphological patterns in the ST and the TTs

(see e.g. Halliday 1961; Matthiessen 1995), it is seen that words here compose groups/phrases, groups/phrases compose clauses, and clauses compose clause complexes, with no line break being used in the ST. Such an organization has been applied throughout the whole book of *Stray Birds* in English. Also, it is important to note that *Stray Birds* was first written by Tagore in Bengali and was later translated into English by Tagore himself. However, unlike the poems written in Bengali, the translated poems were stripped of all the formal beauty of the original, of rhythm and rhymes, etc., thus becoming a prose of a strange speech. Indeed, Tagore himself wondered what has been left in the translated poems without the poetic forms and doubted whether the poems would appeal to the Europeans (Pound 1913).

Although the ST is not arranged in lines, punctuation marks are used to separate the different elements in a clause, notably commas (,), full stops (.), and double quotation marks (""). We find that the choices of punctuation marks follow the conventions in English and no deviated uses are observed. Commas are applied to separate a participant from a process, a process from a participant, a circumstance from a process, or a clause from another clause.

In Table 3.1, we quantify the frequencies of the separations caused by commas.[1] We find that ten poems in the ST separate participant from process, and such separations can only be found under the following circumstances. Firstly, when a Vocative is acting as a participant, e.g. in Poem 2, "O troupe of little vagrants of the world, leave your footprints in my words," the Vocative is separated by a comma. Secondly, when the participants are followed by an embedded phrase, e.g. "Some unseen fingers, like an idle breeze, are playing upon my heart the music of the ripple."

The separation of process from participant in the ST is rarely seen, with only two instances found. One is due to a Vocative that occurs before the participant, e.g. "Listen, **my heart**, to the whisper of the world with which it makes love to you"; and the other is due to the two neighboring participants in one poem, e.g. "Life finds its wealth by **the claims of the world**, and **its worth by the claims of love.**"

The separations of process from circumstance also occur in certain specific occasions, mostly when an Adjunct appears in the middle of the clause, e.g. in "Some unseen fingers, **like an idle breeze**, are playing upon my heart the music of the ripples"; or when two parallel phrases appear together, e.g. "O Beauty, find thyself **in love, not in the flattery of thy mirror.**"

Comparatively, separations between clauses have a larger frequency than the three categories mentioned above, invovling 18 instances in total.

TABLE 3.1 Types of separation in the ST

Type of separation	Poem No.	Freq.
participant-process separation	2, 11, 13, 23, 27, 28, 38, 41, 47, 50	10
process-participant separation	13, 33	2
circumstance-process separation	11, 26, 27, 28, 41, 47	6
clause-clause separation	1, 3, 6, 7, 12, 14, 16, 18, 19, 20, 23, 25, 35, 36, 39, 43, 52, 53	18

The following observations are made: Firstly, when clauses in the ST are not separated, it is because one of the clauses is downranked, as seen in "Listen, my heart, to the whispers of the of the world **with which it makes love to you.**" Secondly, two free clauses are sometimes separated, e.g. "These little thoughts are the rustle of leaves, they have their whisper of joy in my mind," and "What you are you do not see, what you see is your shadow." On the contrary, it is also possible for free clauses not to be separated, such as "My heart beats her waves at the shore of the world and writes upon it her signature in tears with the words …" Thirdly, free clauses are sometimes separated from the bound ones, e.g. "I find my song, when I find my freedom." Fourthly, separations of two free clauses with a comma are quite common in the ST and are seen in 7 poems (Poem 18, 19, 25, 33, 43, 52, and 53). Finally, clauses with similar structures tend to be separated, such as "The bird wishes it were a cloud. The cloud wishes it were a bird."

3.1.2 Analysis of graphological choices in TT1

In Figure 3.1, we use the symbols of foursquare (□) to stand for Chinese characters in the TTs. Following the principle of composition, characters can form words, words form groups or phrases, groups or phrases form clauses, and clauses form clause complexes (cf. Halliday & McDonald 2004). Among the four TTs, the layout of TT1 is most similar to the ST and is of prose style, with no line break being found.

In terms of punctuation, we find that 55 commas are added in TT1, compared with the choices made in the ST. These commas inform readers where to pause while reading the poem. As shown in Example 3.1, the pauses are explicitly marked out with the help of the commas. In this way, readers are guided throughout the reading process.

EXAMPLE 3.1

ST: You smiled and talked to me of nothing and I felt that for this I had been waiting long.
TT1: 你微微地笑着，不同我说什么话，而我觉得，为了这个，我已等待很久了。
PY: nǐ wēi wēi de xiào zhe, bù tóng wǒ shuō shén me huà, ér wǒ jué de, wèi le zhè gè, wǒ yǐ děng dài hěn jiǔ le.
BT: You faintly smiled, not talked much to me, and I felt, for this, I already had been waiting for so long.

(Adapted from Tagore 2010: 22)

TABLE 3.2 Types of separation in TT1

Type of separation	Poem No.	Freq.
participant-process separation	1, 4, 8, 11, 14, 17, 18, 21, 23, 25, 26, 32, 34, 37, 41, 47	16
process-participant separation	37	1
circumstance-process separation	7, 9, 11, 17, 33, 39, 42, 47	8
clause-clause separation	1, 3, 6, 7, 9, 10, 12, 13, 14, 15, 16, 17, 18, 19, 20, 22, 23, 24, 25, 26, 27, 28, 29, 30, 31, 35, 37, 38, 39, 40, 41, 42, 43, 44, 47, 49, 51, 52, 53	39

Similar to the uses of comma in the ST, we find various line breaks caused by the commas in TT1 (i.e. different kinds of separations of grammatical elements). In Table 3.2, we quantify the frequencies of such separations and tabulate the number of poems.

We find 16 separations between participant and process in TT1, which is a larger frequency compared to the frequencies of ten instances in the ST. Example 3.2 illustrates this kind of separation in TT1.

EXAMPLE 3.2

ST: Some unseen fingers, like an idle breeze, are playing upon my heart the music of the ripples.

TT1: 有些看不见的手指，如懒懒的微飔似的，正在我的心上，奏着潺湲的乐声。

PY: yǒu xiē kàn bú jiàn de shǒu zhǐ, rú lǎn lǎn de wēi sī sì de, zhèng zài wǒ de xīn shàng, zòu zhe chán yuán de yuè shēng.

BT: Some unseen fingers, like an idle breeze, are now on my heart, playing the rippling music.

(Adapted from Tagore 2010: 7)

Unlike the separations of participant and process in the ST, which are grammatically necessary, the separations in TT1 are used to separate a Subject that is longer than the Predicator in terms of layout (cf. Chan 2016 for descriptions of the uses of punctuation in Chinese). Examples of such participants include "夏日的飞鸟" (PY: xià rì de fēi niǎo; IG: summer SUB flying bird) and "她的热切的脸" (PY: tā de rè qiè de liǎn; IG: her earnest face). However, commas are not added to separate the participants that are short in length, e.g. "你" (PY: nǐ; IG: you), "我" (PY: wǒ; IG: I), "我们" (PY: wǒ men; IG: we), and "世界" (PY: shì jiè; IG: world). There are some exceptions. In certain cases, long Subjects are not followed by commas, e.g. in "水 里 的 游 鱼 是 沉默的" (PY: shuǐ lǐ de yóu yú shì chén mò de; IG: water in SUB swimming fish be silent), as the Predicator "是" (PY: shì; IG: be) is not long in layout, no comma is used after "水 里 的 游 鱼" (PY: shuǐ lǐ de yóu yú; IG: water in SUB swimming fish).

Another possibility of separation between participant and process is when a Vocative functions as an interpersonal Theme (see Straus, Kaufman & Stern 2014; Chan 2016 for discussions on this kind of layout in English and Chinese). In eight poems (Poem 2, 7, 12, 13, 19, 28, 30, and 38) in TT1, the translator adds commas after the interpersonal Themes realized by Vocatives, among which four equivalent instances of additional commas are found in the ST. Also, Vocatives only appear at the beginning of the lines in TT1, and commas are added after the Vocatives, such as "跳舞 着 的 流水 啊" (PY: tiào wǔ zhe de liú shuǐ a; IG: dancing VPART SUB flowing water MOD). However, in the English ST, Vocatives are not only found at the beginning, but also at the end of clause complexes, as seen in "The sands in your way beg for your song and your movement, **dancing water.**" For Vocatives appearing at the end of the clause complexes, no separation of participant and process is found.

Similar to the ST, separation between process and participant is rarely seen in TT1, with only one instance being found when the Complement/ Goal functions as the Theme and is thus separated from the rest of the clause, i.e. "那 小小的 需要, 他 是 永不 要求, 永不 知道, 永不 记 着 的" (PY: nà xiǎo xiǎo de xū yào, tā shì yǒng bù yāo qiú, yǒng bù zhī dào, yǒng bù jì zhe de; IG: that small need, he be never ask, never know, never remember VPART SUB).

There are eight instances of separation between circumstance and process in TT1. Among these examples, the circumstances include those of Direction, e.g. "世界 对着 它的 爱人" (PY: shì jiè duì zhe tā de ài rén; IG: world to its lover), Reason, e.g. "因 了 爱 的 要求" (PY: yīn le ài de yāo qiú; IG: because ASP love SUB request), and Manner, e.g. "秘密地, 温顺地" (PY: mì mì de, wēn shùn de; IG: secretly, gently). According to the Chinese standards of using punctuations, Adjuncts, which may be located at the beginning or the end of the clause complexes, should be followed or preceded by commas (General Administration of Quality, Inspection and Quarantine Bureau of the People's Republic of China 2011). However, in the grammar of English, no such use of comma is found around the circumstantial elements (Straus, Kaufman & Stern 2014). This explains why fewer instances of separation between circumstance and process are found in the ST.

Separation between clauses are frequently found in TT1, with an occurrence of 39 poems, comparing to 17 poems in the ST. These instances of separation between clauses can be categorized as follows. Firstly, downranked clauses in the ST are separated and become free clauses in TT1 (in Poem 13, 16, and 27) (see Example 3.3).

EXAMPLE 3.3

ST: Listen, my heart, to the whispers to the world [[with which it makes love to you]].

TT1: 静静地听啊，我的心呀，听那"世界"的低语，这是他对你的爱的表示呀。

PY: jìng jìng de tīng a, wǒ de xīn ya, tīng nà "shì jiè" de dī yǔ, zhè shì tā duì nǐ de ài de biǎo shì ya.

BT: Silently listen, my heart, to the world's whisper, this is his love to you.

(Adapted from Tagore 2015: 8)

Secondly, prepositional phrases in the ST are separated and translated as free clauses in TT1 (in Poem 3, 8, 10, 11, 24, 31, 38, and 47) (see Example 3.4).

EXAMPLE 3.4

ST: Her wistful face haunts my dreams like the rain at night.

TT1: 她的热切的脸，如夜雨似的，搅扰着我的梦魂。

PY: tā de rè qiè de liǎn, rú yè yǔ sì de, jiǎo rǎo zhe wǒ de mèng hún.

BT: Her wistful face, like the evening rain, haunts my dreams.

(Adapted from Tagore 2010: 5)

Thirdly, it is possible to separate bound clauses from free clauses in TT1 (in Poem 9, 15, 27, 38, 39, 40, 44, 51, and 53) (see Example 3.5).

EXAMPLE 3.5

ST: We wake up to find that we were dear to each other.

TT1: 我们醒了，却知道我们原是相亲爱的。

PY: wǒ men xǐng le, què zhī dào wǒ men yuán shì xiāng qīn ài de.

BT: We wake up, yet knowing that we used to be dear to each other.

(Adapted from Tagore 2010: 6)

Fourthly, separations can be found between free clauses (in Poem 1, 7, 9, 12, 14, 16, 17, 18, 19, 23, 24, 25, 29, 30, 35, 42, 43, 45, 47, 49, 52, and 53) (see Example 3.6), which conform to the standards of using punctuations in Chinese (e.g. Chan 2016: 580, General Administration of Quality, Inspection and Quarantine Bureau of the People's Republic of China 2011).

EXAMPLE 3.6

ST: These little thoughts are the rustle of leaves; they have their whisper of joy in my mind.
TT1: 这些微思，是绿叶的簌簌之声呀；他们在我的心里，愉悦地微语着。
PY: zhè xiē wēi sī, shì lǜ yè de sù sù zhī shēng ya; tā men zài wǒ de xīn lǐ, yú yuè de wēi yǔ zhe.
BT: These little thoughts, are the rustle of green leaves; they are in my heart, whispering happily.

(Adapted from Tagore 2010: 10)

3.1.3 Analysis of graphological choices in TT2

TT2 is a work created in classical Chinese in the form of classical Chinese poetry, through which the translator expresses his worries about his homeland, patriotism, hatred towards power, and tenderness towards the weak (see Chapter 5). In Figure 3.2, we point out the two layout patterns of TT2. The first pattern is to arrange all Chinese characters in a vertical line, without using any punctuation mark and following the traditional layout of classical Chinese poetry (see Tagore 1931). In addition, according to the second pattern, as seen in Yao (2000), poems are composed in four lines, with each line containing five Chinese characters, normally separated by commas and stops. Among the 50 poems in our data, 35 contain four lines, while the rest are written in 6 lines (Poem 7, 19, 27, 30, 49, 51, 52, and 53), 8 lines (Poem 3, 16, 37, and 44), 10 lines (Poem 26), or 11 lines (Poem 29 and 43).

Separations of grammatical elements in TT2 are rather random, since each line, consisting of five Chinese characters, will sometimes be analyzed as one clause. Divisions of lines are mostly based on the needs for rhyme and on the semantic meaning of the clauses, rather than on grammatical elements.

3.1.4 Analysis of graphological choices in TT3

Graphologically, the translator of TT3 tends to divide the poems into several lines, with each line containing a specific grammatical element of the clause (see Figure 3.1). Also, unlike TT1, which is characterized by the abundant use of punctuation marks, a very limited number of punctuation marks are used in TT3. In our data, double quotation marks are the only punctuation marks used in TT3, i.e. in Poem 12 and Poem 20. Moreover, we find that the separations of the various elements in TT3 are realized either by the choices of spacing between Chinese characters or by the line breaks. In Table 3.3, we tabulate the frequencies of the different kinds of separation.

TABLE 3.3 Types of separation in TT3

Type of separation	Poem No.	Freq.
participant-process separation	1, 2, 3, 4, 7, 8, 9, 10, 11, 12, 13, 14, 17, 18, 19, 21, 23, 24, 25, 26, 27, 28, 29, 32, 34, 35, 38, 39, 41, 44, 47, 48, 50, 51, 52	35
process-participant separation	3, 7, 17, 18, 24, 29, 50, 53	8
circumstance-process separation	3, 7, 9, 24, 30, 33, 37, 42, 43, 44	10
clause-clause separation	1, 2, 3, 6, 7, 8, 9, 10, 11, 12, 13, 14, 15, 16, 17, 18, 19, 20, 21, 23, 25, 26, 27, 28, 29, 30, 32 ,33, 34, 35, 36, 37, 38, 39, 40, 41, 43, 44, 45, 46, 47, 48, 49, 50, 51, 52, 53	47

As shown in the table, in 35 poems, participants are separated from processes with the help of line break (e.g. Poem 1, 2, and 3), comma (e.g. Poem 12), or spacing (e.g. Poem 17). Separations of process from participant as well as those of circumstance from process are not frequently seen in TT3, with only eight and ten examples being found respectively.

The most frequently-occurred separation is clause-clause separation, with 47 instances being found. For example, in Poem 5, one clause, i.e. "强悍的 沙漠 用 火热的 爱情 追求 一 片 草叶" (PY: qiáng hàn de shā mò yòng huǒ rè de ài qíng zhuī qiú yí piàn cǎo yè; IG: rough desert with burning love pursue one MEAS grass) is separated from the remaining clauses and line breaks are frequently observed. Thus, we note that the translator does make graphological considerations and trade-offs are made in terms of separation or non-separation from time to time.

3.1.5 Analysis of graphological choices in TT4

According to Figure 3.1, the layout pattern of TT4 is similar to that of TT3 in that line breaks are observed and no punctuation mark is used. However, TT4 differs from the other TTs in that the translator arranges his translation in several stanzas. In Poem 1, we find two paralleled stanzas, through which the translator purposefully reveals the contrast between stray birds and yellow leaves (see Figure 4.2 for logico-semantic analysis that reveals the contrast).

Similar to the analysis of other TTs, we quantify the different types of separations found in TT4, which reflect how choices of line break are made by the translator (see Table 3.4). Clause-clause separations are most frequently seen in TT4. In most cases, the translator tends to arrange one clause into a new line (see Figure 3.1).

TABLE 3.4 Types of separation in TT4

Type of separation	_Poem No._	_Freq._
participation-process separation	2, 11, 12, 13, 14, 17, 19, 21, 28, 30, 34, 38, 41, 47, 48, 50	16
process-participant separation	11, 14, 17, 28, 41, 43, 50	7
circumstance-process separation	23, 26, 32, 33, 36, 37, 47	7
clause-clause separation	1, 2, 3, 4, 6, 7, 8, 9, 10, 11, 12, 13, 14, 15, 16, 17, 18, 19, 20, 21, 23, 24, 25, 26, 27, 28, 29, 30, 32, 33, 34, 35, 36, 37, 38, 39, 40, 41, 42, 43, 44, 45, 46, 47, 48, 49, 50, 51, 52, 53	50

For participant-process separation, 16 instances are found. Among the participants separated, six are Vocatives separated from the remaining clause, while four are participants separated in different lines to form paralleled constructions. For instance, in "看不见的 手指 无所事事的 风" (PY: kàn bú jiàn de shǒu zhǐ wú suǒ shì shì de fēng; IG: unseen finger idle winds), "无所事事 的 风" (PY: wú suǒ shì shì de fēng; IG: idle winds) is contrasted with "看不见 的 手指" (PY: kàn bú jiàn de shǒu zhǐ; IG: unseen finger), with each nominal group occupying one line of the poem.

Separations of process and participant have a small frequency and are found in six poems. The reason for these separations may be either due to the need for comparison or because the participant of the clause is too long.

For circumstance-participant separation, seven instances are found. TT4 is similar to TT3 in this respect as it does not separate circumstance into a new line. Instead, circumstances are put together with other elements of a clause, as seen in "大漠 因为 迷恋 一 叶 绿 草 而 焦黄" (PY: dà mò yīn wéi mí liàn yí yè lǜ cǎo ér jiāo huáng; IG: desert because love one leaf green grass and yellowish), where "因为 迷恋 一 叶 绿 草" (PY: yīn wéi mí liàn yí yè lǜ cǎo; IG: because love one leaf green grass) is not separated from the rest of the clause.

3.2 Analysis of phonological choices

The phonological analysis focuses on the choices of rhyme in the data. In general, the ST as well as the translations by Zheng Zhenduo (TT1) and Lu Jinde (TT3) are not rhymed, whereas various poems in Yao Hua (TT2) and Feng Tang's translations (TT4) are rhymed on purpose, resulting in a large number of translation shifts in lexicogrammar (see Chapter 4). In this section, we build up a profile of how rhyme choices are realized in the TTs and discuss the translation shifts from the perspective of phonology.

3.2.1 Analysis of phonological choices in the ST

In the ST, the poet neither divides the poems into different lines nor adopts any choice of rhyme, alliteration or consonance. Thus, the ST is free in form and is more prose-like. In his essay titled "Poem and Rhythm," Tagore (2016a) regards prose as an art form that is of equal importance as poem. Although rhythm may help express feelings, it does not represent the totality of a poem. The essence of poetry lies in its emotion, while choices of rhyme would merely play a subsidiary role. He further suggests that rhyme in poetry is never a compulsory choice and a poem is capable of moving its readers with the help of emotion. Following the dimension of stratification in SFL, we can state that Tagore (2016a) emphasizes the choices made on the content plane of language rather than on the expression plane (see Halliday 1978; Halliday & Matthiessen 2014). As a result, by following his standards, Tagore composes his *Stray birds* in paragraphs, with no choice of rhyme being made.

3.2.2 Analysis of phonological choices in TT1

As one of the first Chinese translators of Tagore's poems, Zheng Zhenduo (e.g. 1921, 2004a) believed that poems were translatable and the translation of a poem can be very close to the original. The translation strategy he favored was literal translation rather than free translation. In addition, he pursued the kind of translation that could transplant the whole artistic arrangement from one language to another, and suggested that such transplant happened not only in the arrangements of plot but also in the arrangements of sections, paragraphs or even words in sentences. Therefore, he provided his translation of *Stray Birds* by strictly following the phonological choices in the ST and no attempt of rhyme was made in TT1.

3.2.3 Analysis of phonological choices in TT2

The choice of rhyme is frequent in classical Chinese poetry. In these classical poems, rhyme is based on either oral or written language, depending on the period during which the poetry was written. Before the Tang Dynasty or after the May 4th Movement, rhyme in poetry was based on oral language; whereas from the Tang Dynasty to the May 4th Movement, a strict rhyme scheme was specified to be the standard in *Book of Rhyme* (韵书) (Wang 1958).

In TT2, 18 poems have fixed rhymed patterns (see Table 3.5 and Figure 3.3) and all the rhymed choices appear at the end of the lines with even number. For instance, in a four-line poems, rhymed choices will appear at the end of the second and the fourth lines, e.g. "我身不自见，我见非真**相**。

TABLE 3.5 Frequency of rhymed poems and their rhymed patterns in TT2

Poem No.	Number of lines in the poem	Rhymed lines	Amount of rhymes
11, 20, 32, 35, 36, 40, 45, 46, 47, 48	6	2, 4	1
30, 53	6	2, 4, 6	1
44	8	2, 4, 6	1
26	10	2, 4, 6, 8	2
43	11	2, 4, 6, 8, 10, 11	1
29	12	2, 4, 10, 12	1

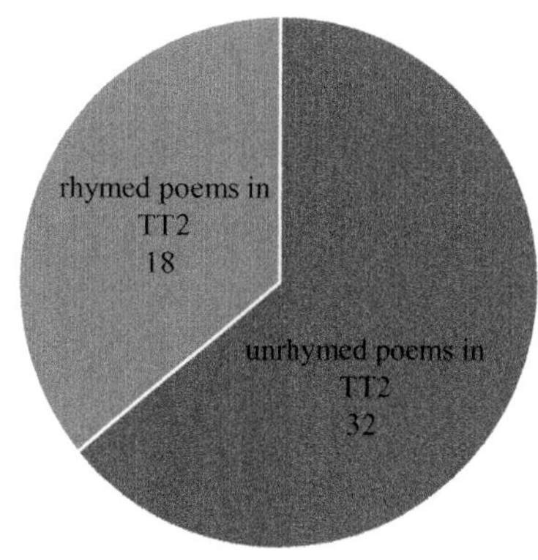

FIGURE 3.3 Percentage of rhymed and unrhymed poems in TT2

如 将 影 悟 身，谓 身 亦 已 **妄**" (PY: wǒ shēn bú zì jiàn, wǒ jiàn fēi zhēn **xiàng**. rú jiāng yǐng wù shēn, wèi shēn yì yǐ **wàng**; IG: my body NEG self see, I see NEG real fact. if DISP shadow understand body, say body also already absurd), where "相" (PY: xiàng; BT: fact) and "妄" (PY: wàng; BT: absurd) rhyme with each other.

3.2.4 Analysis of phonological choices in TT3

Similar to the ST and TT1, no rhymed choice is found in TT3. As the translator of TT3, Lu Jinde (2008), explained in his preface, he was a lover of literature and poetry and translated *Stray Birds* for fun. What he valued most were the ideas, clever thoughts, philosophy, and oriental culture reflected in Tagore's poems. Therefore, he did not take the choices on the expression plane of language into consideration.

3.2.5 Analysis of phonological choices in TT4

In TT4, rhyme was the most important consideration of the translator; therefore, he tried his best to find suitable rhyme patterns (Feng 2015, 2019c). Also, Feng has admitted that rhyme is the most powerful weapon of a poet.

In Table 3.6 and Figure 3.4, it is observed that rhymed choices occupy a large proportion in TT4, with 36 out of 50 poems being rhymed and all rhymed choices located at the end of the lines. Most poems rhyme with a common vowel, such as "花" (PY: huā; BT: flower) and "她" (PY: tā; BT: she) in "大地 的 泪水 让 笑脸 常 开 不 败 如 **花** 如 **她**" (PY: dà dì de lèi shuǐ ràng xiào liǎn cháng kāi bú bài rú **huā** rú **tā**; IG: land SUB tear let smiling face always bloom NEG fall be like **flower** be like **her**). Some poems rhyme with vowels that are similar with each other when pronounced, such as "过" (PY: guò; IG: past) and "歌" (PY: gē; IG: song) in "世界 踏 着 心 的 琴弦 匆 匆 而 **过** 低 徊 的 心 唱 了 很 久 忧伤 的 **歌**" (PY: shì jiè tà zhe xīn de qín xián cōng cōng ér **guò** dī huái de xīn chàng le hěn jiǔ yōu shāng de **gē**; IG: world step VPART heart SUB string quickly and **pass** linger SUB heart sing ASP very long sad SUB **song**). Some poems rhyme with a common initial consonant,

TABLE 3.6 Frequency of rhymed and unrhymed poems in TT4

Category	Poem No.	Freq.
Rhymed poem	1, 2, 3, 4, 7, 9, 11, 13, 14, 15, 16, 17, 18, 19, 21, 23, 24, 26, 27, 28, 29, 30, 33, 34, 36, 37, 38, 39, 41, 42, 43, 44, 47, 49, 52, 53	36
Unrhymed poem	8, 10, 12, 20, 25, 32, 35, 40, 45, 46, 48, 50, 51	13

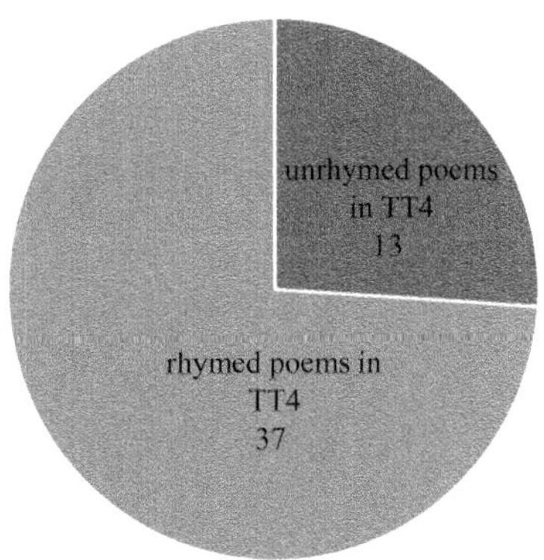

FIGURE 3.4 Percentage of rhymed and unrhymed poems in TT4

such as "泣" (PY: qì; IG: cry) and "去" (PY: qù; IG: go) in "如果 因为 思念 太 阳 而 终 日 哭**泣** 星星 也 将 离 你 而 **去**" (PY: rú guǒ yīn wéi sī niàn tài yang ér zhōng rì kū **qì** xīng xing yě jiāng lí nǐ ér **qù**; IG: if because miss sun then all day cry star also will leave you and go). Further, some poems rhyme with identical Chinese characters, like "自己" (PY: zì jǐ; BT: oneself) in "你 无 法 看到 自己 你 看到 的 是 你 认为 的 自己" (PY: nǐ wú fǎ kàn dào zì **jǐ** nǐ kàn dào de shì nǐ rèn wéi de zì **jǐ**; IG: you no method see self you see SUB be you thought self).

3.3 Summary

In this chapter, we have investigated the choices made on the expression plane of language in the ST and the TTs. As poetry is a specific register that is not only printed in book form but is also possible to be read aloud (see Chapter 5), choices in both graphology and phonology strata were considered in the analysis.

In terms of the graphological analysis, we described the layout patterns in the ST and the four TTs. Also, our description of line breaks was made in accordance with the syntagmatic structures in SFL, and we observed four patterns of line break, viz. participant-process separation, process-participant separation, process-circumstance separation, and clause-clause separation. Figure 3.5 quantifies and summarizes these four kinds of line breaks in the ST and the three TTs except for TT2, where a fixed style has been adopted to arrange the poems in four lines, with each line containing five Chinese characters.

The following comparisons are made. Firstly, the separation of participant from process is not frequently found in the ST, with instances only seen in clauses starting with Vocatives or participants followed by embedded clauses.

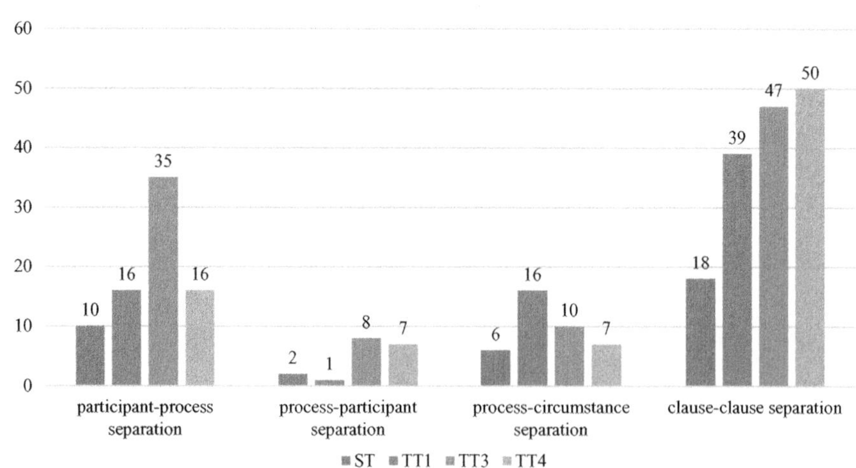

FIGURE 3.5 Frequency of the types of separation in the ST and the TTs

In TT1, more separations of this kind are found, which divide participants that contain more Chinese characters into new lines. The translator of TT3 adopts a unique layout pattern while dividing the lines, according to which more lines are found in a poem. Also, he intentionally chooses to separate participant from process more frequently, with the highest frequency being found among all the TTs. The translator of TT4 chooses a similar layout pattern to that of TT3, with a less frequent occurrence of choosing participant-process separation; moreover, he tends to separate Vocatives, long participants or antithetic patterns into a new line.

Secondly, the frequency of separation of process from participant in the ST and TT1 is not very high. However, in TT3 and TT4, more examples of this kind are found, and the reason is due to the differences between the prose layout in the ST and TT1 and the verse layout characterized with line breaks in TT3 and TT4. The former layout makes it difficult to separate participant from process in the ST and TT1, whereas the latter allows the translators of TT3 and TT4 to separate different grammatical elements into different lines.

Thirdly, separation of process from circumstance is least frequent in the ST, with only six instances; but an increased frequency of this type of separation is seen in the TTs, with frequencies of 8 in TT1, 10 in TT3, and 7 in TT4. In the ST, these separations occur only when phrases or groups are paralleled. However, their occurrences in the TTs have highlighted the circumstances, such as those of Direction, Temporal, Manner, Reason, and Angle.

Fourthly, there is a significant increase in the frequency of clause-clause separation in the TTs, which is related to how downranked clauses, prepositional phrases, bound clauses, and free clauses are separated from the remaining parts of the poems.

The phonological analysis illustrates how Rabindranath Tagore, i.e. the author of the ST, emphasizes emotions and sentiments in the poems rather than the forms or layout patterns. According to Tagore (2016a), despite the form in which a poem is composed, be it prose or verse, with or without rhyme, it is always the emotion that makes it a poem. In TT1 and TT3, Tagore's approach is accepted and taken up by the translators, who follow the phonological pattern in the ST and do not rhyme in their translations. However, by adopting a different view on poetry translation, the translator of TT2 maps his work onto the form of classic Chinese poems, with five characters being arranged in each line. To achieve this goal, various phonological and graphological adjustments were made in TT2 (see also Section 5.4.2). Similarly, the translator of TT4 underscores the effects of rhyme in poetry (Feng 2015, 2019a) in view of which more than half of the poems in TT4 analyzed did rhyme. In TT2 and TT4, such a choice of rhyme in phonology resulted in a large amount of translation shifts or "trade-offs" in lexicogrammar, which will be discussed in Chapter 4.

Note

1 The separations are here described in accordance with the grammatical elements found in the experiential analysis of SFL (see Section 4.2 for experiential analysis from the perspective of process type). Processes are realized by verbal groups and are the central element in the structure of transitivity. Participants, realized by nominal groups, are the elements that are directly involved in the process. Circumstances are not directly involved in the process, and they augment the configuration of process and participants by way of expansion and projection (see Matthiessen 1995; Matthiessen, Teruya & Lam 2010).

4

TRANSLATING ON THE CONTENT PLANE OF LANGUAGE

Lexicogrammatical choices

In this chapter, we examine the choices made on the content plane of language in the ST and the TTs from the perspective of lexicogrammar. Our lexicogrammatical analysis covers both the textual mode of meaning (Sections 4.1 and 4.2) and the experiential mode of meaning (Sections 4.3 and 4.4), involving two lexicogrammatical systems, i.e. THEME and TRANSITIVITY. After the quantitative analysis, we also point out the different types of translation shift and suggest some delicate categories of the shift.

4.1 Analysis of Theme

Characterized as "the element that serves as the point of departure of message," Theme[1] is the textual function that "locates and orients the clause within its context," while the rest of the clause is referred to as Rheme (Halliday & Matthiessen 2014: 89; see Wang 2014; Kim & Matthiessen 2015 for reviews of studies on Theme in translation). In both English and Chinese, three types of Theme are identified, including textual Theme, interpersonal Theme, and topical Theme (for systemic functional descriptions of Mandarin Chinese, see Halliday & McDonald 2004; Li 2007). During the analysis, we frequently found Subject-less clauses in the Chinese TTs, as the Subjects that function as unmarked topical Themes were often omitted in Chinese (Halliday & McDonald 2004). In the present study, such topical Themes in the Subject-less clauses are reinstated with the aim of examining the organization of textual structures. In Example 4.1 from TT2, the Subjects omitted in the second and the third clauses, viz. "飞鸟" (PY: fēi niǎo; IG: flying bird) are analyzed as unmarked topical Themes[2].

EXAMPLE 4.1

飞 鸟 鸣 窗 前，
PY: fēi niǎo míng chuāng qián,
IG: flying bird sing window front,
BT: Flying birds sing in front of the window,
[ø: 飞 鸟] 飞 来
PY: fēi niǎo fēi lái
IG: flying bird fly PV
BT: Flying birds come
[ø: 飞 鸟] 复 飞 去。
PY: fēi niǎo fù fēi qù.
IG: flying bird then fly PV.
BT: flying birds then fly away.

(Adapted from Tagore 1931: 1)

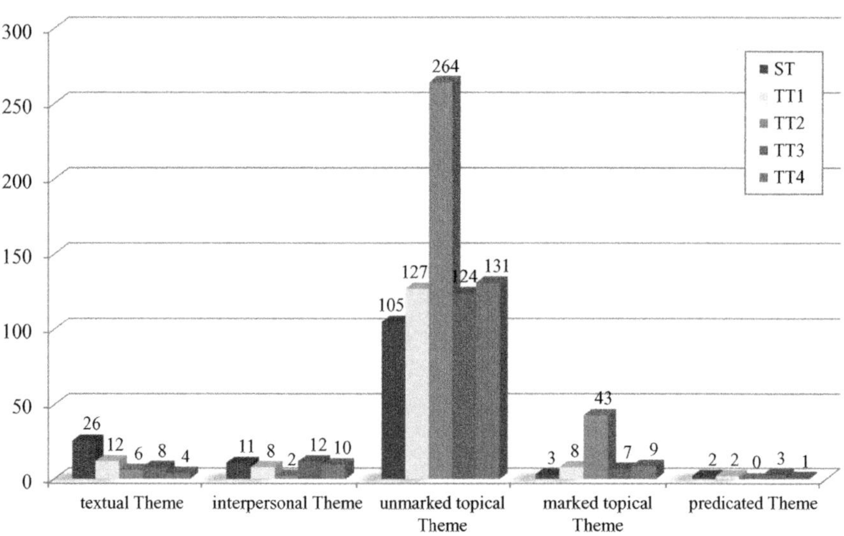

FIGURE 4.1 Frequency of different types of Theme

Following this method, we identify the different types of Themes in the data and calculate their frequencies. Figure 4.1 sketches the occurrence of the Theme choices. From the figure, it is seen that more textual Themes are found in the ST rather than the TTs, while the frequencies in the four TTs range from four to twelve, with TT1 having the largest frequency and TT4 the lowest. In terms of interpersonal Theme, the frequencies in the ST and the TTs are similar, ranging from eight to twelve, except for TT2, which has only two instances of interpersonal Theme. In terms of unmarked topical Theme, the frequency in TT2 is extremely high, while those in the ST and the other TTs are not significantly different. Similarly, in terms of marked topical Themes, the occurrences in TT2 are much larger than those in the ST and the other TTs, while the ST has the smallest number of marked topical Theme. The significantly higher frequency of marked and unmarked topical Themes in TT2 is because the total number of clauses in TT2 almost doubles those in the other TTs. Also, for predicated Themes, their occurrence is not frequent, ranging from zero to three; such choices are not found in TT2 because they are omitted by the translator. From Sections 4.1.1 to 4.1.3, we discuss the findings of Theme analysis in detail.

4.1.1 Analysis of textual Theme

In Table 4.1, we tabulate the frequency of textual Themes in the ST and the TTs. Textual Themes can be realized by continuatives, conjunctions, and conjunctive Adjuncts. Among the three categories, conjunction constitutes the largest proportion, while a limited number of continuatives and conjunctive Adjuncts are found.

The following observations are made. Firstly, few conjunctions are found in the TTs, which is related to the probability nature of using conjunctions in the two languages (cf. Halliday 1991a, 1993; Toury 2004). In English, conjunctions tend to be used to explicitly link the two clause simplexes or clause complexes; while in Chinese, two neighboring clauses are simply juxtaposed, with the logico-semantic relations being left for readers/hearers to infer (cf. Chao 1968; Li & Thompson 1981; Li 2007; Wang 2014). When translating from Chinese to English, translators are likely to add such conjunctions (see Wang & Ma 2020). Conversely, when translating from English to Chinese, fewer conjunctions are found in the TTs.

Example 4.2 shows how conjunctions in the ST are omitted in the TTs, where no conjunction such as "和" (PY: hé; IG: and) and "然后" (PY: rán hòu; IG: and) is used to translate "and" in the ST. In this way, the logico-semantic relationship is changed from explicit in the ST to implicit in the TTs. Also, we find verbal adverbs such as "又" (PY: yòu; IG: again) in TT1 and TT3 and "复" (PY: fù; IG: again) in TT2. These adverbs cohesively link this clause to the previous one and are helpful for readers to understand the logico-semantic relationship between the two clauses (Hu 1994; Peng 2000; cf. Halliday & Hasan 1976).

TABLE 4.1 Frequency of textual Themes

	ST	*TT1*	*TT2*	*TT3*	*TT4*
conjunction	24	11	5	7	4
continuative	0	1	0	1	0
conjunctive Adjunct	0	0	1	0	0
Total	24	12	6	8	4

EXAMPLE 4.2

ST: **and** [ø: stray birds of summer] fly away
TT1: [ø: 夏天 的 飞 鸟] **又** 飞 去 了。
PY: xià tiān de fēi niǎo yòu fēi qù le.
IG: summer SUB flying bird again fly away ASP.
BT: Flying birds of summer again fly away.
TT2: [ø: 飞 鸟] **复** 飞 去。
PY: fēi niǎo fù fēi qù.
IG: flying bird again fly away.
BT: Flying birds again fly away.
TT3: [ø: 夏日 漂泊的 鸟] **又** 飞 走 了
PY: xià rì piāo bó de niǎo yòu fēi zǒu le
IG: summer stray bird again fly away ASP
BT: Stray birds of summer again fly away.
TT4: [ø: 夏日 的 飞 鸟] 消失 在 我 眼 前
PY: xià rì de fēi niǎo xiāo shī zài wǒ yǎn qián
IG: summer SUB flying bird disappear CV my eye front
BT: Flying birds of summer disappear in front of my eyes.
(Adapted from Tagore 1931: 1; 2008: 5; 2010: 2; 2015: 1)

Similar examples of omissions are found in the TTs; the omitted conjunctions include "and," "that," "when," "while," "because," and "if." Among these omissions, six instances of "that" have all been omitted, as it is a conjunction that realizes the hypotactic relationship between clauses in English, and no such conjunction is needed in Chinese (cf. Peng 2000; Li 2007).

Secondly, not all conjunctions as textual Themes in the ST are omitted in the TTs. These conjunctions in the ST mark an enhancing relationship, including "and" (here in the sense of "and then" or "and so," rather than "and also"), "but" (concessive relation), "if," "when," and "because." We find that such conjunctions are often translated in TT1, while none of them is translated in TT3. In Example 4.3, two conjunctions function as textual Themes in the ST, i.e. "if" and "when." The conjunction "if" that reveals the enhancing relation in the ST has been equivalently translated as "如果" (PY: rú guǒ; IG: if) in TT1 and TT4 and "假如" (PY: jiǎ rú; IG: if) in TT3, but is omitted in TT2, where a mood type shift from bound clause in the ST to elemental interrogative in TT2 is observed. The conjunction "when" in the ST is not translated as conjunctions in all the four TTs. Moreover, in TT3 and TT4, we find textual Themes realized by "而" (PY: ér; IG: and), which cohesively link the two clauses and reveal the extending relations explicitly.

EXAMPLE 4.3

ST: **If you shed tears**
when you miss the sun,
TT1: **如果** 错过 了 太阳 时
PY: rú guǒ cuò guò le tài yáng shí
IG: if miss ASP sun time
BT: If you miss the sun,
你 流 了 泪，
PY: nǐ liú le lèi,
IG: you shed ASP tear,
BT: you shed tears,
TT2: 白日 既 西 匿，
PY: bái rì jì xī nì,
IG: sun already west hide,
BT: The sun already hides in the west,
众 星 相 代 明。
PY: zhòng xīng xiāng dài míng.
IG: many stars successively replace light.
BT: many stars replace its light successively.
如何 偏 泪眼，
PY: rú hé piān lèi yǎn,
IG: how just tearful eye,
BT: Why do you just have tearful eyes?
TT3: **假如** 你 为了 思念 太阳
PY: jiǎ rú nǐ wèi le sī niàn tài yáng
IG: if you for miss sun
BT: If you miss the sun,
而 [ø: 你] 落 泪
PY: ér nǐ luò lèi
IG: and you shed tears
BT: and you shed tears.
TT4: **如果** [ø: 你] 因为 思念 太阳
PY: rú guǒ nǐ yīn wéi sī niàn tài yáng
IG: if you because miss sun
BT: If because you miss the sun,
而 [ø: 你] 终 日 哭泣
PY: ér nǐ zhōng rì kū qì
IG: and you all day cry
BT: and you cry all day

(Adapted from Tagore 1931: 1; 2008: 5; 2010: 4; 2015: 6)

In another example, the conjunction "but" functioning as textual Theme in the ST is equivalently translated as "但是" (PY: dàn shì; IG: but) in TT1 (see Example 4.4). However, in TT2, TT3, and TT4, no textual Theme is found and there is no explicit cohesive marker in these three TTs to link the clause with the previous discourse. The translator of TT1 translates such conjunctions equivalently, with all the four occurrences of "but" in the ST being rendered either as "但是" (PY: dàn shì; IG: but), "但" (PY: dàn; IG: but), "而" (PY: ér; IG: and) or "却" (PY: què; IG: but). Comparatively, only one occurrence of "but" is translated in TT3 and TT4, while none of them is translated in TT2. As a result, TT1 has the largest frequency of conjunctions as textual Themes compared to the other three TTs.

Moreover, Example 4.4 reveals a difference between modern Chinese in TT1, TT3, and TT4 as well as classical Chinese in TT2. To equivalently translate the wh- interrogative in the ST in terms of mood type, modal particles are added to the TTs, such as "呢" (PY: ne; IG: MOD) in TT1, "欤" (PY: yú; IG: MOD) in TT2, and "啊" (PY: a; IG: MOD) in TT4. In TT1 and TT4, which are written in modern Chinese, the modal particles are found at the end of the clause; whereas in TT2, which is written in classical Chinese, the particle is seen in the middle of the clause, following the Subject "谁" (PY: shuí; IG: who).

EXAMPLE 4.4

ST: **but** who are you so silent?
TT1: **但是** 你 是 谁 呢，
PY: dàn shì nǐ shì shuí ne,
IG: but you be who MOD,
BT: but who are you
[ø: 你] 那样 沉默 着。
PY: nǐ nà yàng chén mò zhe.
IG: you that silent VPART.
BT: you are silent like that.
TT2: 谁 欤 独 无 言?
PY: shuí yú dú wú yán?
IG: who MOD alone have (NEG) word?
BT: Who has no word?
TT3: 你 是 谁
PY: nǐ shì shuí
IG: you be who
BT: Who are you?
怎么 默不作声

PY: zěn me mò bú zuò shēng
IG: why silent
BT: Why so silent?
TT4: 你 谁 啊,
PY: nǐ shuí a,
IG: you who MOD,
BT: Who are you?
不 说 一 句 话
PY: bù shuō yí jù huà
IG: NEG say one sentence word
BT: You do not say one sentence.

(Adapted from Tagore 1931: 2; 2008: 14; 2010: 13; 2015: 23)

Thirdly, conjunctive Adjuncts are found only in TT2, realized by "及" (PY: jí; IG: when) – a preposition in Chinese that plays a cohesive role (see Example 4.5), which relates the clause to the following one by way of enhancement. In the ST, TT1, and TT4, the poems consist of one clause only. While in TT3, the logico-semantic relationship of enhancement between the two clauses is not marked out explicitly.

EXAMPLE 4.5

ST: God finds himself by creating.
TT1: 上帝 从 创造 中 找到 他自己。
PY: shàng dì cóng chuàng zào zhōng zhǎo dào tā zì jǐ.
IG: God from creation in find himself.
BT: God finds himself from creation.
TT2: 创造 亦 已 成,
PY: chuàng zào yì yǐ chéng,
IG: creation also already complete,
BT: Creation is also already completed,
天帝 匿 无 踪。
PY: tiān dì nì wú zōng.
IG: God hide NEG trace.
BT: God hides himself without any trace.
及 [ø: 天帝] 寻 本来 身,
PY: jí tiān dì xún běn lái shēn,
IG: when God find original body
BT: When God finds his original body

[ø: 本来 身] 却 被 创造 容。
PY: běn lái shēn què bèi chuàng zào róng.
IG: original body but CV creation contain.
BT: but his original body is contained by his creation.
TT3: 上帝 造 了 万物
PY: shàng dì zào le wàn wù
IG: God create ASP everything
BT: God creates everything.
[ø: 上帝] 才 察觉到 他自己
PY: shàng dì cái chá jué dào tā zì jǐ
IG: God VADV realize himself
BT: God then realizes himself.
TT4: 神 在 创造 中 发现 自己
PY: shén zài chuàng zào zhōng fā xiàn zì jǐ
IG: god CV creation in find himself
BT: God finds himself in creation.

(Adapted from Tagore 1931: 3; 2008: 26; 2010: 24; 2015: 46)

4.1.2 Analysis of interpersonal Theme

Table 4.2 tabulates the different realizations of interpersonal Themes, including Vocative, Finite verbal operator, interrogative element, and modal/comment Adjunct. In terms of the total frequency, the largest number of interpersonal Themes are found in TT3 and the smallest number of interpersonal Themes are found in TT2.

Two examples of Vocative markers[3], i.e. "O," are found in the ST, and they are translated variably in the TTs. One of the two Vocative markers is translated equivalently in TT1 (see Example 4.6), while the other is translated equivalently in TT3. In TT2 and TT4, no such equivalence is found. As shown in Example 4.6, "O" is translated as "啊" (PY: a; IG: ah) in TT1, which functions similarly to "哦" (PY: o; IG: oh) and "噢" (PY: o; IG: oh) in Chinese. The Vocative marker here suggests that the poem is addressed to "Beauty" – the

TABLE 4.2 Frequency of interpersonal Themes

	ST	*TT1*	*TT2*	*TT3*	*TT4*
Vocative	5	8	1	10	8
Finite verbal operator	3	—	—	—	—
interrogative element	4	0	1	2	1
modal/comment Adjunct	0	1	0	1	0
Total	11	8	2	12	9

Vocative that functions as the interpersonal Theme in the ST. In this example, we also find the equivalent recreation of this interpersonal Theme in the TTs, including "美 呀" (PY: měi ya; IG: beauty MOD) in TT1, "美 乎" (PY: měi hū; IG: beauty MOD) in TT2, and "美丽" (PY: měi lì; IG: beauty) in TT3, with modal particles such as "呀" (PY: ya; IG: MOD) in modern Chinese and "乎" (PY: hū; IG: MOD) in classical Chinese being used. In TT4, however, the interpersonal Theme "Beauty" in the ST is translated as a topical Theme.

EXAMPLE 4.6

ST: **O** Beauty, find thyself in love, …
TT: **啊**，美 呀，在 爱 中 找 你自己 吧，
PY: a, měi ya, zài ài zhōng zhǎo nǐ zì jǐ ba,
IG: ah, beauty MOD, CV love in find yourself MOD,
BT: Ah Beauty, find yourself in love.
TT2: 美 乎 尔 何 在?
PY: měi hū ěr hé zài?
IG: beauty MOD you where CV?
BT: Beauty, where are you?
爱 中 寻 尔 真。
PY: ài zhōng xún ěr zhēn.
IG: love in find your self.
BT: Find your self in love.
TT3: 美丽 你 要 在 恋爱 中 寻找 自己
PY: měi lì nǐ yào zài liàn ài zhōng xún zhǎo zì jǐ
IG: beauty you need to CV love in find self
BT: Beauty, you need to find yourself in love.
TT4: 美 在 爱 中
PY: měi zài ài zhōng
IG: beauty CV love in
BT: Beauty is in love.

(Adapted from Tagore 1931: 2; 2008: 16; 2010: 15; 2015: 28)

For Vocatives that function as interpersonal Themes in the data, four of them are found in the ST. Also, such Vocatives are added in three of the TTs, except for TT2. As shown in Example 4.7, the Vocative in the ST – "Woman" – is translated as the interpersonal Themes in three of the TTs, namely "妇人" (PY: fù rén; IG: woman) in TT1, "女郎" (PY: nǚ láng; IG: lady) in TT3, and "姑娘" (PY: gū niang; IG: girl) in TT4, whereas the lexical meanings of "Woman" have been slightly changed in TT3 and TT4. Additionally, the translators of TT1, TT3, and TT4 not only retain the interpersonal Theme, but also equivalently recreate the field of exploring, i.e. to express the poet's emotions to the woman. However, by omitting the interpersonal Theme and translating it as a topical Theme, the translator of TT2 has recreated the field of activity as reporting, i.e. to report on how the housekeeper did her job (see Section 5.1).

EXAMPLE 4.7

ST: **Woman**, when you move about in your household service
TT1: **妇人**，你 在 料理 家 事 的 时候，
PY: fù rén, nǐ zài liào lǐ jiā shì de shí hou,
IG: woman you CV do household service SUB time,
BT: Woman, when you are doing your household service,
TT2: 健 妇 日 当 家，
PY: jiàn fù rì dāng jiā,
IG: robust woman day manage family,
BT: A robust woman manages the family every day,
TT3: **女郎** 当 你 在 做 家 事 时
PY: nǚ láng dāng nǐ zài zuò jiā shì shí
IG: lady when you CV do household service time
BT: Lady, when you do household service,
TT4: **姑娘** 你 在 屋子 里 忙
PY: gū niang nǐ zài wū zi lǐ máng
IG: girl you CV room in busy
BT: Girl, when you are busy in the room
(Adapted from Tagore 1931: 3; 2008: 22; 2010: 20; 2015: 38)

Vocatives functioning as interpersonal Themes in the TTs can be added by the translators or translated from Rhemes in the ST. For instance, in Example 4.8, the translators of TT3 and TT4 have each added one Vocative as the interpersonal Theme, namely "心 哪" (PY: xīn na; IG: heart MOD) in TT3 and "心 呐" (PY: xīn na; IG: heart MOD) in TT4. These Vocatives are both translated from "my heart" in the ST, which functions as Vocative but constitutes part of the Rheme. In the four TTs, only TT1 closely follows the Theme/ Rheme pattern in the ST, with the Vocative – "我的 心 呀" (PY: wǒ de xīn ya; IG: my heart MOD) being rendered as part of the Rheme. When these Vocatives are explicitly translated, readers would know whom the poem is addressed to. In TT2, however, no Vocative is found in Theme or Rheme position and the field of activity is changed from enabling to reporting, i.e. from instructing the addressee to perform a certain act to reporting the narrator's mental state (see also Section 5.1).

EXAMPLE 4.8

ST: Listen, my heart, to the whispers of the world…
TT1: 静静地 听，我的 心 呀，
PY: jìng jìng de tīng, wǒ de xīn ya,
IG: silently listen, my heart MOD,
BT: Silently listen, my heart,
听 那 "世界" 的 低语，
PY: tīng nà "shì jiè" de dī yǔ,
IG: listen that "world" SUB murmur,
BT: listen to the world's murmur,
TT2: 静 听
PY: jìng tīng
IG: silently listen
BT: Silently listen
复 静 听，⁴
PY: fù jìng tīng,
IG: again silently listen,
BT: silently listen again,
静 中 呼 我 心。
PY: jìng zhōng hū wǒ xīn.
IG: silence in call my heart.
BT: You call my heart in silence.
TT3: **心 哪** 请 聆 听 天 地 对 你 的 窸窣 细语
PY: xīn na qǐng líng tīng tiān dì duì nǐ de xī sū xì yǔ
IG: heart MOD please listen heaven earth to you SUB rustling murmur
BT: Heart, please listen to the rustling murmur from heaven and earth to you.
TT4: **心 呐** 听 吧…
PY: xīn na tīng ba …
IG: heart MOD listen MOD…
BT: Heart, listen…
(Adapted from Tagore 1931: 3; 2008: 9; 2010: 8; 2015: 13)

Three Finite verbal operators that function as interpersonal Themes are found in the ST. However, as a result of the typological difference between English and Chinese, Finites are not identified in the Chinese TTs (Halliday & McDonald 2004; Li 2007). As shown in Example 4.9, "Do not" functions as the interpersonal Theme in the ST, and the mood type of this clause is imperative: jussive. In TT1, TT3, and TT4, the imperative mood is maintained. These imperatives in Chinese are marked out by "不 要" (PY: bú yào; IG: not do) in TT1 and TT4 as well as "别" (PY: bié; IG: do not) and "要" (PY: yào; IG: do) in TT3, which all function as topical Themes. In TT2, however, the command to the addressees for not blaming the food in the ST has become milder and is changed into a wish.

EXAMPLE 4.9

ST: Do not blame your food
because you have no appetite.
TT1: 不 要 因为 你自己 没 有 胃口，
PY: bú yào yīn wéi nǐ zì jǐ méi yǒu wèi kǒu,
IG: NEG do because yourself not have appetite
BT: Do not because you yourself have no appetite,
而 去 责备 你的 食物。
PY: ér qù zé bèi nǐ de shí wù.
IG: and CV blame your food
BT: and blame your food.
TT2: 病 来
PY: bìng lái
IG: sick CPART
BT: when man is sick
胃 失 调，
PY: wèi shī tiáo
IG: stomach lose balance
BT: the stomach loses balance
转 觉
PY: zhuǎn jué
IG: then feel
BT: then he feels
食 无 味。
PY: shí wú wèi.
IG: food   have (NEG)   taste.
BT: food has no taste.
物 味 何尝 改，
PY: wù wèi hé cháng gǎi,
IG: food taste never change,
BT: Food taste never changes,
愿
PY: yuàn
IG: wish
BT: food wishes
君 无 责备。
PY: jūn wú zé bèi.

IG: you   have (NEG)   blame.
BT: you do not blame.
TT3: 别 怪
PY: bié guài
IG: do (NEG)   blame
BT: Do not blame
食物 不 好 吃
PY: shí wù bù hǎo chī
IG: food not good taste
BT: the food does not taste good
要 怪
PY: yào guài
IG: should blame
BT: You should blame
自己 没 胃口
PY: zì jǐ méi wèi kǒu
IG: yourself   have (NEG)   appetite
BT: yourself has no appetite.
TT4: 没 食欲 的 时候
PY: méi shí yù de shí hou
IG: have (NEG)   appetite SUB time
BT: When you have no appetite,
不 要 责备 你的 食物
PY: bú yào zé bèi nǐ de shí wù
IG: not do blame your food
BT: do not blame your food.

(Adapted from Tagore 1931: 3; 2008: 23; 2010: 21; 2015: 40)

Interrogative elements that function as interpersonal Themes in the ST are never translated equivalently in the TTs. In the English ST, these wh- elements function as both interpersonal Themes and unmarked topical Themes. In the Chinese TT, as observed by Li (2007: 118), "this type of interrogative is structurally characterized by the presence of a question-word in the clause" and the question-word is either a nominal or an adverbial. In most cases, the question elements in Chinese are not given a thematic textual status (cf. Matthiessen 2004). As seen in Example 4.10, "what language," the interpersonal Theme in the ST, is translated as "什么" (PY: shén me; IG: what), "什么 话" (PY: shén me huà; IG: what language), and "哪种 语言" (PY: nǎzhǒng yǔyán; IG: which language) in TT1, TT3, and TT4 respectively, which all function as part of the Rhemes in the TTs. In TT2, no mood type of elemental interrogative is found, with no interrogative element being used.

EXAMPLE 4.10

ST: "What language is thine, O sea?"
TT1: "海 水 呀，你 说 的 是 什么？"
PY: "hǎi shuǐ ya, nǐ shuō de shì shén me?"
IG: "sea water MOD, you say SUB be what?"
BT: "Sea water, what do you say?"
TT2: 无 住 海潮 音，
PY: wú zhù hǎi cháo yīn,
IG: NEG stop tide sound,
BT: The tide sound does not stop,
日 夜 作 疑语。
PY: rì yè zuò yí yǔ.
IG: day night ask question.
BT: it asks question day and night.
TT3: "大海 啊，你 说 的 是 什么 话？"
PY: "dà hǎi a, nǐ shuō de shì shén me huà?"
IG: "sea MOD, you speak SUB be what language?"
BT: "Sea, what is the language you speak?"
TT4: "沧海，你 用 的 是 哪种 语言？"
PY: "cāng hǎi, nǐ yòng de shì nǎ zhǒng yǔ yán?"
IG: "sea, you use SUB be which kind language?"
BT: "Sea, which kind of language do you use?"

(Adapted from Tagore 1931: 2; 2008: 8; 2010: 7; 2015: 12)

Modal/comment Adjuncts that function as interpersonal Themes are not found in the ST, TT2 and TT4. However, such interpersonal Themes are added to TT1 and TT3, which include "请" (PY: qǐng; IG: please) in TT1 and TT3 as well as "难道" (PY: nán dào; IG: MADV) in TT3. As previously illustrated in Example 4.8, "请" (PY: qǐng; IG: please), a politeness marker is added to the imperative clauses in TT1 and TT3 respectively (cf. Chen 1989). In Example 4.11, "难道" (PY: nán dào; IG: MADV), a modal/comment Adjunct is added in TT3 with the purpose of emphasis. The mood type is also changed from declarative in the ST to polar interrogative in TT3, with the speech function being changed from statement to question, which is in fact a rhetorical question that does not require an answer.

EXAMPLE 4.11

ST: you also miss the stars.
TT1: 那么 你 也 要 错过 群 星 了。

PY: nà me nǐ yě yào cuò guò qún xīng le.
IG: then you also will miss group star ASP.
BT: then you will also miss the group of stars.
TT2: 独自 拥 愁城。
PY: dú zì yōng chóu chéng.
IG: alone own sorrow.
BT: you own your sorrow alone.
TT3: **难道** 你 没有 错过 群 星 吗?
PY: nán dào nǐ méi yǒu cuò guò qún xīng ma?
IG: MADV you   have (NEG)   miss group star MOD?
BT: Haven't you really missed the group of star?
TT4: 星星 也 将 离 你
PY: xīng xing yě jiāng lí nǐ
IG: star also will leave you
BT: Star will also leave you
而 去
PY: ér qù
IG: and go
BT: and go.

(Adapted from Tagore 1931: 1; 2008: 5; 2010: 4; 2015: 6)

4.1.3 Analysis of topical Theme

In Table 4.3, we quantify the frequency of topical Themes, including those that conflate with participant, process or circumstance. Also, predicated Themes are found in the data, which involve a particular combination of choices of Theme and information (cf. Li 2007; Halliday & Matthiessen 2014).

Based on the frequencies of topical Themes and their realizations, the following observations are made. Firstly, more participants functioning as topical Themes are found in the TTs, especially in TT2, as a result of the increase in the number of clauses in the TTs. In Example 4.12, there is only one topical Theme in the ST, which is realized by the participant – "life." However, in the

TABLE 4.3 Frequency of topical Themes

	ST	*TT1*	*TT2*	*TT3*	*TT4*
participant	101	128	259	128	128
process	6	7	6	6	5
circumstance	3	4	42	8	11
predicated Theme	2	2	0	3	1
Total	112	141	307	145	145

TTs, we find more topical Themes, especially those realized by participants, such as "生命" (PY: shēng mìng; IG: life) in TT1, "生" (PY: shēng; IG: life) and "厥 值" (PY: jué zhí; IG: its value) in TT2, and "生命" (PY: shēng mìng; IG: life) in TT4. The topical Themes in TT3 are realized by circumstances, i.e. "因着 世间 的 需要" (PY: yīn zhe shì jiān de xū yào; IG: because world SUB need) and "因着 爱" (PY: yīn zhe ài; IG: because love), which form a contrast between the two clauses.

EXAMPLE 4.12

ST: **Life** finds its wealth by the claims of the world, and its worth by the claims of love.

TT1: **生命** 因了 "世界" 的 要求，得到 他的 资产，

PY: shēng mìng yīn le "shì jiè" de yāo qiú, dé dào tā de zī chǎn,

IG: life because world SUB claim obtain his property,

BT: Because of the world's claim, life obtains his property,

[ø: 生命] 因了 爱 的 要求，得到 他的 价值。

PY: shēng mìng yīn le ài de yāo qiú, dé dào tā de jià zhí.

IG: life because love SUB claim obtain his worth.

BT: Because of love's claim, life obtains his worth.

TT2: **生** 因 世 所 需，乃 得 其 资产。

PY: shēng yīn shì suǒ xū, nǎi dé qí zī chǎn.

IG: life because world VPART need, then obtain his property.

BT: Life then obtains his property because of the world's need.

[ø: 生] 若 无 爱 相要，

PY: shēng ruò wú ài xiāng yāo,

IG: life if   have (NEG)   love invitation,

BT: If life has no invitation from love,

厥 值 殊 难 算。

PY: jué zhí shū nán suàn.

IG: its value very hard calculate.

BT: its value is very hard to be calculated.

TT3: **因着 世间 的 需要** 生命 才 成为 财富

PY: yīn zhe shì jiān de xū yào shēng mìng cái chéng wéi cái fù

IG: because world SUB need life become wealth

BT: Because of the world's need, life becomes wealth.

因着 爱 生命 才 变得 有价值

PY: yīn zhe ài shēng mìng cái biàn dé yǒu jià zhí

IG: because love life then become valuable

BT: Because of love, life becomes valuable.

TT4: [ø: 生命] 从 世 所 愿
PY: shēng mìng cóng shì suǒ yuàn
IG: life follow world VPART wish
BT: Life follows the world's wish.
生命 有 了 金钱
PY: shēng mìng yǒu le jīn qián
IG: life have ASP money
BT: Life has money.
[ø: 生命] 从 爱 所 愿
PY: shēng mìng cóng ài suǒ yuàn
IG: life follow love VPART wish
BT: Life follows love's wish.
生命 有 了 金线
PY: shēng mìng yǒu le jīn xiàn
IG: life have ASP golden thread
BT: Life has golden thread.

(Adapted from Tagore 1931: 3; 2008: 20; 2010: 18; 2015: 33)

Secondly, the addition of topical Themes in the TTs is related to how comparisons realized by "like" in the ST is translated. As shown in Example 4.13, "like the longings of the earth" in the ST is analyzed as an Adjunct. In TT1, TT2, and TT3, however, such comparisons are rendered as processes of "如" (PY: rú; IG: be like) in TT1, "若" (PY: ruò; IG: be like) in TT2, and "好像" (PY: hǎo xiàng; IG: be like) in TT4, and the process types are analyzed as relational: identifying. We also note that "如" (PY: rú; IG: be like) and "好像" (PY: hǎo xiàng; IG: be like) are commonly used in modern Chinese, while "若" (PY: ruò; IG: be like) is only seen in TT2 in classical Chinese. In TT4, such comparisons in the ST are often translated in an implicit way, with processes being omitted. According to Example 4.13, the two nominal groups, i.e. "树" (PY: shù; IG: tree) and "大地 的 渴望" (PY: dà dì de kě wàng; IG: earth SUB longing) in TT4 are compared with each other. Although no process is found, it is still analyzed as a clause in this study.

In addition, the translation of "tiptoe" – a circumstance that constitute part of the Rheme in the ST is also related to the additions of topical Themes in the TTs, because it is translated as various processes, including "竖" (PY: shù; IG: erect) from "竖 趾" (PY: shù zhǐ; IG: erect toe) in TT1, "翘企" (PY: qiào qǐ; IG: stand) in TT2, "踮" (PY: diǎn; IG: stand) from "踮 着 脚尖" (PY: diǎn zhe jiǎo jiān; IG: stand VPART tiptoe) in TT3, as well as "踮" (PY: diǎn; IG: stand) from "踮 着 脚" (PY: diǎn zhe jiǎo; IG: stand VPART foot) in TT4.

EXAMPLE 4.13

ST: **The trees**, like the longings of the earth, stand a-tiptoe
[ø: **the trees**] to peep at the heaven.
TT1: 群 树 如 表示 大地 的 愿望 似的，
PY: qún shù rú biǎo shì dà dì de yuàn wàng sì de,
IG: group tree be like express earth SUB wish   as if,
BT: The group of trees are as if expressing the earth's wish,
[ø: **群树**] 竖 趾
PY: qún shù shù zhǐ
IG: group tree erect toe
BT: the group of trees erect their toes,
[ø: **群 树**] 立 着，
PY: qún shù lì zhe,
IG: group tree stand VADV,
BT: the group of trees stand,
[ø: **群 树**] 向 天空 窥望。
PY: qún shù xiàng tiān kōng kuī wàng.
IG: group tree to sky peep.
BT: the group of trees peep to the sky.
TT2: 大地 有 热忱，
PY: dà dì yǒu rè chén,
IG: earth have ardor,
BT: The earth has its ardor,
万 木 意 若 示。
PY: wàn mù yì ruò shì.
IG: many tree mood   be like   show.
BT: The many trees are like showing their mood.
一一 攒 天空，
PY: yī yī cuán tiān kōng,
IG: each gather sky,
BT: Each gathers to the sky,
[ø: **万 木**] 窥望
PY: wàn mù kuī wàng
IG: many tree peep
BT: Many trees peep.
[ø: **万 木**] 以 翘企。
PY: wàn mù yǐ qiào qǐ.
IG: many tree to stand.
BT: Many trees stand.
TT3: 森林 踮 着 脚尖

PY: sēn lín diǎn zhe jiǎo jiān
IG: forest tiptoe VPART tiptoe
BT: Forest walks on tiptoe,
[ø: 森林] 抬着头
PY: sēn lín tái zhe tóu
IG: forest raise VPART head
BT: forest raises its head,
[ø: 森林] 向上 探看
PY: sēn lín xiàng shàng tàn kàn
IG: forest upward look
BT: forest looks upward,
[ø: 森林] 好像是 大地 对 上天 的 思念
PY: sēn lín hǎo xiàng shì dà dì duì shàng tiān de sī niàn
IG: forest   be like   earth to heaven SUB yearning
BT: forest is like the earth's yearning to heaven.
TT4: 树 大地 的 渴望
PY: shù dà dì de kě wàng
IG: tree land SUB yearning
BT: Tree is the land's yearning.
[ø: 树] 踮着 脚
PY: shù diǎn zhe jiǎo
IG: tree tiptoe VPART foot
BT: Tree stands on tiptoe.
[ø: 树] 偷窥 天堂
PY: shù tōu kuī tiān táng
IG: tree peep heaven
BT: Tree peeps into the heaven.

(Adapted from Tagore 1931: 3; 2008: 24; 2010: 22; 2015: 41)

Thirdly, downranked clauses in the ST are often translated as several clauses in the TTs; this method of translation further increases both the frequencies of topical Themes realized by participants and the number of clauses in the TTs. In Example 4.14, the poem in the ST consists of one clause only, while the poem in the four TTs are expanded to five, twelve, six, and five clauses respectively. The minor processes, such as "stops," "nods," and "goes" in the downranked clause complex in the ST – "where the world like a passer-by stops for a moment, nods to me and goes," are all translated as processes in free clauses in the TTs. Also, the circumstance in the downrandked clause complex in the ST, which is realized by "like a passer-by," has been translated as free clauses in the TTs (cf. Example 4.13).

EXAMPLE 4.14

ST: I sit at my window this morning [[[where the world like a passer-by stops for a moment, || nods to me || and goes]]].
TT1: 我 今 晨 坐 在 窗 前，
PY: wǒ jīn chén zuò zài chuāng qián,
IG: I this morning sit CV window front,
BT: I sit in front of the window this morning,
"世界" 如 一 个 过路 的 人 似的，
PY: "shì jiè" rú yí gè guò lù de rén sì de,
IG: world   be like   one MEAS   pass by   SUB person   as if,
BT: The world is like a passer-by,
[ø: "世界"] 停留 了 一会，
PY: "shì jiè" tíng liú le yí huì,
IG: world stop ASP moment,
BT: The world stops for a moment,
[ø: "世界"] 又 走 过去 了。
PY: "shì jiè" yòu zǒu guò qù le.
IG: world then walk away ASP.
BT: The world then walks away.
TT2: 晨兴 百 无 营，
PY: chén xīng bǎi wú yíng,
IG: morning very   have (NEG)   affair,
BT: In the morning I have nothing to do,
坐 我 绮窗 前。
PY: zuò wǒ qǐ chuāng qián.
IG: sit I window front.
BT: I sit in front of the window.
[ø: 绮窗 前] 似 有 行客 过，
PY: qǐ chuāng qián sì yǒu xíng kè guò,
IG: window front seem have traveler pass,
BT: In front of the window a traveler seems passed by,
[ø: 行客] 徘徊
PY: xíng kè pái huái
IG: traveler hesitate
BT: The traveler hesitates
[ø: 行客] 结 我 缘。
PY: xíng kè jié wǒ yuán.
IG: traveler form me ties.
BT: The traveler forms some ties with me.

[ø: 行客] 顾 我
PY: xíng kè gù wǒ
IG: traveler   look at   me
BT: The traveler looks at me.
[ø: 行客] 点头
PY: xíng kè diǎn tóu
IG: traveler nod
BT: The traveler nods.
[ø: 行客] 去，
PY: xíng kè qù,
IG: traveler leave,
BT: The traveler leaves,
[ø: 行客] 一往
PY: xíng kè yì wǎng
IG: traveler   go away
BT: The traveler goes away.
[ø: 行客] 不 复 延。
PY: xíng kè bú fù yán.
IG: traveler not again invite.
BT: The traveler cannot be invited again.
生世 只 如此，
PY: shēng shì zhǐ rú cǐ,
IG: life only such,
BT: Life is only as such,
[ø: 我] 感 之
PY: wǔ gǎn zhī
IG: I feel this
BT: I feel this.
[ø: 我] 辄 喟然。
PY: wǒ zhé wèi rán.
IG: I MOD sigh.
BT: I sigh.
TT3: 今 晨 我 坐 在 窗 前
PY: jīn chén wǒ zuò zài chuāng qián
IG: this morning I sit CV window front
BT: This morning I sit in front of the window
[ø: 我] 看到
PY: wǒ kàn dào
IG: I see
BT: I see
世界 像 一 位 过客

PY: shì jiè xiàng yí wèi guò kè
IG: world   be like   one MEAS passer-by
BT: the world is like a passer-by.
[ø: 世界] 在 我 面前 驻足 片刻
PY: shì jiè zài wǒ miàn qián zhù zú piàn kè
IG: world CV my front stop moment
BT: The world stops in front of me for a moment.
[ø: 世界] 点点头
PY: shì jiè diǎn diǎn tóu
IG: world nod
BT: The world nods.
[ø: 世界] 便 离开 了
PY: shì jiè biàn lí kāi le
IG: world then leave ASP
BT: The world then leaves.
TT4: 我 今 晨 坐 在 窗 前，
PY: wǒ jīn chén zuò zài chuāng qián,
IG: I today morning sit CV window front,
BT: I sit in front of the window this morning.
"世界" 如 一 个 过路 的 人 似的，
PY: "shì jiè" rú yí gè guò lù de rén sì de,
IG: "world"   be like   one MEAS pass-by SUB person   as if,
BT: The world is like one person who pass-by.
[ø: "世界"] 停留 了 一会，
PY: "shì jiè" tíng liú le yí huì,
IG: "world" stop ASP moment,
BT: The world stops for a moment.
[ø: "世界"] 向 我 点点 头
PY: "shì jiè" xiàng wǒ diǎn diǎn tóu
IG: "world" to me nod head
BT: The world nods to me.
[ø: "世界"] 又 走 过去 了。
PY: "shì jiè" yòu zǒu guò qù le.
IG: "world" then walk away ASP.
BT: The world then walks away

(Adapted from Tagore 1931: 2; 2008: 10; 2010: 9; 2015: 16)

Fourthly, in both the ST and the TTs, most processes that function as topical Themes are found in imperative clauses, and these imperatives are translated equivalently in terms of mood in TT1, TT3, and TT4. As shown in Example 4.15, "seat" – a process in the ST functions as the unmarked topical Theme. In TT1, TT3, and TT4, we find processes like "不 要" (PY: bú yào; IG: not do), which signals the imperative mood in the Chinese TTs and are here analyzed as the unmarked topical Themes. In TT2, however, only declaratives are found, while there is no imperative to warn and instruct the addressee. Such a difference is closely related to the variation in terms of the contextual parameter of field, i.e. the change of field of activity from enabling to reporting (see Section 5.1).

EXAMPLE 4.15

ST: **Do not** seat your love upon a precipice because it is high.

TT1: **不 要** 因为 峭壁 是 高的，
PY: bú yào yīn wéi qiào bì shì gāo de,
IG: not do because precipice be high,
BT: Do not because the precipice is high,

而 **让** 你的 爱情 坐 在 峭壁 上。
PY: ér ràng nǐ de ài qíng zuò zài qiào bì shàng.
IG: and let your love sit CV cliff on.
BT: and let your love sit on the cliff.

TT2: **恩爱** 常 相 结，
PY: ēn ài cháng xiāng jié,
IG: love often each other tie,
BT: Love is often tied with each other,

[ø: **恩爱**] 却 缘 平 地
PY: ēn ài què yuán píng dì
IG: love but   be along   flat ground
BT: but love is along the flat ground,

[ø: **恩爱**] 起。
PY: ēn ài qǐ.
IG: love rise.
BT: love rises.

[ø: **恩爱**] 跻 之 绝壁 顶，
PY: ēn ài jī zhī jué bì ding,
IG: love rise it precipice top,
BT: Love rises to the top of the precipice,

[ø: **这**] 只 令 此 情 死。
PY: zhè zhǐ lìng cǐ qíng sǐ.
IG: this only CV this love die.
BT: this only let this love die.

TT3: **不 要** 把 爱情 置放 在 悬崖 上
PY: bú yào bǎ ài qíng zhì fàng zài xuán yá shàng
IG: not do DISP love place CV precipice on
BT: Do not place love on a precipice.

因为 [ø: **悬崖**] 太 高 了

PY: yīn wéi xuán yá tài gāo le
IG: because precipice too high ASP
BT: Because the precipice is too high.
TT4: **不 要** 将 爱 托付 给 悬崖
PY: bú yào jiāng ài tuō fù gěi xuán yá
IG: not do DISP love entrust to precipice
BT: Do not entrust love to precipice,
只是 因为 **悬崖** 够 高 啊
PY: zhǐ shì yīn wéi xuán yá gòu gāo a
IG: only because precipice enough high MOD
BT: only because the precipice is high enough.

(Adapted from Tagore 1931: 2; 2008: 10; 2010: 9; 2015: 15)

Fifthly, processes that function as topical Themes are also seen in declarative clauses in TT2, and such topical Themes are analyzed as marked choices. As previously shown in Example 4.14, the unmarked choice of "坐 我 绮窗 前" (PY: zuò wǒ qǐ chuāng qián; IG: sit I window front) is in fact "我 坐 绮窗 前" (PY: wǒ zuò qǐ chuāng qián; IG: I sit window front), with "坐" (PY: zuò; IG: sit) functioning as a marked topical Theme.

Sixthly, a limited number of circumstances are found in the ST, while more of them are found in the TTs. In general, circumstances are analyzed as marked topical Themes in both the ST and the TTs. As illustrated in Example 4.16, "once," a circumstance, functions as the marked topical Theme in the ST. In the four TTs, marked topical Themes realized by circumstances are also found, including "有一次" (PY: yǒu yí cì IG: once) in TT1, "梦 中" (PY: mèng zhōng; IG: dream in) in TT2, "曾经" (PY: céng jīng; IG: once) in TT3, and "做梦 时" (PY: zuò mèng shí; IG: dream time) in TT4. Among these four choices of circumstances in the TTs, those in TT1 and TT3 are equivalent to the choice in the ST, while those in TT2 and TT4 are translated from "dreamt" in the ST, which functions as part of the Rheme in the first clause.

EXAMPLE 4.16

ST: **Once** we dreamt
that **we** were strangers.
TT1: **有一次,** 我们 梦见
PY: yǒu yí cì, wǒ men mèng jiàn
IG: once, we dream
BT: Once we dream
大家 都 是 不 认识 的。
PY: dà jiā dōu shì bú rèn shi de.

IG: we all be NEG know SUB.
BT: we are all not known to each other.
TT2: **梦 中** [ø: 我们] 曾 相遇，
PY: mèng zhōng wǒ men céng xiàng yù,
IG: dream in we once meet,
BT: In dream we once met,
[ø: 我们] 都 道
PY: wǒ men dōu dào
IG: we all say
BT: we all say
[ø: 我们] 不 相 识。
PY: wǒ men bù xiāng shí.
IG: we not   each other   known.
BT: we are not known to each other.
TT3: **曾经** 在 梦 中 你 我 都 是 陌生人
PY: céng jīng zài mèng zhōng nǐ wǒ dōu shì mò shēng rén
IG: once CV dream in you I both be stranger
BT: Once in dream, you and I are both strangers.
TT4: **做梦 时** 我们 距离 非常 遥远
PY: zuò mèng shí wǒ men jù lí fēi cháng yáo yuǎn
IG: dream time our distance very far
BT: In dream, our distance is very far.

(Adapted from Tagore 1931: 2; 2008: 7; 2010: 6; 2015: 9)

Seventhly, some interrogative elements in both the ST and the TTs are ana-lyzed as circumstances that function as topical Themes. However, these topical Themes are unmarked choices rather than marked, such as "why" in Example 4.17. In the Chinese TTs, equivalents of "why" are often found in the Rhemes, such as "为什么" (PY: wèi shén me; IG: why) in TT1 and TT4, "孰" (PY: shú; IG: which) in TT2, and "怎么" (PY: zěn me; IG: how) in TT3. Such difference in terms of the syntagmatic order of the interrogative elements is due to the typological variation between English and Chinese. Also, we note that "孰" (PY: shú; IG: which) is a lexical choice in classical Chinese and is only found in TT2.

EXAMPLE 4.17

ST: I cannot tell
why this heart languishes in silence.
TT1: 我 不 能 说 出
PY: wǒ bù néng shuō chū
IG: I NEG can speak out

BT: I cannot speak out

这心 为什么 那样 默默地 颓 着。

PY: zhè xīn wèi shén me nà yàng mò mò de tuí zhe.

IG: this heart why that quietly decline VPART.

BT: why this heart declines quietly like that.

TT2: [ø: 我] 收 视

PY: wǒ shōu shì

IG: I focus vision

BT: I focus my vision

[ø: 我] 坐观 心,

PY: wǒ zuò guān xīn,

IG: I   sit by   heart,

BT: I sit by my heart,

[ø: 我] 难 言

PY: wǒ nán yán

IG: I hard tell

BT: I'm hard to tell

心 孰 为。

PY: xīn shú wéi.

IG: heart what do.

BT: what heart does.

TT3: 我 不 知

PY: wǒ bù zhī

IG: I NEG know

BT: I don't know

怎么 说 才 好

PY: zěn me shuō cái hǎo

IG: how say VADV good

BT: how should I say

这 颗 心 不知不觉 在 憔悴

PY: zhè kē xīn bù zhī bù jué zài qiáo cuì

IG: this MEAS heart unconsciously CV wither

BT: this heart withers unconsciously.

TT4: 我 不 知道

PY: wǒ bù zhī dào

IG: I NEG know

BT: I don't know

这 心 为什么 在 寂寞 中 枯焦

PY: zhè xīn wèi shén me zài jì mò zhōng kū jiāo

IG: this heart why CV loneliness in wither

BT: why this heart withered in loneliness.

(Adapted from Tagore 1931: 3; 2008: 22; 2010: 20; 2015: 37)

Eighthly, we find that circumstances can function as unmarked topical Themes in the TTs. For instance, in TT3 from Example 4.18, the circumstance – "在 人 的 心 中" (PY: zài rén de xīn zhōng; IG: CV man SUB heart in) is analyzed as the unmarked topical Theme in the clause, whose process type is existential or relational: existential according to the description in Halliday and McDonald (2004). The existential process is realized by the verbal group "有" (PY: yǒu; IG: be), with "在 人 的 心 中" (PY: zài rén de xīn zhōng; IG: CV man SUB heart in) being the Location and the nominal group "海 的 宁静 大地 的 籁音 和 空 中 的 歌曲" (PY: hǎi de níng jìng dà dì de lài yīn hé kōng zhōng de gē qǔ; IG: sea SUB silence earth SUB heaven sound and air in SUB song) being the Existent. In TT1 and TT4, topical Themes like "人类" (PY: rén lèi; IG: mankind) and "人" (PY: rén; IG: man) are translated equivalently from "Man" in the ST. In TT2, however, the choices of topical Themes are not equivalent to that in the ST, involving various additions of marked topical Themes, such as "惟" (PY: wéi; IG: only), "潜 时" (PY: qián shí; IG: diving time), "逐 时" (PY: zhú shí; IG: chasing time), and "喜 时" (PY: xǐ shí; IG: happy time).

We also note that some lexical choices of nominal groups in TT4 deviate from those in the ST, although these nominal groups do not occupy thematic position. For instance, "noise" and "music" in the ST are rendered as "肉欲" (PY: ròu yù; IG: carnal desire) and "神曲" (PY: shén qǔ; IG: divine song), which have reminded the readers of sex and lust (see also Section 5.2).

EXAMPLE 4.18

ST: But Man has in him the silence of the sea, the noise of the earth and the music of the air.

TT1: 但是 **人类** 却 兼有 了 海 里 的 沉默，地上 的 喧闹，与 空 中 的 音乐。

PY: dàn shì rén lèi què jiān yǒu le hǎi lǐ de chén mò, dì shàng de xuān nào, yǔ kōng zhōng de yīn yuè.

IG: but man but combine ASP sea in SUB silence, earth on SUB noise, and air in SUB music.

BT: But man combines the silence of the sea, the noise of the earth and the music of the air.

TT2: **惟** 人 乃 并兼，

PY: wéi rén nǎi bìng jiān,

IG: only man then combine,

BT: Only man then combines everything,

一**身** 备 众 有；

PY: yì shēn bèi zhòng yǒu;

IG: himself own others have;
BT: Himself owns what others have;
潜时 墨 可 守,
PY: qián shí mò kě shǒu,
IG: diving time convention can stick,
BT: During diving time, man can stick to the convention,
逐时 险 可 走,
PY: zhú shí xiǎn kě zǒu,
IG: running time danger can   rush into,
BT: During running time, man can   rush into danger,
喜时 弦 可 手。
PY: xǐ shí xián kě shǒu.
IG: happy time string can play.
BT: During happy time, man can play the string.
TT3: 但 **在 人 的 心 中** 却 兼 有 海 的 宁静 大地 的 籁 音 和 空 中 的 歌曲
PY: dàn zài rén de xīn zhōng què jiān yǒu hǎi de níng jìng dà dì de lài yīn hé kōng zhōng de gē qǔ
IG: but CV man SUB heart in but combine sea SUB silence land SUB heaven sound and air in SUB song
BT: but in the man's heart, there combines the silence of the sea, the heavenly sound of the land, and the song of the air.
TT4: **人** 同时 拥有 海 的 静寂 地 的 肉 欲 天 的 神 曲
PY: rén tóng shí yōng yǒu hǎi de jìng jì dì de ròu yù tiān de shén qǔ
IG: man simultaneously possess sea SUB silence earth SUB carnal desire sky SUB divine song
BT: Man simultaneously possess the silence of the sea, the carnal desire of the earth, and the divine song of the sky.

(Adapted from Tagore 1931: 3; 2008: 25; 2010: 23; 2015: 43)

In terms of the predicated Themes in the data, two of them are found in the ST and TT1, three are found in TT3, and one is found in TT4. There is no predicated Theme in TT2 because the form of the poetry does not allow the translator to make that choice[5]. As shown in Example 4.19, "It is the tears of the earth," a predicated Theme in the ST, is translated equivalently in TT1 and TT3 with the help of a copula "是" (PY: shì; IG: be) at the beginning of the clause (cf. Li 2007). However, among the two choices of predicated Theme in the ST, the other one has not been translated equivalently in TT1, TT2, and TT4. Thus, we find omissions of predicated Theme in TT1, TT2, and TT4 (see Section 4.2.2).

EXAMPLE 4.19

ST: **It is the tears of the earth** that keep her smiles in bloom.
TT1: 是 "地" 的 泪点，使 她的 微笑 保持 着 青春 不 谢。
PY: shì "dì" de lèi diǎn, shǐ tā de wēi xiào bǎo chí zhe qīng chūn bú xiè.
IG: be "earth" SUB tear, CV her smile keep VADV young not wither.
BT: It is the tear of the earth that keep her smile in young and not withered.
TT2: [ø: 她] 独 坐
PY: tā dú zuò
IG: she alone sit
BT: She sits alone.
意 含 涕，
PY: yì hán tì,
IG: expression contain tear,
BT: Her expression contains tears.
[ø: 她] 欢 来
PY: tā huān lái
IG: she happy MOD
BT: when she is happy,
[ø: 她] 一 展 眉。
PY: tā yì zhǎn méi.
IG: she unfold eyebrow.
BT: she unfolds her eyebrow.
[ø: 涕] 沃 如 华 上 露，
PY: tì wò rú huá shàng lù,
IG: tear fertile   be like   flower on dew,
BT: Her tears are fertile, like dew on a flower,
自 泽 盛 开 枝。
PY: zì zé shèng kāi zhī.
IG: own raindrop   be in bloom   branch.
BT: Her own raindrops are in bloom on the branch.
TT3: 是 大地 的 泪水 让 她的 笑容 开成 花朵
PY: shì dà dì de lèi shuǐ ràng tā de xiào róng kāi chéng huā duǒ
IG: be earth SUB tear let her smile bloom VADV flower
BT: It is the tears of the earth that let her smile bloom into flower.
TT4: 大地 的 泪水 让 笑脸 常 开
PY: dà dì de lèi shuǐ ràng xiào liǎn cháng kāi
IG: earth SUB tear let smiling face often bloom
BT: The tear of the earth let the smiling face often bloom.
[ø: 笑 脸] 不 败
PY: xiào liǎn bú bài
IG: smiling face NEG fade

BT: The smiling face does not fade.

[ø: 笑 脸] 如 花

PY: xiào liǎn rú huā

IG: smiling face   be like   flower

BT: The smiling face is like flower.

[ø: 笑 脸] 如 她

PY: xiào liǎn rú tā

IG: smiling face   be like   her

BT: The smiling face is like her.

(Adapted from Tagore 1931: 1; 2008: 25; 2010: 3; 2015: 4)

TABLE 4.4 Frequency of marked and unmarked topical Themes

	ST	*TT1*	*TT2*	*TT3*	*TT4*
marked topical Theme	3	6	43	6	9
unmarked topical Theme	105	131	264	133	134
Total	108	137	307	139	143

Table 4.4 tabulates the frequencies of unmarked and marked topical Theme. In all of the four TTs, especially TT2, we find an increase in the frequencies of marked topical Theme, which are generally realized by circumstances. Also, we find other conflations with marked topical Themes, such as Complement and process. Example 4.20 shows how Complement – "what you are" functions as a marked topical Theme in the ST. Instead of choosing the Subject "you" as the unmarked topical Theme, "what you are" – the Complement within the interpersonal structure of the clause, is here selected as the marked topical Theme. In TT1, TT3, and TT4, "你" (PY: nǐ; IG: you) functions as the unmarked topical Themes; whereas in TT2, "我 身" (PY: wǒ shēn; my body) and "我 见" (PY: wǒ jiàn; IG: I see) are selected as unmarked topical Themes, which involve translation shifts of Theme substitution (see Section 4.2.3).

EXAMPLE 4.20

ST: **What you are** you do not see,

TT1: 你 看 不 见 你的 真相，

PY: nǐ kàn bú jiàn nǐ de zhēn xiàng,

IG: you see not PV your truth,

BT: You do not see your truth.

TT2: 我 身 不 自 见，

PY: wǒ shēn bú zì jiàn,

IG: my body not self see,
BT: My body cannot see itself,
我 见 非 真相。
PY: wǒ jiàn fēi zhēn xiàng.
IG: I see NEG truth.
BT: What I see is not the truth.
TT3: 你 是 什么 样 的 人
PY: nǐ shì shén me yàng de rén
IG: you be what kind SUB person
BT: What kind of person are you?
你 看 不 见
PY: nǐ kàn bú jiàn
IG: you see not PV
BT: You do not see.
TT4: 你 无法 看到 自己
PY: nǐ wú fǎ kàn dào zì jǐ
IG: you unable see self
BT: You are unable to see yourself.

(Adapted from Tagore 1931: 2; 2008: 11; 2010: 10; 2015: 18)

Processes can also be selected as marked topical Themes. Such examples are only found in TT2, which is written in classical Chinese. In Example 4.21, the Subject of the clause – "海潮 音" (PY: hǎi cháo yīn; IG: tide sound) functions as the Rheme, while "无 住" (PY: wú zhù; IG: NEG stop) – the process of negative polarity serves as the marked topical Theme. In TT1, TT3, and TT4, the dialogic mode in the ST has been equivalently preserved, as these three TTs and the ST are all written in the form of dialogue between human being and the sea (see Section 5.3). Therefore, the topical Themes are all equivalently recreated, as seen in "what language" and "my language" in the ST, "你 说 的" (PY: nǐ shuō de; IG: you say SUB) and "我 说 的" (PY: wǒ shuō de; IG: I say SUB) in TT1 and TT3, and "你 用 的" (PY: nǐ yòng de; IG: you use SUB) and "我 用 的" (PY: wǒ yòng de; IG: I use SUB) in TT4.

EXAMPLE 4.21

ST: "What language is thine, O sea?"
"[ø: My language is] The language of eternal question."
TT1: "海 水 呀，你 说 的 是 什么?"
PY: "hǎi shuǐ ya, nǐ shuō de shì shén me?"
IG: "sea water MOD, you say SUB be what?"
BT: Sea water, what do you say?

"[ø: 我 说 的] 是 永恒的 疑问。"
PY: "wǒ shuō de shì yòng héng de yí wèn."
IG: "I say SUB be eternal question."
BT: What I say is the eternal question.
TT2: **无 住** 海潮 音，
PY: wú zhù hǎi cháo yīn,
IG: NEG stop tide sound,
BT: The tide sound does not stop,
[ø: 海潮 音] 日 夜 作 疑语。
PY: hǎi cháo yīn rì yè zuò yí yǔ.
IG: tide sound day night make question.
BT: the tide sound makes questions day and night.
TT3: "大海 啊，你 说 的 是 什么 话?"
PY: "dà hǎi a, nǐ shuō de shì shén me huà?"
IG: "sea MOD, you say SUB be what language?"
BT: "Sea, what is the language you say?"
"[ø: 我 说 的] 是 问 一 个 永远 不明白的 问题。"
PY: "wǒ shuō de shì wèn yí gè yòng yuǎn bù míng bai de wèn tí."
IG: "I say SUB be ask one MEAS forever unclear question."
BT: "What I say is to ask a forever unclear question."
TT4: "沧海，你 用 的 是 哪 种 语言?"
PY: "cāng hǎi, nǐ yòng de shì nǎ zhǒng yǔ yán?"
IG: "ocean, you use SUB be which kind language?"
BT: "Ocean, which is the language you use?"
"[ø: 我 用 的 是] 永 不 止息 的 探问。"
PY: "wǒ yòng de shì yǒng bù zhǐ xī de tàn wèn."
IG: "I use SUB be never NEG stop SUB question."
BT: "What I use is the never stopped question."

(Adapted from Tagore 1931: 2; 2008: 8; 2010: 7; 2015: 12)

Choices of marked topical Themes can be related to the translators' consideration of the rhymed choices made on the expression plane of language. Such examples are only found in TT4, where rhymed lines are found (see Section 3.2.5). As shown in Example 4.22, the ST, TT1, and TT3 are not rhymed; but in TT4, "人" (PY: rén; IG: man) and "伸" (PY: shēn; IG: stretch) at the end of two lines rhyme with each other. The Complement – "将 灯 背 在 身后 的 人" (PY: jiāng dēng bēi zài shēn hòu de rén; IG: DISP lantern carry CV back SUB man) is analyzed here as the marked topical Theme of the clause. We can consider this choice as a motivated one, as the unmarked textual choice will be "阴影 在 将 灯 背 在 身后 的 人 面 前 延伸" (PY: yīn yǐng zài jiāng dēng bēi zài shēn hòu de rén miàn qián yán shēn; IG: shadow CV DISP lantern carry CV back SUB man face front extend), which is equivalent to the ST in terms of Theme choice.

EXAMPLE 4.22

ST: They throw their shadows before them who carry their lantern on their back.

TT1: 那些 把 灯 背 在 他们的 背上 的 人，把 他们的 影子 投 到 他们 前面 去。

PY: nà xiē bǎ dēng bēi zài tā men de bèi shàng de rén, bǎ tā men de yǐng zi tóu dào tā men qián miàn qù.

IG: those DISP lantern carry CV their shoulder SUB person, DISP their shadow throw CV their front PV.

BT: Those who carry lantern on their shoulder throw their shadow to their front.

TT2: 暮夜 [ø: 人] 笼 灯

PY: mù yè rén lóng dēng

IG: night man carry lantern

BT: At night a man carries a lantern.

[ø: 人] 行，

PY: rén xíng,

IG: man walk,

BT: The man walks,

忽尔 [ø: 人] 背 其 光。

PY: hū ér rén bèi qí guāng.

IG: suddenly man   turn back to   his light.

BT: Suddenly man turns back to his light.

此 身 似 可 匿，

PY: cǐ shēn sì kě nì,

IG: this body seem can hide,

BT: This body seems can be hide.

前 影 故 彰彰。

PY: qián yǐng gù zhāng zhāng.

IG: front shadow so obvious.

BT: So the front shadow is obvious.

TT3: 把 提灯 放 在 后面 的 人 把 阴影 放 在 前面

PY: bǎ tí dēng fàng zài hòu miàn de rén bǎ yīn yǐng fàng zài qián miàn

IG: DISP lantern carry CV back SUB person DISP shadow carry CV front

BT: The person who carries his lantern on his back carries his shadow at his front.

TT4: 将 灯 背 在 身后 的 人 阴影 在 她们 面前 延伸

PY: jiāng dēng bēi zài shēn hòu de rén yīn yǐng zài tā men miàn qián yán shēn

IG: DISP lantern carry CV back SUB person shadow CV their front extend

BT: For the persons who carry their lantern on their backs, their shadows extend to their front.

(Adapted from Tagore 1931: 2; 2008: 13; 2010: 12; 2015: 21)

In Section 4.1, we report on the general frequencies of different Theme choices in the data and discuss some patterns found in the ST and the TTs in quantitative terms. In Section 4.2, we will introduce the different kinds of Theme shift.

4.2 Theme shift

When Theme shift takes place, the translators' thematic choices remain in the textual metafunction and the actual choices in the TTs diverge from those in the ST (Matthiessen 2014b). Table 4.5 shows the delicate types of Theme shift, including Theme addition, Theme omission, and Theme substitution (For more discussions on Theme shift, see Wang 2017; Wang & Ma 2020). In terms of the total occurrence of Theme shift, TT2 has the largest frequency, TT3 and TT4 contribute a large proportion of the shifts, while TT1 has the smallest frequency among all the TTs. From Sections 4.2.1 to 4.2.3, we elaborate on the three kinds of Theme shift in detail.

TABLE 4.5 Different types of Theme shift

Type of theme shift			TT1	TT2	TT3	TT4
Theme addition	textual Theme	conjunction	7	5	1	1
	interpersonal Theme	modal/comment Adjunct	1	0	2	0
		Vocative	4	0	5	5
		interrogative element	0	1	0	0
	topical Theme	participant	28	154	36	40
		process	1	4	2	1
		circumstance	1	29	1	1
Theme omission	textual Theme	conjunction	17	24	17	22
		continuative	1	2	1	2
	interpersonal Theme	Finite verbal operator	3	3	3	3
		interrogative element	4	4	4	3
		Vocative	0	3	1	1
	topical Theme	participant	1	19	6	7
		process	0	4	0	0
		circumstance	0	0	0	0
Theme substitution			17	32	24	28
Total			85	284	102	114

4.2.1 Theme addition

Theme addition means that extra Themes are added to the TTs, including addition of textual Theme, interpersonal Theme, and topical Theme.

4.2.1.1 Addition of textual Theme

As textual Themes can be realized by conjunction, continuative, and conjunctive Adjunct, these three categories have the potential to be added as textual Themes in the TTs. In our data, only conjunctions are added as textual Themes to the TTs. These added conjunctions have explicitly marked out the hypotactic or paratactic relationship between the two adjacent clauses. Different from studies on translation from Chinese to English where various textual Themes are added (e.g. Wang 2017), only a small number of such conjunctions are found here. These conjunctions include "那么" (PY: nà me; IG: then) and "而" (PY: ér; IG: and) in TT1, "如" (PY: rú; IG: if), "而" (PY: ér; IG: and), "及" (PY: jí; IG: when), and "因" (PY: yīn; IG: because) in TT2, "若" (PY: ruò; IG: if) in TT3, and "然后" (PY: rán hòu; IG: and) in TT4.

In Example 4.23, "及" (PY: jí; IG: when) functions as a textual Theme in TT2. The clause "及 寻 本来 身" (PY: jí xún běn lái shēn; IG: when   look for original body) is a bound one, which is hypotactically related to the preceding clause – "却 被 创造 容" (PY: què bèi chuàng zào róng; IG: but PASS creation contain), and the logico-semantic relation between the two clauses is that of enhancing, as the conjunction "及" (PY: jí; IG: when) reflects the sequence of time. This logico-semantic relation is not found in the ST and is added here in TT2. The poem in the ST consists of one clause only and is translated equivalently as one clause in both TT1 and TT4. In TT3, however, two clauses are used to translate the poem, involving the addition of a logico-semantic type, and the logical connector is omitted.

EXAMPLE 4.23

ST: God finds himself by creating.
TT1: 上帝 从 创造 中 找到 他自己。
PY: shàng dì cóng chuàng zào zhōng zhǎo dào tā zì jǐ.
IG: God from creation in find himself.
BT: God finds himself from creation.
TT2: 创造 亦 已 成，
PY: chuàng zào yì yǐ chéng,
IG: creation also already complete,

BT: Creation has already been completed,
天帝 匿 无 踪。
PY: tiān dì nì wú zōng.
IG: God hide NEG trace.
BT: God hides his trace.
及 寻 本来 身,
PY: jí xún běn lái shēn,
IG: when look for original body,
BT: When he looks for his original body
[ø: 本来 身] 却 被 创造 容。
PY: běn lái shēn què bèi chuàng zào róng.
IG: original body but PASS creation contain.
BT: but his original body is contained by creation.
TT3 上帝 造 了 万物
PY: shàng dì zào le wàn wù
IG: God create ASP everything
BT: God created everything.
[ø: 上帝] 才 察觉 到 他自己
PY: shàng dì cái chá jué dào tā zì jǐ
IG: God then realize PV himself
BT: God then realized himself.
TT4: 神 在 创造 中 发现 自己
PY: shén zài chuàng zào zhōng fā xiàn zì jǐ
IG: God CV creation in find himself
BT: God finds himself in creation.

(Adapted from Tagore 1931: 3; 2008: 26; 2010: 24; 2015: 46)

4.2.1.2 Addition of interpersonal Theme

In terms of interpersonal Themes, modal/comment Adjuncts, Vocatives and interrogative elements are added to the TTs, with a limited amount of such additions being found in the data.

Additions of modal/comment Adjuncts as interpersonal Themes are found in TT1 and TT3, including "请" (PY: qǐng; IG: please) in TT1, "难道" (PY: nán dào; IG: MADV) and "请" (PY: qǐng; IG: please) in TT3. We note that "请" (PY: qǐng; IG: please) is added to imperatives in both TT1 and TT3. The addition of "难道" (PY: nán dào; IG: MADV) in TT3 is further related to the mood shift from declarative in the ST to polar interrogative in TT3 (see Example 4.11); whereas in TT1, TT2, and TT4, the declarative mood is equivalently translated.

For Vocatives added as interpersonal Themes in the TTs, they are only found in TT1, TT3, and TT4. These Vocatives signal the addressee of the poem and are translated from the Rhemes in the ST, but no Vocative is added in TT2, as most poems in TT2 report the events and goings-on rather than to be addressed to a certain addressee of the poem.

Only one occurrence of the addition of interrogative element as interpersonal Theme is found. As shown in Example 4.24, the added interpersonal Theme – "如何" (PY: rú hé; IG: why) is from an elemental interrogative clause in TT2. Similar to "为什么" (PY: wèi shén me; IG: why), "如何" (PY: rú hé; IG: why) is here used to initiate a question. Also, we find that the projected clause in the ST – "My dear, dear sister" is omitted in TT2, but it is equivalently translated in the other three TTs as minor clauses.

EXAMPLE 4.24

ST: the moon rises,
and the glass lamp, with a bland smile, calls her,
"My dear, dear sister."
TT1: 但 当 明月 出来 时,
PY: dàn dāng míng yuè chū lái shí,
IG: but when moon appear time,
BT: But when the moon appears,
玻璃 灯 却 温和地 微笑 着,
PY: bō li dēng què wēn hé de wēi xiào zhe,
IG: glass lamp yet blandly smile VPART,
BT: the glass lamp yet blandly smiles,
叫 明月 为——
PY: jiào míng yuè wéi
IG: call moon as
BT: calls the moon as
"我 亲爱的, 亲爱的 姊姊。"
PY: "wǒ qīn ài de, qīn ài de zǐ zi."
IG: "my dear, dear sister."
BT: "My dear dear sister."
TT2: 如何 明 月 来,
PY: rú hé míng yuè lái,
IG: why bright moon come,
BT: why when the bright moon comes,
[ø: 玻璃 灯] 暗然
PY: bō li dēng àn rán
IG: glass lamp eclipsed
BT: the glass lamp becomes eclipsed,
[ø: 玻璃 灯] 乃 低 首。
PY: bō li dēng nǎi dī shǒu.

IG: glass lamp then lower head.
BT: the glass lamp then lowers his head.
TT3: 当 月亮 升起 时
PY: dāng yuè liang shēng qǐ shí
IG: when moon rise time
BT: When the moon rises,
玻璃 灯 媚笑着 对着 月亮 说
PY: bō li dēng mèi xiào zhe duì zhe yuè liang shuō
IG: glass lamp obsequiously to moon say
BT: the glass lamp obsequiously says to the moon,
我 亲爱的 亲爱的 姐姐
PY: wǒ qīn ài de qīn ài de jiě jie
IG: my dear dear sister
BT: my dear dear sister
TT4: 夜 来
PY: yè lái
IG: night come
BT: Night comes,
月 升
PY: yuè shēng
IG: moon rise
BT: the moon rises,
玻璃 灯 满脸 笑容
PY: bō li dēng mǎn liǎn xiào róng
IG: glass lamp face smile
BT: the glass lamp's face is filled with smile
"我 亲爱的，亲爱的 姐妹。"
PY: "wǒ qīn ài de, qīn ài de jiě mèi."
IG: "my dear, dear sister."
BT: "My dear dear sister."

(Adapted from Tagore 1931: 4; 2008: 30; 2010: 28; 2015: 53)

4.2.1.3 Addition of topical Theme

For topical Themes added to the TTs, they are either participant, process, or circumstance. Most additions are participants and most of them are added to TT2. The following observations can be made in terms of the addition of participants as topical Themes.

Firstly, downranked clauses in the ST tend to be translated as more clauses in the TTs, as a result of which more topical Themes added. In Example 4.25, the downranked or embedded clause in the ST – "that answers the storms" has been translated as additional clauses in all the four TTs, with additions of topical Themes being found, including "我们" (PY: wǒ men; IG: we) in TT1 and TT3 as well as "树 树" (PY: shù shù; IG: tree tree) in TT2. A marked topical Theme realized by a circumstance, i.e. "对 狂 风 啊" (PY: duì kuáng fēng a; IG: to fierce wind MOD) is found in TT4, which is due to the translator's concern of rhyming "沙" (PY: shā; IG: rustle) with "话" (PY: huà; IG: word).

EXAMPLE 4.25

ST: We, the rustling leaves, have a voice [[that answers the storms]],
TT1: 我们，萧萧的 树叶，都 有 声响，
PY: wǒ men, xiāo xiāo de shù yè, dōu yǒu shēng xiǎng,
IG: we rustling leaf all have sound,
BT: We rustling leaves all have sound,
[ø: 我们] 回答 那 暴风雨，
PY: wǒ men huí dá nà bào fèng yǔ,
IG: we answer that storm,
BT: we answer that storm,
TT2: 树 树 迎 风 雨，
PY: shù shù yíng fēng yǔ,
IG: tree tree greet wind rain,
BT: The trees greet the wind and rain.
[ø: 树 树] 萧萧 声 互 答。
PY: shù shù xiāo xiāo shēng hù dá.
IG: tree tree rustling sound   each other   answer.
BT: The trees answers each other with rustling sounds.
TT3: 我们 这些 叶子 用 窸窣的 声音
PY: wǒ men zhè xiē yè zi yòng xī sū de shēng yīn
IG: we these leaf use rustling sound
BT: We leaves use rustling sound,
[ø: 我们] 来 回答 暴风雨
PY: wǒ men lái huí dá bào fèng yǔ
IG: we to answer storm
BT: we answer the storm.
TT4: 我们 是 沙沙 作 响 的 叶子
PY: wǒ men shì shā shā zuò xiǎng de yè zi
IG: we be rustling make sound SUB leaf
BT: We are the rustling leaves.
对 狂 风 啊 我们 沙沙
PY: duì kuáng fēng a wǒ men shā shā
IG: to fierce wind MOD we rustle
BT: To the fierce wind, we rustle.

(Adapted from Tagore 1931: 2; 2008: 14; 2010: 13; 2015: 23)

Secondly, when translating similes that compare one thing with another in the ST, additional clauses are found in the analysis, leading to additions of topical Themes realized by participants. For instance, in Example 4.26, "like a hill stream among its pebbles" in the ST is not analyzed as a clause because no process such as "be like" is found. However, in the four TTs, we find equivalents of the relational: identifying process of "be like" being translated, including "正如" (PY: zhèng rú; IG: be like) in TT1 and TT2, "好像" (PY: hǎo xiàng; IG: be like) in TT3, and "像" (PY: xiàng; IG: be like) in TT4. In TT1 and TT2, the additions of the relational: identifying process have led to the increase of topical Themes realized by participants, i.e. "你的 手足" (PY: nǐ de shǒu zú; IG: your limb) in TT1 and "语 喁喁" (PY: yǔ yú yú; IG: talk   low voice) in TT2. In TT3 and TT4, we find alterations of process type from material process realized by "sing" in the ST to relational: identifying realized by "好像" (PY: hǎo xiàng; IG: be like) and "像" (PY: xiàng; IG: be like) in TT3 and TT4. Therefore, no addition of topical Theme is found in TT3 and TT4.

EXAMPLE 4.26

ST: Woman, when you move about in your household service
your limbs sing like a hill stream among its pebbles.
TT1: 妇人，你 在 料理 家事 的 时候，
PY: fù rén, nǐ zài liào lǐ jiā shì de shí hou,
IG: woman, you CV manage housework SUB time,
BT: Woman, when you manage housework,
你的 手足 歌唱 着，
PY: nǐ de shǒu zú gē chàng zhe,
IG: your limb sing VPART
BT: you limbs sing,
[ø: 你的 手足] 正如 山 间 的 溪 水 歌唱 着 在 小石 中 流过。
PY: nǐ de shǒu zú zhèng rú shān jiān de xī shuǐ gē chàng zhe zài xiǎo shí zhōng liú guò.
IG: your limb just   be like   hill between SUB stream water sing VPART CV pebble in pass.
BT: your limbs are just like stream water between hills passing pebbles.
TT2: 健妇 日 当家，
PY: jiàn fù rì dāng jiā,
IG: diligent woman day manage house,
BT: Diligent woman manages the house everyday,
唇边 语 喁喁。
PY: chún biān yǔ yú yú.
IG: lip talk   low voice.

BT: her lips talk in a low voice.
[ø: 语 喁喁] 正 如 山涧 鸣，
PY: yǔ yú yú zhèng rú shān jiàn míng,
IG: talk   low voice   just   be like   stream singing,
BT: The talk in a low voice is just like stream singing,
[ø: 山涧] 流过 小 石 中。
PY: shān jiàn liú guò xiǎo shí zhōng.
IG: stream pass small stone in.
BT: the stream passes the small stone.
TT3: 女郎 当 你 在 做 家事 时
PY: nǚ láng dāng nǐ zài zuò jiā shì shí
IG: lady when you CV do housework time
BT: Lady, when you do housework,
你的 手脚 就 好像 山溪 在 卵石 间 游唱
PY: nǐ de shǒu jiǎo jiù hǎo xiàng shān xī zài luǎn shí jiān yóu chàng
IG: your limb just   be like   stream CV pebble between sing
BT: your limbs are just like the stream singing between pebbles.
TT4: 姑娘 你 在 屋子 里 忙
PY: gū niang nǐ zài wū zi lǐ máng
IG: girl you CV room in busy
BT: Girl, you are busy in the room,
你的 手臂 像 泉水 在 山 石 间 流淌
PY: nǐ de shǒu bì xiàng quán shuǐ zài shān shí jiān liú tǎng
IG: your limb   be like   stream CV mountain rock between flow
BT: your limbs are like the stream flowing between mountain rocks.
(Adapted from Tagore 1931: 3; 2008: 22; 2010: 20; 2015: 38)

Thirdly, in order to map the translation of *Stray Birds* onto the form of classical Chinese poetry, the translator of TT2 has added a very large number of clauses, resulting in the additions of topical Themes. In terms of the frequency of participants added as topical Themes, 154 of them are found in TT2, representing four or five times of their frequency in the other three TTs (see Table 4.5). In Example 4.27, three clauses are observed in the ST and TT4, four in TT1 and TT3, and 14 in TT2. We find that ten clauses are added to TT2. The first two topical Themes in the ST, i.e. "my heart," are translated equivalently as "我 心" (PY: wǒ xīn; IG: my heart) in TT2, and the third topical Theme in the ST, i.e. "I" is replaced by "伊" (PY: yī; IG: she). The other 11 topical Themes, which are realized by two participants and nine circumstances, are added by the translator of TT2, including "茫茫 人 海 中" (PY: máng máng rén hǎi zhōng; IG: vast people sea in), "我 心" (PY: wǒ xīn; IG: my heart), "岸边" (PY: àn biān; IG: bank), "题语" (PY: tí yǔ; IG: signature), and "伊"

(PY: yī; IG: she). To recreate a classical poem, the translator of TT2 has to make various changes to the experiential meaning (see Section 4.3 and 4.4 for more discussions). In TT1, one topical Theme "我的 心" (PY: wǒ de xīn; IG: my heart) is added. In TT3, there are two substitutions of topical Themes and one addition. In TT4, equivalence of topical Themes is maintained.

EXAMPLE 4.27

ST: My heart beats her waves at the shore of the world
and [ø: my heart] writes upon it her signature in tears with the words,
"I love thee."
TT1: 我的 心 冲激 着 她的 波浪
PY: wǒ de xīn chōng jī zhe tā de bō làng
IG: my heart beat VPART her wave
BT: My heart beats her waves,
[ø: 我的 心] 在 "世界" 的 海岸 上，蘸 着 眼泪
PY: wǒ de xīn zài "shì jiè" de hǎi àn shàng, zhàn zhe yǎn lèi
IG: my heart CV "world" SUB shore on, dip VPART tear
BT: my heart dips her tears at the shore of the world,
[ø: 我的 心] 在 上边 写 着 她的 题记：
PY: wǒ de xīn zài shàng biān xiě zhe tā de tí jì:
IG: my heart CV on write VPART her signature:
BT: my heart writes her signature on it:
"我 爱 你。"
PY: "wǒ ài nǐ."
IG: "I love you."
BT: I love you.
TT2: 我 心 冲
PY: wǒ xīn chōng
IG: my heart dash
BT: My heart dashes
[ø: 我 心] 以 动，为 伊 心 上 波。
PY: wǒ xīn yǐ dòng, wèi yī xīn shàng bō.
IG: my heart to beat, for her heart on ripple.
BT: my heart beats for the ripple on her heart.
茫茫 人 海 中，[ø: 我 心] 着 岸
PY: máng máng rén hǎi zhōng, wǒ xīn zhuó àn
IG: vast people sea in, my heart hit shore
BT: In the vast sea of people, my heart hits the shore
[ø: 我 心] 潜
PY: wǒ xīn qián

IG: my heart dive

BT: my heart dives,

[ø: 我 心] 相 摩。

PY: wǒ xīn xiāng mó.

IG: my heart VADV rub.

BT: my heart rubs it.

岸边 似 有 题，

PY: àn biān sì yǒu tí,

IG: bank seem have signature,

BT: At the bank there seems to be signature,

题语 复 如何?

PY: tí yǔ fù rú hé?

IG: signature then what?

BT: what is then the signature?

[ø: 题语] 直 道 伊 心 曲，

PY: tí yǔ zhí dào yī xīn qǔ,

IG: signature directly tell her heart melody,

BT: The signature directly tells the melody of her heart,

[ø: 伊] 爱 我

PY: yī ài wǒ

IG: she love me

BT: she loves me

[ø: 伊] 了 无 他。

PY: yī liǎo wú tā.

IG: she completely   have (NEG)   him

BT: She completely does not have him in her heart.

[ø: 我 心] 不 假 笔 与 墨，

PY: wǒ xīn bù jiǎ bǐ yǔ mò,

IG: my heart NEG use pen and ink,

BT: My heart does not use pen and ink,

[ø: 我 心] 亦 弗 琢 与 磨。

PY: wǒ xīn yì fú zhuó yǔ mó.

IG: my heart also   need (NEG)   polish and ponder.

BT: my heart also does not need polish and ponder.

[ø: 我 心] 惟 将 情 蘸 泪，

PY: wǒ xīn wéi jiāng qíng zhàn lèi,

IG: my heart only DISP love dip tear,

BT: My heart only dips love in tears,

[ø: 我 心] 大书 滋 滂沱。

PY: wǒ xīn dà shū zī páng tuó.

IG: my heart write more pouring.

BT: my heart writes with more pouring tears.

TT3: 我 心 中 的 浪潮 冲拍 着 这 世界
PY: wǒ xīn zhōng de làng cháo chōng pāi zhe zhè shì jiè
IG: my heart in SUB wave beat VPART this world
BT: The waves in my heart beats this world,
[ø: 我 心 中 的 浪潮] 用 泪水 签名 在 海岸
PY: wǒ xīn zhōng de làng cháo yòng lèi shuǐ qiān míng zài hǎi àn
IG: my heart in SUB wave use tear sign CV shore
BT: the waves in my heart signs at the shore with tears,
[ø: 我 心 中 的 浪潮] 写 下 的 尽 是
PY: wǒ xīn zhōng de làng cháo xiě xià de jìn shì
IG: my heart in SUB wave write down SUB all be
BT: All the waves in my heart write down is
我 爱 你
PY: wǒ ài nǐ
IG: I love you
BT: I love you.
TT4: 我的 心 起伏 在 尘世 的 岸边
PY: wǒ de xīn qǐ fú zài chén shì de àn biān
IG: my heart fluctuate CV world SUB bank
BT: My heart fluctuates at the bank of the world,
[ø: 我的 心] 用 泪水 签下 印记
PY: wǒ de xīn yòng lèi shuǐ qiān xià yìn jì
IG: my heart with tear sign mark
BT: my heart signs its marks with tears
"我 爱 你"
PY: "wǒ ài nǐ"
IG: "I love you"
BT: "I love you."

(Adapted from Tagore 1931: 3; 2008: 17; 2010: 16; 2015: 29)

Fourthly, to create his own style of translation, the translator of TT4 has added a large number of topical Themes, especially those realized by participants. In Example 4.28, the translator of TT4 tries to establish a contrast between the two stanzas, with one focusing on "夏日 的 飞 鸟" (PY: xià rì de fēi niǎo; IG: summer SUB flying bird) and the other on "秋天 的 黄 叶" (PY: qiū tiān de huáng yè; IG: autumn SUB yellow leaf) (see Figure 4.2). In order to do so, clauses that are not found in the ST are added, including "[ø: 夏日 的 飞 鸟] 笑" (PY: xià rì de fēi niǎo xiào; IG: summer SUB flying bird laugh), "[ø: 夏日 的 飞 鸟] 翩跹" (PY: xià rì de fēi niǎo xiào piān xiān; IG: summer SUB flying bird flutter), "[ø: 秋天 的 黄 叶] 无 笑" (PY: qiū tiān de huáng yè wú xiào; IG: autumn SUB yellow leaf have [NEG] laugh) and "[ø: 秋天 的 黄 叶] 无 翩跹" (PY: qiū tiān de huáng yè wú piān xiān; IG: autumn SUB yellow

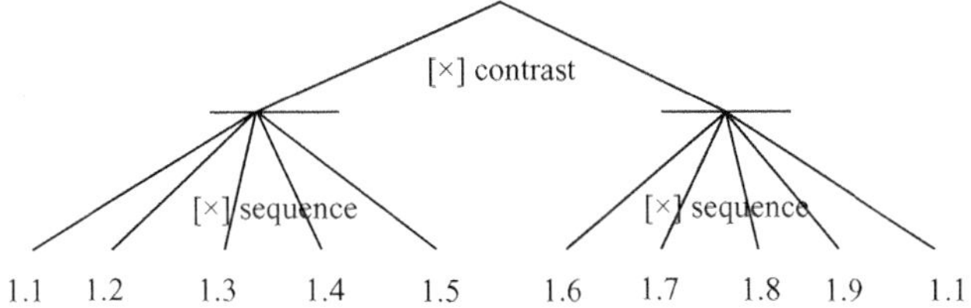

FIGURE 4.2 An RST analysis of TT4 in Example 4.28

leaf   have [NEG]   laugh fluttering). As a result of such additions, various topical Themes realized by the participants are added. In TT3, the addition of one topical Theme realized by "秋天 的 黄 叶" (PY: qiū tiān de huáng yè; IG: autumn SUB yellow leaf) is also found in the last clause, which is translated from "with a sigh" – a prepositional phrase in the ST.

EXAMPLE 4.28

ST: Stray birds of summer come to my window
[ø: stray birds of summer] to sing
and [ø: stray birds of summer] fly away.
And yellow leaves of autumn, <<which have no songs,>> flutter
which have no songs
and [ø: yellow leaves of autumn] fall there with a sigh.
TT1: 夏天 的 飞 鸟，飞 到 我 窗 前
PY: xià tiān de fēi niǎo, fēi dào wǒ chuāng qián
IG: summer SUB flying bird, fly to my window front
BT: Flying birds of summer fly to the front of my window,
[ø: 夏天 的 飞 鸟] 唱歌，
PY: xià tiān de fēi niǎo chàng gē,
IG: summer SUB flying bird sing,
BT: flying birds of summer sing,
[ø: 夏天 的 飞 鸟] 又 飞 去 了。
PY: xià tiān de fēi niǎo yòu fēi qù le.
IG: summer SUB flying bird then fly away ASP.
BT: flying birds of summer then fly away.
秋天 的 黄 叶，它们 没 有 什么 可 唱，
PY: qiū tiān de huáng yè, tā men méi yǒu shén me kě chàng,
IG: autumn SUB yellow leaf, they not have what can sing,
BT: Yellow leaves of autumn, they have nothing to sing,
[ø: 秋天 的 黄 叶] 只 叹息 一 声，
PY: qiū tiān de huáng yè zhǐ tàn xī yì shēng,
IG: autumn SUB yellow leaf only sigh one sound,

BT: yellow leaves of autumn only sigh for once,

[ø: 秋天 的 黄 叶] 飞落 在 那里。

PY: qiū tiān de huáng yè fēi luò zài nà lǐ.

IG: autumn SUB yellow leaf drop CV there.

BT: yellow leaves of autumn drop there.

TT2: 飞 鸟 鸣 窗 前,

PY: fēi niǎo míng chuāng qián,

IG: flying bird sing window front,

BT: Flying birds sing in front of the window,

[ø: 飞 鸟] 飞来

PY: fēi niǎo fēi lái

IG: flying bird come

BT: flying birds come,

[ø: 飞 鸟] 复 飞去。

PY: fēi niǎo fù fēi qù.

IG: flying bird then go.

BT: flying irds then go.

红 叶 了 无 言,

PY: hóng yè liǎo wú yán,

IG: red leaf completely have (NEG) word,

BT: Red leaves have completely no words,

[ø: 红 叶] 飞落

PY: hóng yè fēi luò

IG: red leaf drop

BT: red leaves drop,

[ø: 红 叶] 知 何处。

PY: hóng yè zhī hé chù.

IG: red leaf know where.

BT: red leaves does not know where.

TT3: 夏日 漂泊的 鸟 飞 到 我的 窗 前

PY: xià rì piāo bó de niǎo fēi dào wǒ de chuāng qián

IG: summer stray bird fly to my window front

BT: Stray birds of summer fly to the front of my window,

[ø: 夏日 漂泊的 鸟] 唱歌

PY: xià rì piāo bó de niǎo chàng gē

IG: summer stray bird sing

BT: stray birds of summer sing,

[ø: 夏日 漂泊的 鸟] 又 飞走 了

PY: xià rì piāo bó de niǎo yòu fēi zǒu le

IG: summer stray bird then fly away ASP

BT: stray birds of summer then fly away.

秋天 的 黄 叶 它 无歌 可 唱

PY: qiū tiān de huáng yè tā wú gē kě chàng

IG: autumn SUB yellow leaf it no song can sing
BT: Yellow leaves of autumn, it can sing no song,
[ø: 秋天 的 黄 叶] 抖动着 坠落
PY: qiū tiān de huáng yè dǒu dòng zhe zhuì luò
IG: autumn SUB yellow leaf tremblingly drop
BT: yellow leaves of autumn drop tremblingly,
[ø: 秋天 的 黄 叶] 触 地
PY: qiū tiān de huáng yè chù dì
IG: autumn SUB yellow leaf touch ground
BT: yellow leaves of autumn touch the ground
[ø: 秋天 的 黄叶] 一 声 叹息
PY: qiū tiān de huáng yè yì shēng tàn xī
IG: autumn SUB yellow leaf one sound sigh
BT: yellow leaves of autumn sigh for once.
TT4: 夏日 的 飞 鸟 来 到 我 窗 前
PY: xià rì de fēi niǎo lái dào wǒ chuāng qián
IG: summer SUB flying bird come to my window front
BT: Flying birds of summer come to the front of my window,
[ø: 夏日 的 飞 鸟] 歌
PY: xià rì de fēi niǎo gē
IG: summer SUB flying bird sing
BT: flying birds of summer sing,
[ø: 夏日 的 飞 鸟] 笑
PY: xià rì de fēi niǎo xiào
IG: summer SUB flying bird laugh
BT: flying birds of summer laugh,
[ø: 夏日 的 飞 鸟] 翩跹
PY: xià rì de fēi niǎo piān xiān
IG: summer SUB flying bird flutter
BT: flying birds of summer flutter,
[ø: 夏日 的 飞 鸟] 消失 在 我 眼前
PY: xià rì de fēi niǎo xiāo shī zài wǒ yǎn qián
IG: summer SUB flying bird disappear CV my front
BT: flying birds of summer disappear in front of me.
秋 天 的 黄 叶 一 直 在 窗 前
PY: qiū tiān de huáng yè yì zhí zài chuāng qián
IG: autumn SUB yellow leaf always CV window front
BT: Yellow leaves of autumn are always in front of the window,
[ø: 秋天 的 黄 叶] 无 歌
PY: qiū tiān de huáng yè wú gē
IG: autumn SUB yellow leaf   have (NEG)   song
BT: yellow leaves of autumn have no song,
[ø: 秋天 的 黄 叶] 无 笑

PY: qiū tiān de huáng yè wú xiào
IG: autumn SUB yellow leaf   have (NEG)   laughter
BT: yellow leaves of autumn have no laughter,
[ø: **秋天的黄叶**] 无 翩跹
PY: qiū tiān de huáng yè wú piān xiān
IG: autumn SUB yellow leaf   have (NEG)   fluttering
BT: yellow leaves of autumn have no fluttering,
[ø: 秋天 的 黄 叶] 坠落 在 我 眼前
PY: qiū tiān de huáng yè zhuì luò zài wǒ yǎn qián
IG: autumn SUB yellow leaf drop CV my front
BT: yellow leaves of autumn drop drop in front of me.

(Adapted from Tagore 1931: 1; 2008: 3; 2010: 2; 2015: 1)

Fifthly, most additions of topical Themes realized by participants are unmarked and only two additions of marked topical Themes that are realized by participants are found in TT2. As seen in Example 4.29, three clauses are used by the translator of TT2 to translate one clause in the ST. In the final clause in TT2, "歌声" (PY: gē shēng; IG: song sound) functions as the marked topical Theme. It is the Complement/Actor in the clause, and the unmarked form of this clause is "随时 奏 歌 声" (PY: suí shí zòu gē shēng; IG: any time play song sound). In the other three TTs, the topical Theme in the ST – "the bird," which is realized by a participant, is translated as participants, i.e. "空 中 的 飞 鸟" (PY: kōng zhōng de fēi niǎo; IG: air in SUB flying bird) in TT1, "空 中 的 鸟儿" (PY: kōng zhōng de niǎo er; IG: air in SUB bird) in TT3, and "鸟" (PY: niǎo; IG: bird) in TT4.

EXAMPLE 4.29

ST: the bird in the air is singing.
TT1: 空 中 的 飞 鸟 是 歌唱 着 的;
PY: kōng zhōng de fēi niǎo shì gē chàng zhe de;
IG: air in SUB flying bird be sing VPART SUB;
BT: the bird in the air is singing.
TT2: 好 鸟 飞
PY: hǎo niǎo fēi
IG: good bird fly
BT: good bird flies,
与 [ø: 好 鸟] 鸣,
PY: yǔ hǎo niǎo míng,
IG: and good bird sing,

BT: and good bird sings,

歌 声 随时 奏。

PY: gē shēng suí shí zòu.

IG: song sound   any time   play.

BT: sound of the song plays any time.

TT3: 空 中 的 鸟儿 婉转

PY: kōng zhōng de niǎo er wǎn zhuǎn

IG: air in SUB bird   sweetly sing

BT: the birds in the air sing sweetly.

TT4: 鸟 鸣 天 上

PY: niǎo míng tiān shàng

IG: bird sing sky in

BT: birds sing in the sky.

(Adapted from Tagore 1931: 3; 2008: 25; 2010: 23; 2015: 43)

In terms of the addition of topical Theme realized by process, the frequency is not huge. In most cases, such additions are related to the additions of imperatives in the TTs. As shown in Example 4.30, imperatives are added in the TTs and are translated from the circumstance – "not in the flattery of thy mirror." In the ST, the unmarked topical Theme is realized by "find," which is a process. In TT1, TT2, and TT3, additional processes functioning as topical Themes are added, including "不要" (PY: bú yào; IG: do not) in TT1, "不 堪" (PY: bù kān; IG: NEG bear) in TT2, and "不要" (PY: bú yào; IG: do not) in TT3. We also note that no imperative clause is found in TT4.

EXAMPLE 4.30

ST: O Beauty, find thyself in love, not in the flattery of thy mirror.

TT1: **啊**, 美 呀, 在 爱 中 找 你自己 吧,

PY: a, měi ya, zài ài zhōng zhǎo nǐ zì jǐ ba,

IG: ah, beauty MOD, CV love in find yourself MOD,

BT: Ah Beauty, find yourself in love,

不要 到 你 镜子 的 谄谀 中 去 找 呀。

PY: bú yào dào nǐ jìng zi de chǎn yú zhōng qù zhǎo ya.

IG: do not   CV your mirror SUB flattery in CV find MOD.

BT: Don't find in the flattery of your mirror.

TT2: 美 乎 尔 何 在?

PY: měi hū ěr hé zài?

IG: beauty MOD you where CV?

BT: Beauty, where are you?

爱 中 寻 尔 真。

PY: ài zhōng xún ěr zhēn.

IG: love in find your self.

BT: In love, find your self.

不 堪 明镜 时,

PY: bù kān míng jìng shí,

IG: NEG bear mirror time,

BT: when you cannot bear the mirror,

[ø: 明镜] 依 样

PY: míng jìng yī yàng

IG: mirror follow appearance

BT: the mirror follows the appearance

[ø: 明镜] 会 阿 人。

PY: míng jìng huì ē rén.

IG: mirror can flatter people.

BT: mirror can flatter people.

TT3: 美丽 你 要 在 恋爱 中 寻找 自己

PY: měi lì nǐ yào zài liàn ài zhōng xún zhǎo zì jǐ

IG: beauty you   need to   CV love in find self

BT: Beauty, you need to find yourself in love.

不要 在 镜子 中 寻找 谄媚

PY: bú yào zài jìng zi zhōng xún zhǎo chǎn mèi

IG: do not   CV mirror in find flattery

BT: Do not find flattery in the mirror.

TT4: 美 在 爱 中

PY: měi zài ài zhōng

IG: beauty CV love in

BT: Beauty is in love.

[ø: 美] 不 在 镜 中

PY: měi bú zài jìng zhōng

IG: beauty NEG CV mirror in

BT: Beauty is not in the mirror.

(Adapted from Tagore 1931: 2; 2008: 16; 2010: 15; 2015: 28)

In TT2, processes functioning as unmarked topical Themes are also found in declarative clauses besides imperatives. In Example 4.31, two processes functioning as topical Themes are observed in TT2, i.e. "有" (PY: yǒu; IG: have) and "试看" (PY: shì kàn; IG: try see). While "试看" (PY: shì kàn; IG: try see) is used in an imperative clause – "试 看 晓 来 烟" (PY: shì kàn xiǎo lái yān; IG: try see dawn SUB smoke), "有" (PY: yǒu; IG: have) is used in a declarative clause, whose process type is analyzed as existential in this study.

EXAMPLE 4.31

ST: The mystery of creation is like the darkeness of night ——
it is great.
Delusions of knowledge are like the fog of the morning.
TT1: 创造 的 神秘，<< >> —— 是 伟大的。
PY: chuàng zào de shén mì, shì wěi dà de.
IG: creation SUB mystery, be great.
BT: The mystery of creation is great,
[ø: 创造 的 神秘] << 有如 夜间 的 黑暗，>>
PY: chuàng zào de shén mì yǒu rú yè jiān de hēi àn,
IG: creation SUB mystery   be like   night SUB darkness,
BT: the mystery of creation is like darkness of the night,
而 知识 的 幻影，不过 如 晨 间 之 雾。
PY: ér zhī shí de huàn yǐng, bú guò rú chén jiān zhī wù.
IG: and knowledge SUB delusion, just   be like   morning in SUB fog.
BT: And delusions of knowledge are just like fog of the moning.
TT2: 伟 哉 造化 力，神秘 长 夜 玄。
PY: wěi zāi zào huà lì, shén mì cháng yè xuán.
IG: great MOD creation power, mysterious long night profound.
BT: The great power of creation is like the mysterious and profound long night,
[ø: 你] 不 信
PY: nǐ bú xìn
IG: you NEG believe
BT: you don't believe
有 知 妄，
PY: yǒu zhī wàng,
IG: be knowledge unfounded,
BT: there is unfounded knowledge,
试 看 晓 来 烟。
PY: shì kàn xiǎo lái yān.
IG: try see dawn SUB smoke.
BT: try to see the smoke at dawn.
TT3: 造化 的 奥妙 好像 黑暗 之于 夜晚
PY: zào huà de ào miào hǎo xiàng hēi àn zhī yú yè wǎn
IG: creation SUB mystery   be like   darkness to night
BT: The mystery of creation is like darkness to the night.
[ø: 造化 的 奥妙] 无边地 巨大
PY: zào huà de ào miào wú biàn de jù dà
IG: creation SUB mystery boundlessly huge
BT: the mystery of creation is boundlessly huge.
知识 的 困惑 则 有如 大雾 之于 清晨

PY: zhī shí de kùn huò zé yǒu rú dà wù zhī yú qīng chén
IG: knowledge SUB bewilderment then be like fog to morning
BT: Bewilderment of knowledge is then like fog to the morning.
TT4: 创造 的 隐秘 夜晚 无穷无尽的 黑暗
PY: chuàng zào de yǐn mì yè wǎn wú qióng wú jìn de hēi àn
IG: creation SUB mystery night endless darkness
BT: The mystery of creation [ø: is like] the endless darkness at night.
已知的 虚幻 早晨 的 雾气
PY: yǐ zhī de xū huàn zǎo chén de wù qì
IG: known illusion morning SUB fog
BT: Known illusion [ø: is like] fog in the morning
[ø: 已知的 虚幻] 飞快 消散
PY: yǐ zhī de xū huàn fēi kuài xiāo sàn
IG: known illusion quickly disappear
BT: known illusion disappears quickly.

(Adapted from Tagore 1931: 2; 2008: 6; 2010: 8; 2015: 14)

The added circumstances functioning as topical Themes are found in all the four TTs, but mostly in TT2, with only one instance being found in TT1, TT3, and TT4. In Example 4.32, two topical Themes realized by circumstances are added in TT2, namely "汲汲" (PY: jí jí; IG: in haste) and "混混" (PY: hùn hùn; IG: ceaselessly), which form a contrast in the two lines of the poem. Also, several topical Themes are added in TT2, while only the first two topical Themes, i.e. "生 者" (PY: shēng zhě; IG: alive people), are translated from "man" and "he" in the ST. As a result of the additions of the six clauses in TT2, we find six additional topical Themes, among which four are realized by participants and two are realized by circumstances. In TT1, TT3, and TT4, the two topical Themes in the ST are equivalently translated, while only the addition of topical Themes realized by participants are found, including "他" (PY: tā; IG: he) in TT1 and "人" (PY: rén; IG: man) in TT4.

EXAMPLE 4.32

ST: **Man** does not reveal himself in his history,
he struggles up through it.
TT1: 人 在 他的 历史 中 表现 不 出 他自己,
PY: rén zài tā de lì shǐ zhōng biǎo xiàn bù chū tā zì jǐ,
IG: man CV his history in reveal NEG out himself,
BT: Man does not reveal himself in his history,

他 在 历史 中 奋斗 着
PY: tā zài lì shǐ zhōng fèn dòu zhe
IG: he CV history in struggle VPART
BT: he struggles in history,
[ø: 他] 露出 头角。
PY: tā lòu chū tóu jiǎo.
IG: he show talent.
BT he shows talent.
TT2: 生 者 积
PY: shēng zhě jī
IG: alive people accumulate
BT: The alive people accumulate
[ø: 生 者] 为 人,
PY: shēng zhě wéi rén,
IG: alive people become man,
BT: The alive people become man.
死 者 陈
PY: sǐ zhě chén
IG: dead people stale
BT: The dead people stale.
[ø: 死 者] 为 史。
PY: sǐ zhě wéi shǐ.
IG: dead people becomes history.
BT: The dead people become history.
生 随 死 俱 去,
PY: shēng suí sǐ jù qù,
IG: life with death both go,
BT Life and death both go,
甚 事 足 立 己。
PY: shèn shì zú lì jǐ.
IG: what affair worthwhile exist oneself.
BT: What affair is worthwhile for oneself to exist.
汲汲 欲 自 见,
PY: jí jí yù zì jiàn,
IG: in haste   want to   oneself see,
BT: In haste, one wants to see oneself,
混混 去 无 己。
PY: hùn hùn qù wú jǐ.
IG: ceaselessly CV   have (NEG)   oneself.
BT: Ceaselessly there is no oneself.
TT3: 人 无法 在 历史 中 突显 什么
PY: rén wú fǎ zài lì shǐ zhōng tū xiǎn shén me

IG: man cannot CV history in reveal something
BT: Man cannot reveal anything in history,
人 只是 在 历史 的 洪流 里 挣扎 而已
PY: rén zhǐ shì zài lì shǐ de hóng liú lǐ zhēng zhá ér yǐ
IG: man only CV history SUB current in struggle only
BT: man only struggle in the current of history.
TT4: 人 在 历史 里 湮没 无 闻
PY: rén zài lì shǐ lǐ yān mò wú wén
IG: man CV history in oblivion not hear
BT: Man is unknown in history,
人 总是 努力
PY: rén zǒng shì nǔ lì
IG: man always struggle
BT: man always struggles,
[ø: 人] 超越 现存
PY: rén chāo yuè xiàn cún
IG: man surpass   current situation
BT: man surpasses the current situation.
(Adapted from Tagore 1931: 4; 2008: 29; 2010: 27; 2015: 52)

The translators of TT3 and TT4 have added marked topical Themes realized by circumstances to create two parallel lines in a poem. For instance, in Example 4.33, two circumstances functioning as marked topical Themes are found in TT3, namely "因着 世间 的 需要" (PY: yīn zhe shì jiān de xū yào; IG: because world in SUB need) and "因着 爱" (PY: yīn zhe ài; IG: because love); the first marked topical Theme is a substitution of "life" in the ST, while the second one is added by the translator. Further, we note that all four translators render part of the Rheme in the ST – "and its worth by the claims of love" as free clauses, resulting in the additions of various topical Themes.

EXAMPLE 4.33

ST: **Life** finds its wealth by the claims of the world, and its worth by the claims of love.
TT1: **生命** 因了 "世界" 的 要求，得到 他的 资产，
PY: shēng mìng yīn le "shì jiè" de yāo qiú, dé dào tā de zī chǎn,
IG: life because "world" SUB claim, obtain his property,
BT: Because of the world's claim, life obtains his property,

[ø: 生命] 因了 爱 的 要求，得到 他的 价值。
PY: shēng mìng yīn le ài de yāo qiú, dé dào tā de jià zhí.
IG: life because love SUB claim, obtain his worth.
BT: Because of love's claim, life obtains his worth.
TT2: 生 因 世 所 需，乃 得 其 资产。
PY: shēng yīn shì suǒ xū, nǎi dé qí zī chǎn.
IG: life because world VPART need, then obtain his property.
BT: Because of the world's need, life then obtains his property.
[ø: 生] 若 无 爱 相要，
PY: shēng ruò wú ài xiāng yāo,
IG: life if   have (NEG)   love invitation,
BT: If life has no invitation from love,
厥 值 殊 难 算。
PY: jué zhí shū nán suàn.
IG: its value very hard calculate.
BT: its value is very hard to be calculated.
TT3: 因着 世间 的 需要 生命 才 成为 财富
PY: yīn zhe shì jiān de xū yào shēng mìng cái chéng wéi cái fù
IG: because world SUB need life then become wealth
BT: Because of the world's need, life becomes wealth.
因着 爱 生命 才 变得 有价值
PY: yīn zhe ài shēng mìng cái biàn de yǒu jià zhí
IG: because love life then become valuable
BT: Because of love, life becomes valuable.
TT4 [ø: 生命] 从 世 所 愿
PY: shēng mìng cóng shì suǒ yuàn
IG: life follow world VPART wish
BT: Life follows the world's wish.
生命 有 了 金钱
PY: shēng mìng yǒu le jīn qián
IG: life have ASP money
BT: Life has money.
[ø: 生命] 从 爱 所 愿
PY: shēng mìng cóng ài suǒ yuàn
IG: life follow love VPART wish
BT: Life follows love's wish.
生命 有 了 金线
PY: shēng mìng yǒu le jīn xiàn
IG: life have ASP golden thread
BT: Life has golden thread.

                    (Adapted from Tagore 1931: 3; 2008: 20; 2010: 18; 2015: 33)

4.2.2 Theme omission

Different kinds of Theme can be omitted. There are three kinds of Theme omission, i.e. omission of textual Theme, interpersonal Theme, and topical Theme.

4.2.2.1 Omission of textual Theme

The omitted textual Themes are mostly conjunctions (see Section 4.1.1) and the largest number of such omissions are found in TT2. In the data, the frequently-omitted textual Themes include "and," "when," and "that." Example 4.34 shows how "and" is omitted in the TTs. Although no lexical equivalent of "and" is found in the TTs, such as "而且" (PY: ěr qiě; IG: and) and "并且" (PY: bìng qiě; IG: and), the logico-sematic relation of extension in the ST is maintained in TT1, TT2, and TT4. However, in TT3, all logico-semantic relations between the clauses are omitted, and the whole poem composed of four clauses in the ST is translated as a one-clause poem, with a prepositional phrase functioning as the marked topical Theme.

EXAMPLE 4.34

ST: You smile **and** [ø: you] talked to me of nothing
TT1: 你 微微地 笑 着，
PY: nǐ wēi wēi de xiào zhe,
IG: you slightly smile VPART,
BT: You smile slightly,
不 同 我 说 什么 话，
PY: bù tóng wǒ shuō shén me huà,
IG: NEG with me say what word,
BT: you do not say anything with me,
TT2: 伊人 但 微笑，
PY: yī rén dàn wēi xiào,
IG: she only smile,
BT: She only smiles,
了 无 一 语 付。
PY: liǎo wú yì yǔ fù.
IG: completely   have (NEG)   one word given.
BT: she completely has no word.
TT3: 为了 你 对 我 随兴 的 闲聊 与 笑语 我 可是 苦 等 了 多少 的 日 夜 啊
PY: wéi le nǐ duì wǒ suí xìng de xián liáo yǔ xiào yǔ wǒ kě shì kǔ děng le duō shǎo de rì yè a

IG: for you to me casual chat and cheerful talk I EMPH painfully wait ASP many
SUB day night MOD
BT: For your casual chat and   cheerful talk   to me, I have painfully waited for
many days and nights.
TT4: 你 对 我 微笑
PY: nǐ duì wǒ wēi xiào
IG: you to me smile
BT: You smile to me
不 语
PY: bù yǔ
IG: NEG talk
BT: you do not talk.

(Adapted from Tagore 1931: 3; 2008: 24; 2010: 22; 2015: 42)

Textual Themes realized by "that" are all omitted in the TTs due to the typological difference between English and Chinese (cf. Li 2007). In the English ST, "that" links the free clause and the bound clause, with logico-semantic relations of projection or expansion being involved. However, in the Chinese TTs, the conjunction, viz. "that," is not needed to connect the two clauses. Example 4.35 illustrates how omissions of "that" take place in the TTs, while the projection of idea in the ST is translated equivalently in the TTs.

EXAMPLE 4.35

ST: The light that plays, like a naked child, among the green leaves happily knows not **that** man can lie.
TT1: 光 如 一 个 裸体的 孩子，
PY: guāng rú yí gè luǒ tǐ de hái zi,
IG: light   be like   one MEAS naked child,
BT: The light is like a naked child,
[ø: 光] 快快活活地 在 绿 叶 当中 游戏，
PY: guāng kuài kuài huó huó de zài lǜ yè dāng zhōng yóu xì
IG: light happily CV green leaf in play
BT: the light happily plays in the green leaves,
他 不 知道
PY: tā bù zhī dào
IG: he NEG know
BT: he does not know,
人 是 会 欺诈的。

PY: rén shì huì qī zhà de
IG: man be can deceptive
BT: man is deceptive.
TT2: 鲜鲜 白日 光，灼 如 脱 襁 婴；
PY: xiān xiān bái rì guāng, zhuó rú tuō qiǎng yīng;
IG: bright day light, burn like   take off   swaddling clothes   baby;
BT: The bright day light burns like a baby taken off its swaddling clothes;
跳跃 绿 阴 中，
PY: tiào yuè lǜ yīn zhōng,
IG: jump green shade in,
BT: the bright day light jumps in the green shade
不 自 禁 其 情。
PY: bú zì jìn qí qíng.
IG: NEG oneself control its feeling.
BT: the bright day light cannot control its feeling.
未 识 床头 人，
PY: wèi shí chuáng tóu rén,
IG: NEG know bedside man,
BT: the bright day light does not know the man at his bedside,
昼 卧
PY: zhòu wò
IG: day sleep
BT: the man at his bedside sleeps at day
作 么 生!
PY: zuò me shēng!
IG: do what living!
BT: the man at his bedside does what living.
TT3: 阳光 好像 裸体的 幼童
PY: yáng guāng hǎo xiàng luǒ tǐ de yòu tóng
IG: sunshine   be like   naked child
BT: The sunshine is like a naked child,
在 绿 叶 间 快乐地 耍玩
PY: zài lǜ yè jiān kuài lè de shuǎ wán
IG: CV green leaf between happily play
BT: the sunshine happily plays between green leaves
全 不 知
PY: quán bù zhī
IG: completely NEG know
BT: the sunshine completely does not know
大人 要 隐藏 什么
PY: dà rén yào yǐn cáng shén me
IG: adult want hide what

BT: what adults want to hide.
TT4: 光 玩耍 着 绿色的 叶子
PY: guāng wán shuǎ zhe lǜ sè de yè zi
IG: light play VPART green leaf
BT: The light plays green leaves
如同 一 个 光着的 孩子
PY: rú tóng yí gè guāng zhe de hái zi
IG: be like   one MEAS naked child
BT: the light is like a naked child
懵然 不 知
PY: měng rán bù zhī
IG: completely NEG know
BT: the light completely does not know
世 间 有 很多 骗子
PY: shì jiān yǒu hěn duō piàn zi
IG: world in be many liar
BT: in the world there are many liars.

(Adapted from Tagore 1931: 2; 2008: 16; 2010: 15; 2015: 27)

We find that textual Themes realized by "because," "but" and "if" in the ST are more likely to be explicitly translated in the TTs. However, exceptions are more likely to be found in TT2. As shown in Example 4.36, the textual Theme realized by "if" is omitted in TT2, while "if" is translated equivalently as "如果" (PY: rú guǒ; IG: if), "假如" (PY: jiǎ rú; IG: if), and "如果" (PY: rú guǒ; IG: if) respectively in the other three TTs.

EXAMPLE 4.36

ST: **If** you shed tears
when you miss the sun,
TT1: **如果** 错过 了 太阳 时
PY: rú guǒ cuò guò le tài yang shí
IG: if miss ASP sun time
BT: If you miss the sun,
你 流 了 泪，
PY: nǐ liú le lèi,
IG: you shed ASP tear,
BT: you shed tears,
TT2: 白日 既 西 匿，
PY: bái rì jì xī nì,
IG: sun already west hide,

BT: The sun already hides in the west,

众 星 相 代 明。

PY: zhòng xīng xiāng dài míng.

IG: many stars successively replace light.

BT: The many stars replace its light successively.

如何 偏 泪 眼，

PY: rú hé piān lèi yǎn,

IG: how just tearful eye,

BT: Why do you have tearful eyes?

TT3: **假如** 你 为了 思念 太阳

PY: jiǎ rú nǐ wèi le sī niàn tài yang

IG: if you to miss sun

BT: If you miss the sun,

而 [ø:你] 落 泪

PY: ér nǐ luò lèi

IG: and you shed tears

BT: and you shed tears.

TT4: **如果** [ø:你] 因为 思念 太阳

PY: rú guǒ nǐ yīn wéi sī niàn tài yang

IG: if you because miss sun

BT: If because you miss the sun,

而 [ø: 你] 终 日 哭泣

PY: ér nǐ zhōng rì kū qì

IG: and you all day cry

BT: and you cry all day,

(Adapted from Tagore 1931: 1; 2008: 5; 2010: 4; 2015: 6)

In the present study, there are few omissions of textual Themes realized by continuatives. Instances of this type are all related to the omission of "o" in Poem 2 and 28. Translators can make their own choices on whether to keep the continuative in the ST as the textual Theme or not. As a result, in TT1, "o" is omitted in Poem 2, but is translated equivalently in Poem 28. The opposite occurs in TT3, i.e. "o" is omitted in Poem 28, but is translated equivalently in Poem 2. In TT2 and TT4, the two occurrences of "o" are both omitted (see Example 4.30).

4.2.2.2 Omission of interpersonal Theme

The omissions of interpersonal Theme are associated with omissions of three categories, i.e. omission of Finite, interrogative element, and Vocative. As previously discussed in Section 4.1.2, omissions of Finite verbal operator in the

TTs are due to the typological variations between English and Chinese, as there is no system of FINITE in Chinese.

Omissions of Vocatives functioning as interpersonal Themes are due to the translators' preferences. These omissions are mostly found in TT2. For instance, in Example 4.37, the interpersonal Theme "Moon" is translated as "月儿 啊" (PY: yùe er a; IG: moon MOD), "月亮" (PY: yùe liang; IG: moon), and "月亮" (PY: yùe liang; IG: moon) respectively in the other three TTs, while no such interpersonal Theme is seen in TT2. The poems in TT1, TT3, and TT4 are addressed to the moon, but the poem in TT2 is a description of the scenery and the mental states, and a change of field of activity from sharing to reporting is involved here (see Section 5.1).

EXAMPLE 4.37

ST: "Moon, for what do you wait?"
TT1: "月儿 啊，你 在 等 什么 呢?"
PY: "yùe er a, nǐ zài děng shén me ne?"
IG: "moon MOD, you CV   wait for   what MOD?"
BT: "Moon, what are you waiting for?"
TT2: 夜 静
PY: yè jìng
IG: night silent
BT: The night is silent,
月 未 落，
PY: yùe wèi luò,
IG: moon NEG set,
BT: the moon does not set,
迟迟 何 所 待?
PY: chí chí hé suǒ dài?
IG: so long   what to wait?
BT: what are you waiting for so long?
TT3: 月亮 你 在 等 什么
PY: yùe liang nǐ zài děng shén me
IG: moon you CV wait what
BT: Moon, what are you waiting for?
TT4: "月亮，为什么 你 在 等待?"
PY: "yùe liang, wèi shén me nǐ zài děng dài?"
IG: "moon, why you CV wait?"
BT: "Moon, why do you wait?"

(Adapted from Tagore 1931: 3; 2008: 17; 2010: 16; 2015: 30)

The omissions of interrogative elements functioning as interpersonal Themes in the TTs are all related to the translation strategies of wh- interrogatives from English to Chinese. In the English ST, the wh- elements function as both interpersonal Themes and unmarked topical Themes; whereas in Chinese, the interrogative elements do not have to be in thematic position (cf. Li 2007). In TT4, an exception is found when the wh- interrogative is analyzed as both the interpersonal Theme and part of the topical Theme. When translating "Moon, for what do you wait?" as "月亮，为什么 你 在 等待?" (PY: yuè liang, wèi shén me nǐ zài děng dài; IG: moon why you CV wait), "为什么" (PY: wèi shén me; IG: why), the interrogative element, is found in thematic position. In Chinese, it is also possible to choose "为什么" (PY: wèi shén me; IG: why) as part of the Rheme, and the clause will be "月亮，你 为什么 在 等待?" (PY: yuè liang, nǐ wèi shén me zài děng dài; IG: moon you why CV wait).

4.2.2.3 Omission of topical Theme

Omissions of topical Themes in the TTs are mostly found in TT2, where omissions of topical Themes realized by participants and processes take place; however, in the other three TTs, the topical Themes omitted are all realized by participants. In terms of frequency, TT2 has the largest number of such omissions (see Table 4.5), while a much smaller number of omissions are found in the other three TTs. No omission of circumstance is found in the data, and omissions of topical Themes realized by process are only observed in TT2. In Example 4.38, "leave," which is a topical Theme realized by a process in the ST, is translated as processes in TT1 and TT4, i.e. "留下" (PY: liú xià; IG: leave) and "混到" (PY: hùn dào; IG: mix). In TT2, no topical Theme is realized by processs, with the topical Theme in the ST being omitted.

EXAMPLE 4.38

ST: O troupe of little vagrants of the world, **leave** your footprints in my words.
TT1: 世界 上 的 一 队 小小的 漂泊者 啊，请 **留下** 你们的 足迹 在 我的 文字 里。
PY: shì jiè shàng de yí duì xiǎo xiǎo de piāo bó zhě a, qǐng liú xià nǐ mén de zú jì zài wǒ de wén zì lǐ.
IG: world on SUB one group little vagrant MOD, please leave your footprint CV my word in.
BT: One group of little vagrants in the world, please leave your footprints in my words.
TT2: [ø: 人] 生世 等 萍聚，

PY: rén shēng shì děng píng jù,
IG: man life wait union,
BT: Man in life wait for union,
[ø: 人] 漂泊
PY: rén piāo bó
IG: man wander
BT: Man wanders.
[ø: 人] 终 何 依。
PY: rén zhōng hé yī.
IG: man finally what   rely on.
BT: What does man finally rely on?
萍 去
PY: píng qù
IG: union leave
BT: when union leaves
踪 仍 在,
PY: zōng réng zài,
IG: trace still exist,
BT: its trace still exists,
临 流 歌 芳菲。
PY: lín liú gē fāng fēi.
IG: beside stream sing fragrance.
BT: Beside the stream, man sings fragrantly.
TT3: 哦 人 世 间 这 群 渺小 的 流浪者 把 你们 的 足迹 留 在 我 的 诗文 上 吧
PY: o rén shì jiān zhè qún miǎo xiǎo de liú làng zhě bǎ nǐ men de zú jì liú zài wǒ de shī wén shàng ba
IG: o human world in this group little vagrant CV your footprint leave CV my poetry on MOD
BT: O, this group of little vagrants in human world, leave your footprints in my poems.
TT4: 现 世 里 孤孤单单的 小 混蛋 啊 **混到** 我的 文字 里
PY: xiàn shì lǐ gū gū dān dān de xiǎo hún dàn a hùn dào wǒ de wén zì lǐ
IG: this life in lonely little bastard MOD mix my word in
BT: Little lonely bastards in this world, mix in my words.
留下 你们的 痕迹 吧
PY: liú xià nǐ men de hén jì ba
IG: leave your print MOD
BT: Leave your prints.

(Adapted from Tagore 1931: 1; 2008: 3; 2010: 2; 2015: 2)

Omissions of topical Themes realized by participants are related to omissions of clauses in the TTs. As seen in Example 4.39, the topical Theme in the second clause in the ST – "我们" (PY: wǒ men; IG: we) is omitted in TT3 and TT4. The translators of TT3 and TT4 have combined two clauses into one clause, thus omitting one of the two topical Themes.

EXAMPLE 4.39

ST: **Once** we dreamt
that **we** were strangers.
TT1: **有一次，**我们 梦见
PY: yǒu yí cì, wǒ men mèng jiàn
IG: once, we dream
BT: Once we dream
大家 都 是 不 认识 的。
PY: dà jiā dōu shì bú rèn shi de.
IG: we all be NEG know SUB.
BT: we are all not known to each other.
TT2: **梦 中** [ø: 我们] 曾 相遇，
PY: mèng zhōng wǒ men céng xiāng yù,
IG: dream in we once meet,
BT: In dream we once met,
[ø: **我们**] 都 道
PY: wǒ men dōu dào
IG: we all say
BT: we all say
[ø: **我们**] 不 相 识。
PY: wǒ men bù xiāng shí.
IG: we NEG each other know.
BT: we do not know each other
TT3: **曾经** 在 梦 中 你 我 都 是 陌生人
PY: céng jīng zài mèng zhōng nǐ wǒ dōu shì mò shēng rén
IG: once CV dream in you I both be stranger
BT: Once in dream, you and I are both strangers.
TT4: **做梦 时** 我们 距离 非常 遥远
PY: zuò mèng shí wǒ men jù lí fēi cháng yáo yuǎn
IG: dream time our distance very far
BT: During dreams, our distance is very far.

(Adapted from Tagore 1931: 2; 2008: 7; 2010: 6; 2015: 9)

4.2.3 Theme substitution

Theme substitution takes place when the Theme in the TTs is translated from the Rheme in the ST or other elements not found in the ST. In our data, TT2 and TT4 have the highest frequency of Theme substitution, while TT1 and TT3 have a relatively smaller number of such shifts. For instance, in Example 4.40, the Theme in the ST, i.e. "they," is replaced by "中心" (PY: zhōng xīn; IG: center), "小思小想" (PY: xiǎo sī xiǎo xiǎng; IG: little idea little thought), and "我心里" (PY: wǒ xīn lǐ; IG: my mind in) in TT2, TT3, and TT4 respectively, which are all translated from part of the Rheme in the ST. In TT1, however, the translator makes an equivalent choice by translating "they" in the ST as "他们" (PY: tā men; IG: they).

EXAMPLE 4.40

ST: **they** have their whisper of joy in my mind.
TT1: **他们** 在 我的 心里，愉悦地 微语 着。
PY: tā men zài wǒ de xīn lǐ, yú yuè de wēi yǔ zhe
IG: they CV my mind, happily whisper VPART
BT: They whisper happily in my mind.
TT2: **中心** 似 相 语，
PY: zhōng xīn sì xiāng yǔ,
IG: center seem　each other　talk,
BT: In the center they seem to talk with each other,
TT3: [ø: **小思小想**] 说出的 是 快乐的 悄悄话
PY: xiǎo sī xiǎo xiǎng shuō chū de shì kuài lè de qiāo qiāo huà
IG: little idea little thought told be happy whisper
BT: What little ideas and thoughts told are happy whispers.
TT4: **我 心里** 欢喜 不 止
PY: wǒ xīn lǐ huān xǐ bù zhǐ
IG: my mind happy NEG stop
BT: My mind does not stop from being happy.
(Adapted from Tagore 1931: 2; 2008: 11; 2010: 10; 2015: 17)

The translators, especially those of TT2 and TT4, often make creative choices when substituting the topical Themes in the ST. As illustrated in Example 4.41, the topical Theme in the ST – "his weapons" is further elaborated as "他的 刀 剑" (PY: tā de dāo jiàn; IG: his knife sword) in TT1, "锋铓" (PY: fēng máng; IG: spearhed) in TT2, and "剑" (PY: jiàn; IG: sword) in TT4. An equivalent choice is made by the translator of TT3 by translating "his weapons" as "武器" (PY: wǔ qì; IG: weapon).

EXAMPLE 4.41

ST: When his weapons win
TT1: 当 他的 刀 剑 胜利 时
PY: dāng tā de dāo jiàn shèng lì shí
IG: when his knife sword win time
BT: when his knife and sword win,
TT2: 锋铓 有 胜 时，
PY: fēng máng yǒu shèng shí,
IG: spearhead have win time,
BT: The spearhead has its time to win,
TT3: 当 武器 战胜 的 时候
PY: dāng wǔ qì zhàn shèng de shí hou
IG: when weapon win SUB time
BT: When it is time for weapon to win,
TT4: 剑 胜 了
PY: jiàn shèng le
IG: sword win ASP
BT: The sword has won.

(Adapted from Tagore 1931: 3; 2008: 26; 2010: 24; 2015: 45)

4.3 Analysis of process type

The system of TRANSITIVITY offers resources to construe our experiences of the flow of events as quanta of change (Halliday & Matthiessen 1999, 2014). In this way, human experience is construed into several process types in various languages, among which material, mental, and relational are considered as major types; behavioral, verbal, and existential are regarded as minor types (Matthiessen 1999).

In order to compare the two languages involved, we differentiate six process types in Chinese drawing on the systemic functional descriptions (cf. Tam 1979; Long 1981; Halliday & McDonald 2004; Li 2007; Long & Peng 2012). Two points can be made here:

Firstly, our criterion for distinguishing behavioral processes from mental processes is whether the verb can project or not. If it cannot, it would be considered as a behavioral process. For instance, "你 流 了 泪" (PY: nǐ liú le lèi; IG: you shed ASP tear) is analyzed as behavioral process because the process "流" (PY: liú; IG: shed) cannot project.

Secondly, as the verb "有" (PY: yǒu; IG: have) can be used in both existential and relational: possessive clauses, we have to distinguish them in the analysis. In an existential clause, only one participant – the Existent – can be found, such as "行客" (PY: xíng kè; IG: passenger) in "[ø: 绮窗 前] 似 有 行客 过"

TABLE 4.6 Frequency of process types

process type		ST	TT1	TT2	TT3	TT4
material		47	58	149	58	55
relational	attributive	15	24	73	18	27
	identifying	19	23	19	29	29
mental		11	11	38	15	18
behavioral		7	8	4	5	4
verbal		11	15	20	16	10
existential		0	0	3	0	1
Total		110	137	306	139	141

(PY: qǐ chuāng qián sì yǒu xíng kè guò; IG: window front seem have passenger pass). However, in a relational: possessive clause, there can be another participant. As seen in "秋天 的 黄叶，他们 没 有 什么" (PY: qiū tiān de huáng yè, tā men méi yǒu shén me; IG: autumn SUB yellow leaves, they NEG have what), two participants are found, namely "他们" (PY: tā mén; IG: they) – the Carrier and "什么" (PY: shén me; IG: what) – the Attribute.

Table 4.6 provides a profile of the process types in the data. It can be seen that more process types are found in the TTs, especially in TT2. The following reasons account for the addition of process type.

Firstly, the embedded or downranked clauses in the ST tend to be translated as free clauses in the TTs. As shown in Example 4.42, "where the world like a passer-by stops for a moment, nods to me and goes," which is a downranked clause, is expanded into five, twelve, six, and five clauses respectively in the TTs, while each clause contains one process.

EXAMPLE 4.42

ST: I sit at my window this morning [[[where the world like a passer-by stops for a moment, || nods to me || and goes]]]. (process type: material)
TT1: 我 今 晨 坐 在 窗 前，(process type: material)
PY: wǒ jīn chén zuò zài chuāng qián,
IG: I this morning sit CV window front,
BT: I sit in front of the window this morning,
"世界" 如 一 个 过路 的 人 似的，(process type: relational: identifying)
PY: "shì jiè" rú yí gè guò lù de rén sì de,
IG: "world" be like one MEAS pass by SUB person as if,
BT: The world is like a passer-by,
[ø: "世界"] 停留 了 一会，(process type: material)
PY: "shì jiè" tíng liú le yí hui,

IG: "world" stop ASP moment,

BT: The world stops for a moment

[ø: "世界"] 向 我 点点头， (process type: material)

PY: "shì jiè" xiàng wǒ diǎn diǎn tóu,

IG: "world" to me nod,

BT: The world nods to me,

[ø: "世界"] 又 走 过去 了。(process type: material)

PY: "shì jiè" yòu zǒu guò qù le.

IG: "world" then walk away ASP.

BT: The world then walks away.

TT2: 晨兴 百 无 营， (process type: relational: attributive)

PY: chén xīng bǎi wú yíng,

IG: morning very NEG affair,

BT: In the morning I have nothing to do,

坐 我 绮窗 前。(process type: material)

PY: zuò wǒ qǐ chuāng qián.

IG: sit I window front.

BT: I sit in front of the window.

[ø: 绮窗 前] 似 有 行客 过， (process type: existential)

PY: qǐ chuāng qián sì yǒu xíng kè guò,

IG: window front seem have traveler pass,

BT: In front of the window a traveler seems passed by,

[ø: 行客] 徘徊 (process type: material)

PY: xíng kè pái huái

IG: traveler hesitate

BT: The traveler hesitates

[ø: 行客] 结 我 缘。(process type: material)

PY: xíng kè jié wǒ yuán.

IG: traveler form my ties.

BT: The traveler forms some ties with me.

[ø: 行客] 顾 我 (process type: behavioral)

PY: xíng kè gù wǒ

IG: traveler   look at   me

BT: The traveler looks at me.

[ø: 行客] 点头 (process type: behavioral)

PY: xíng kè diǎn tóu

IG: traveler nod

BT: The traveler nods.

[ø: 行客] 去， (process type: material)

PY: xíng kè qù,

IG: traveler leave,

BT: The traveler leaves,

[ø: 行客] 一往 (process type: material)
PY: xíng kè yì wǎng
IG: traveler   go away
BT: The traveler goes away.
[ø: 行客] 不 复 延。(process type: material)
PY: xíng kè bú fù yán.
IG: traveler NEG again invite.
BT: The traveler cannot be invited again.
生世 只 如此，(process type: relational: attributive)
PY: shēng shì zhǐ rú cǐ,
IG: life only such,
BT: Life is only as such,
[ø: 我] 感 之 (process type: mental)
PY: wǒ gǎn zhī
IG: I feel this
BT: I feel this.
[ø: 我] 辄 喟然。(process type: relational: attributive)
PY: wǒ zhé wèi rán.
IG: I MOD sigh.
BT: I sigh.
TT3: 今 晨 我 坐 在 窗 前 (process type: material)
PY: jīn chén wǒ zuò zài chuāng qián
IG: this morning I sit CV window front
BT: This morning I sit in front of the window
[ø: 我] 看到 (process type: mental)
PY: wǒ kàn dào
IG: I see
BT: I see
世界 像 一 位 过客 (process type: relational: attributive)
PY: shì jiè xiàng yí wèi guò kè
IG: world   be like   one MEAS passer-by
BT: the world is like a passer-by.
[ø: 世界] 在 我 面前 驻足 片刻 (process type: material)
PY: shì jiè zài wǒ miàn qián zhù zú piàn kè
IG: world CV my front stop moment
BT: The world stops in front of me for a moment.
[ø: 世界] 点点头 (process type: material)
PY: shì jiè diǎn diǎn tóu
IG: world nod
BT: The world nods.
[ø: 世界] 便 离开 了 (process type: material)

PY: shì jiè biàn lí kāi le
IG: world then leave ASP
BT: The world then leaves.
TT4: 新的 一 天 我 坐 在 窗 前 (process type: material)
PY: xīn de yì tiān wǒ zuò zài chuāng qián
IG: new one day I sit CV window front
BT: In a new day I sit at the window.
世界 如 过客 (process type: relational: attributive)
PY: shì jiè rú guò kè,
IG: world   be like   passer-by
BT: The world is like a passer-by.
[ø: 世界] 在 我 面前 走过 (process type: material)
PY: shì jiè zài wǒ miàn qián zǒu guò
IG: world CV my front   pass by
BT: The world passed by in front of me.
[ø: 世界] 停 了 (process type: material)
PY: shì jiè tíng le
IG: world stop ASP
BT: The world stops.
[ø: 世界] 点头 (process type: material)
PY: shì jiè diǎn tóu
IG: world nod
BT: The world nods.
[ø: 世界] 又 走 了 (process type: material)
PY: shì jiè yòu zǒu le
IG: world then leave ASP
BT: The world then leaves.

(Adapted from Tagore 1931: 2; 2008: 10; 2010: 9; 2015: 16)

Secondly, as seen in Example 4.42, some circumstances in the ST such as "like a passer-by," tend to be translated as free clauses in the TTs, with additional processes realized by verbal groups like "如" (PY: rú; IG: be like), "似" (PY: sì; IG: be like), "像" (PY: xiàng; IG: be like), and "如" (PY: rú; IG: be like) being added in the four TTs.

Thirdly, extra process types are added by the translators for considerations such as to make up a certain rhyme or to map the translation onto a certain kind of poetic form (see Chapter 3). In Example 4.43, the translator of TT2 adapts the poem in the ST to the classical style of Chinese poetry and adds five process types. Written in this classical form, the Chinese characters rhyme with words at the end of the lines, such as "涕" (PY: tì; IG: tear), "眉" (PY: méi; IG: eyebrow) and "枝" (PY: zhī; IG: branch), with a rhyme scheme of "a a b a." Also, the translator of TT4 employs three additional process types, namely "败" (PY: bài; IG: fall), "如" (PY: rú; IG: be like), and "如" (PY: rú; IG: be like), the last two forming a couplet by making a comparison. Consequently, the rhyme scheme of this poem in TT4 is "a a b b," although the ST is not rhymed. In TT1 and TT3, however, the material process type in the ST has been translated equivalently.

EXAMPLE 4.43

ST: It is the tears of the earth that keep her smiles in bloom. (process type: material)

TT1: 是 "地" 的 泪点，使 她的 微笑 保持 着 青春 不 谢。(process type: material)

PY: shì "dì" de lèi diǎn, shǐ tā de wēi xiào bǎo chí zhe qīng chūn bú xiè.

IG: be earth SUB tear CV her smile keep VPART young not wither.

BT: It is the tear of the earth that keep her smile young and not withered.

TT2: [ø: 她] 独 坐 (process type: material)

PY: tā dú zuò

IG: she alone sit

BT: She sits alone.

意 含 涕，(process type: relational: attributive)

PY: yì hán tì,

IG: expression contain tear,

BT: Her expression contains tears.

[ø: 她] 欢 来 (process type: relational: attributive)

PY: tā huān lái

IG: she happy MOD

BT: when she is happy,

[ø: 她] 一 展 眉。(process type: material)

PY: tā yì zhǎn méi.

IG: she unfold eyebrow.

BT: she unfolds her eyebrow.

[ø: 涕] 沃 如 华 上 露，(process type: relational: identifying)

PY: tì wò rú huá shàng lù,

IG: tear fertile   be like   flower on dew,

BT: Her tears are fertile, like dew on a flower,

自 泽 盛开 枝。(process type: material)

PY: zì zé shèng kāi zhī.

IG: own raindrop   be in bloom   branch.

BT: Her own raindrops are in bloom on the branch.

TT3: 是 大地 的 泪水 让 她的 笑容 开 成 花朵 (process type: material)

PY: shì dà dì de lèi shuǐ ràng tā de xiào róng kāi chéng huā duǒ

IG: be earth SUB tear let her smile bloom VADV flower

BT: It is the tears of the earth that let her smile bloom into flower.
TT4: **大地 的 泪水** 让 笑 脸 常 开 (process type: material)
PY: dà dì de lèi shuǐ ràng xiào liǎn cháng kāi
IG: earth SUB tear let smiling face often bloom
BT: The tear of the earth let the smiling face often bloom.
[ø: **笑 脸**] 不 败 (process type: material)
PY: xiào liǎn bú bài
IG: smiling face NEG fade
BT: The smiling face does not fade.
[ø: **笑 脸**] 如 花 (process type: relational: identifying)
PY: xiào liǎn rú huā
IG: smiling face   be like   flower
BT: The smiling face is like flower.
[ø: **笑 脸**] 如 她 (process type: relational: identifying)
PY: xiào liǎn rú tā
IG: smiling face   be like   her
BT: The smiling face is like her.

(Adapted from Tagore 1931: 1; 2008: 4; 2010: 3; 2015: 4)

Apart from the additions of material and relational process types illustrated above, there are the additions of mental and verbal processes. For instance, in Example 4.44, verbal processes are added in TT1 and TT3, with the processes "叹息" (PY: tàn xī; IG: sigh) being translated from "sigh" in the ST, which constitutes part of the prepositional phrase "with a sigh." In addition, a mental process is added in TT2.

EXAMPLE 4.44

ST: and fall there with a sigh. (process type: material)
TT1: 只 叹息 一 声，(process type: verbal)
PY: zhǐ tàn xī yì shēng,
IG: only sigh one sound,
BT: only sigh once,
飞落 在 那里。(process type: material)
PY: fēi luò zài nà lǐ.
IG: drop CV there.
BT: drop there.
TT2: 红 叶 了 无言，(process type: relational: attributive)
PY: hóng yè liǎo wú yán,
IG: red leaf completely   have (NEG)   word,

BT: Red leaves have completely no word,
飞落 (process type: material)
PY: fēi luò
IG: drop
BT: red leaves drop
知 何处。(process type: mental)
PY: zhī hé chù.
IG: know where.
BT: red leaves know where.
TT3: 抖动着 坠落 (process type: material)
PY: dǒu dòng zhe zhuì luò
IG: tremblingly drop
BT: tremblingly drop,
触 地 (process type: material)
PY: chù dì
IG: touch ground
BT: touch the ground,
一 声 叹息 (process type: verbal)
PY: yì shēng tàn xī
IG: one sound sigh
BT: sigh for once
TT4: 坠落 在 我 眼 前 (process type: material)
PY: zhuì luò zài wǒ yǎn qián
IG: drop CV my eye front
BT: drop in front of my eyes
                    (Adapted from Tagore 1931: 1; 2008: 3; 2010: 2; 2015: 1)

In the TTs, the frequencies of most process types, viz. material, relational, mental, verbal, and existential, have been increased. However, the frequency of the behavioral process has been decreased in TT2, TT3, and TT4, especially in TT2, where adaptations are made and process types are changed to a large extent. In Example 4.45, the behavioral process in the ST is substituted by relational in TT2, with "泪 眼" (PY: lèi yǎn; IG: tearful eye) being used to describe the states of the addressee.

EXAMPLE 4.45

ST: If you shed tears (process type: behavioral)
TT1: 你 流 了 泪，(process type: behavioral)
PY: nǐ liú le lèi,
IG: you shed ASP tear,

> BT: you shed tears,
> TT2: 如何 偏 泪 眼，(process type: relational: attributive)
> PY: rú hé piān lèi yǎn,
> IG: how just tearful eye,
> BT: Why do you have tearful eyes?
> TT3: 而 落 泪 (process type: behavioral)
> PY: ér luò lèi
> IG: and shed tear
> BT: and shed tears.
> TT4: 而 终 日 哭泣 (process type: behavioral)
> PY: ér zhōng rì kū qì
> IG: and all day cry
> BT: and cry all day,
>
> (Adapted from Tagore 1931: 1; 2008: 5; 2010: 4; 2015: 6)

The quantitative distribution here throws light on the process types that are often added or omitted in the TTs. In the next section, we quantify and discuss the process type shifts (Matthiessen 2014b).

4.4 Process type shift

Similar to Table 4.5, which tabulates the various categories of Theme shift, Table 4.7 summarizes the types of process type shift. When these shifts take place, the choices made by the four translators are within the domain of experiential metafunction. Three kinds of process type shift are identified, including process type addition, omission, and substitution.

According to Table 4.7, TT2 has the largest number of process type shifts due to the large number of process type additions and omissions. To map Tagore's original *Stray Birds* to the form of classical Chinese poetry, the translator has to make various changes to the experiential mode of meaning. Despite the changes, readers who are fond of classical poetry may think the translator has infused beauty into the translation (cf. Cheng 2004; Mao 2004; Xu 2018).

TT1 has the smallest number of process type shifts. This refelects the strategies suggested by the translator – Zheng Zhenduo (1921, 2004a, 2004b), who applies a word-to-word way of translating poems. This also explains why Zheng's version is regarded as a classic, as it is congruent with the norms of poetry translation in China, where readers expect a "faithful" translation of poetry.

The occurrence of process type shift in TT3 is between TT1 and TT4. In other words, much freer choices are made in TT3, if compared to TT1, while

TABLE 4.7 Different types of process type shift

Types of process type shift		TT1	TT2	TT3	TT4
process type addition	material	9	129	15	15
	relational: attributive	3	54	6	8
	relational: identifying	11	12	7	10
	mental	2	27	3	3
	verbal	2	19	6	3
	behavioral	1	2	0	1
	existential	0	4	0	0
process type omission	material	1	25	1	3
	relational: attributive	1	9	1	1
	relational: identifying	0	11	0	0
	mental	0	1	2	2
	verbal	0	8	1	0
	behavioral	0	2	1	0
	existential	0	0	0	0
process type substitution		9	4	19	30
Total		39	307	62	76

TT4 is further translated in a free manner. Moreover, TT4 has the second largest number of process type shifts, which further reflect the large number of changes of process type made by the translator – Feng Tang; but the amount of changes in TT4 is not huge compared those in TT2.

4.4.1 Process type addition

Process type addition means that an additional process type is added to the TTs. Example 4.42 serves as an illustration of this kind of shift. In terms of the total frequency, the largest amount of process type addition is found in TT2. Material process is most frequently added in the TTs, especially in TT2, TT3, and TT4. Relational process ranks the second frequent. These quantitative findings further explore the probability of process type and are related to the conception of probability in language (cf. Halliday 1991a; Halliday & James 1993; Matthiessen 1999, 2006).

The addition of process type can be related to the following five factors, which are to some extent similar to Theme addition we previously discussed. Firstly, when an additional clause is added to the TTs, if the clause added is a major one, we can expect an addition of process type. For instance, in Example 4.46, the clause in the ST has been translated as two clauses in TT1, TT3, and TT4. Different process types have been added, namely relational: attributive in TT1 and TT3 as well as verbal in TT4. The addition of process type is rendered from "silent" in the ST.

EXAMPLE 4.46

ST: but who are you so silent? (process type: relational: identifying)
TT1: 但是 你 是 谁 呢， (process type: relational: identifying)
PY: dàn shì nǐ shì shuí ne,
IG: but you be who MOD,
BT: but who are you
[ø:你] 那样 沉默 着。(process type: relational: attributive)
PY: nǐ nà yàng chén mò zhe.
IG: you that silent VPART.
BT: you are silent like that.
TT2: 谁 欤 独 无 言? (process type: relational: attributive)
PY: shuí yú dú wú yán?
IG: who MOD alone   have (NEG)   word?
BT: Who has no word?
TT3: 你 是 谁 (process type: relational: identifying)
PY: nǐ shì shuí
IG: you be who
BT: Who are you?
怎么 默不作声 (process type: relational: attributive)
PY: zěn me mò bú zuò shēng
IG: why silent
BT: Why so silent?
TT4: 你 谁 啊， (process type: relational: identifying)
PY: nǐ shuí a,
IG: you who MOD,
BT: Who are you?
不 说 一 句 话? (process type: verbal)
PY: bù shuō yí jù huà
IG: NEG say one sentence word
BT: You do not say one sentence.

(Adapted from Tagore 1931: 1; 2008: 5; 2010: 4; 2015: 23)

Secondly, all the four translators tend to translate downranked clauses as major clauses, which is a move to a wider environment of translation in terms of rank (see Matthiessen 2001). In Example 4.42, the downranked clause has been translated as several additional clauses in all the four TTs, resulting in additions of process types.

Thirdly, groups/phrases or words can be translated as clauses, which shows how the translators move along the rank scale of the lexicogrammar while making choices. In Example 4.47, "in my mind," which is a prepositional phrase in the ST, has been translated as two clauses in TT2 and TT3, i.e. "中心 似 相 语" (PY: zhōng xīn sì xiāng yǔ; IG: center seem   each other   talk) and "冒 出 我的 心 坎" (PY: mào chū wǒ de xīn kǎn; IG: emerge from my heart bottom), resulting in the additions of a verbal process and a material process in the two TTs. However, in TT1 and TT4, "in my mind" has been translated as prepositional phrases, i.e. "在 我的 心 里" (PY: zài wǒ de xīn lǐ; IG: CV my mind in) and "我 心 里" (PY: wǒ xīn lǐ; IG: my mind in), with no change being made in terms of rank scale.

EXAMPLE 4.47

ST: they have their whisper of joy in my mind. (process type: relational: attributive)

TT1: 他们 在 我的 心 里，愉悦地 微语 着。(process type: verbal)

PY: tā men zài wǒ de xīn lǐ, yú yuè de wēi yǔ zhe.

IG: they CV my mind in, happily whisper VADV.

BT: They whisper happily in my mind.

TT2: 中心 似 相 语，(process type: verbal)

PY: zhōng xīn sì xiāng yǔ,

IG: center seem   each other   talk,

BT: In the center they seem to talk with each other.

愉悦 不 可 名。(process type: verbal)

PY: yú yùe bù kě míng.

IG: happiness NEG can tell.

BT: The happiness cannot be told.

TT3: [ø: 小 思 小 想] 冒 出 我的 心 坎 (process type: material)

PY: xiǎo sī xiǎo xiǎng mào chū wǒ de xīn kǎn

IG: little idea little thought emerge from my heart bottom

BT: Little ideas and thoughts emerge from the bottom of my heart.

说出的 是 快乐的 悄悄话 (process type: relational: identifying)

PY: shuō chū de shì kuài lè de qiāo qiāo huà

IG: told be happy whisper

BT: What was uttered are happy whispers.

TT4: 我 心 里 欢喜 不 止 (process type: relational: attributive)

PY: wǒ xīn lǐ huān xǐ bù zhǐ

IG: my mind in happy NEG stop

BT: My mind does not stop from being happy.

(Adapted from Tagore 1931: 1; 2008: 5; 2010: 4; 2015: 23)

Fourthly, the translators can add repetitive lines to the poems, forming a paralleled construction, leading to the additions of process types. As shown in TT4 in Example 4.43, "常 开" (PY: cháng kāi; IG: often bloom) and "不 败" (PY: bú bài; IG: NEG fade) are similar in their experiential meaning and are both analyzed as material process types. In TT1 and TT3, equivalence of process type has been maintained; whereas in TT2, various process types have been added and some of them are not found in the ST.

Fifthly, the consideration of making choices on the expression plane of language, such as the choice of rhyme, can also lead to the additions of process types. These instances can only be found in TT2 and TT4, where rhymed poems are found (see Section 3.2). In Example 4.48, equivalent choices of the relational process are found in TT1 and TT3. However, in TT2 and TT4, we find additional process types, i.e. two relational: attributive and one mental process in TT2 as well as two mental, one relational: attributive, and one verbal process in TT4. As a result of these additions, both two TTs are characterized with their rhyme schemes. In TT2, end rhymes are found in "意" (PY: yì; IG: intension), "知" (PY: zhī; IG: knowledge), and "记" (PY: jì; IG: remember) following the rhyme scheme of "a b b b." In TT4, "需要" (PY: xū yào; IG: need), "要" (PY: yào; IG: want), "明了" (PY: míng liǎo; IG: understood), and "忘掉" (PY: wàng diào; IG: forget) rhyme with the "ao" sound and the rhyme scheme is "a a a b b."

EXAMPLE 4.48

ST: It is for small needs it never asks, or knows or remembers. (process type: relational: attributive)

TT1: 那 小小的 需要，他 是 永不 要求，永不 知道，永不 记着 的。(process type: relational: attributive)

PY: nà xiǎo xiǎo de xū yào, tā shì yǒng bù yāo qiú, yǒng bù zhī dào, yǒng bú jì zhe de.

IG: that small need he be never asked never known never remembered SUB

BT: That small needs are never asked, never known, never remembered.

TT2: 毫末 亦 有 需, (process type: relational: attributive)

PY: háo mò yì yǒu xū,

IG: trivial matter   also have need,

BT: Trivial matters also have needs,

总 无 相 要 意。(process type: relational: attributive)

PY: zǒng wú xiāng yào yì.

IG: always   have (NEG)   each other   require intension.

BT: trivial matters always have no intension to require others.

来 者 长 无 知, (process type: relational: attributive)

PY: lái zhě cháng wú zhī,

IG: come people often   have (NEG)   knowledge,
BT: People came often have no knowledge,
往 者 终 何 记。(process type: mental)
PY: wǎng zhě zhōng hé jì.
IG: go people   after all   why remember.
BT: why after all will people went remember?
TT3: 这 颗 心 不知 不觉 在 憔悴 只是 因为 一些 不 敢 提 的 小 要求 一些 不 足 闻 问 的 小事 或者 一些 想 不 起来 的 记忆 (process type: relational: attributive)
PY: zhè kē xīn bù zhī bù jué zài qiáo cuì zhǐ shì yīn wéi yì xiē bù gǎn tí de xiǎo yāo qiú yì xiē bù zú wén wèn de xiǎo shì huò zhě yì xiē xiǎng bù qǐ lái de jì yì
IG: this MEAS heart unconsciously CV wither only because some NEG dare pro-pose SUB small need some NEG deserve ask SUB or some remember NEG PV SUB memory
BT: This heart unconsciously withers only because of some small needs dare not proposed, some trivials do not deserve to be asked, or some memory not remembered.
TT4: 为了 那些 细小的 需要 (process type: relational: attributive)
PY: wèi le nà xiē xì xiǎo de xū yào
IG: want those small need
BT: It wants those small needs,
从没 说 (process type: relational: verbal)
PY: cóng méi shuō
IG: never say
BT: It never says
要 (process type: mental)
PY: yào
IG: want
BT: it wants
从不 明了 (process type: relational: attributive)
PY: cóng bù míng liǎo
IG: never understood
BT: it is never understood,
总 想 忘掉 (process type: relational: mental)
PY: zǒng xiǎng wàng diào
IG: always want forget
BT: it always wants to forget
(Adapted from Tagore 1931: 3; 2008: 22; 2010: 20; 2015: 37)

4.4.2 Process type omission

When process type omission takes place, the process type in the ST is omitted and left untranslated in the TT. In terms of the total frequency, the occurrence of process type omission in TT3 and TT4 is smaller compared to the occurrence of process type addition and process type substitution (see Table 4.5). In TT2, however, a larger number of process type omissions are found compared to process type substitution.

Process type omission is found when the translator reorganizes the ST by omitting several clauses. In Example 4.49, process type omission is observed in TT2 and TT4. In TT2, two process types, i.e. one mental process and one material process, have been omitted. In TT4, three process types are omitted, including two material processes and one mental process. While recreating the poem from English to Chinese, the translators of TT2 and TT4 choose to completely ignore some process types or to translate the processes as minor processes at the rank of group/phrase. In this example, two prepositional phrases, i.e. "梦 中" (PY: mèng zhōng; IG: dream in) in TT2 and "做梦 时" (PY: zuò mèng shí; IG: dream time) in TT4 are both translated from "dreamt" in the ST, which is analyzed as a mental process. However, in TT1 and TT3, equivalences of process type are found, with no change being made in this respect.

EXAMPLE 4.49

ST: Once we dreamt (process type: mental)
that we were strangers. (process type: relational: identifying)
We wake up (process type: material)
to find (process type: mental)
that we were dear to each other. (process type: relational: attributive)
TT1: 有一次，我们 梦见 (process type: mental)
PY: yǒu yí cì, wǒ men mèng jiàn
IG: once, we dream
BT: Once we dreamt
大家 都 是 不 认识 的。(process type: relational: identifying)
PY: dà jiā dōu shì bú rèn shi de.
IG: we all be NEG know SUB.
BT: we were all not known to each other.
我们 醒 了，(process type: material)
PY: wǒ men xǐng le,
IG: we wake up ASP,
BT: We woke up
却 知道 (process type: mental)
PY: què zhī dào
IG: but realize
BT: but we realized
我们 原是 相 亲爱的。(process type: relational: attributive)
PY: wǒ men yuán shì xiāng qīn ài de.

IG: we   use to be   each other   dear.
BT: we used to be dear to each other.
TT2: 梦 中 曾 相遇，(process type: material)
PY: mèng zhōng céng xiāng yù,
IG: dream in once meet,
BT: In dream we once met,
都 道 (process type: verbal)
PY: dōu dào
IG: all say
BT: we all say
不 相 识。(process type: mental)
PY: bù xiāng shí.
IG: NEG   each other   known.
BT: we are not known.
那 知 醒 时 情，(process type: mental)
PY: nǎ zhī xǐng shí qíng,
IG: NEG know awake time feeling,
BT: we don't know the feeling while awake,
原 是 漆 和 墨。(process type: relational: identifying)
PY: yuán shì qī hé mò.
IG: used be paint and ink.
BT: we used to be paint and ink.
TT3: 曾经 在 梦 中 你 我 都 是 陌生人 (process type: relational: identifying)
PY: céng jīng zài mèng zhōng nǐ wǒ dōu shì mò shēng rén
IG: once CV dream in you I both be stranger
BT: Once in dream, you and I are both strangers.
梦 醒 (process type: material)
PY: mèng xǐng
IG: dream   wake up
BT: you and I wake up
方 知 (process type: mental)
PY: fāng zhī
IG: just realize
BT: you and I just realize
我们 是 何等 亲密 (process type: relational: attributive)
PY: wǒ men shì hé děng qīn mì
IG: we be so close
BT: we are so close.
TT4: 做梦 时 我们 距离 非常 遥远 (process type: relational: attributive)
PY: zuò mèng shí wǒ men jù lí fēi cháng yáo yuǎn
IG: dream time our distance very far
BT: During dreams, our distance is very far.

醒来 时 我们 在 彼此 的 视野 里 取暖 (process type: relational: attributive)
PY: xǐng lái shí wǒ men zài bǐ cǐ de shì yě lǐ qǔ nuǎn
IG: wake up   time we CV   each other   SUB vision in warm
BT: At waking up time, we warm each other in our vision.

(Adapted from Tagore 1931: 2; 2008: 7; 2010: 6; 2015: 9)

Some patterns of process type omission are found:

Firstly, in TT2, omissions are mostly related to the large number of clause omission. When certain clauses in the ST are ignored and left untranslated in TT2, the process types are omitted. As previously illustrated in Example 4.49, the omissions of the two process types in TT2 and TT4 are due to the omissions of the two clauses.

Secondly, in TT2 and TT4, while translating some relational: identifying processes from the ST, no process such as "是" (PY: shì; IG: be), "如" (PY: rú; IG: be like) or "像" (PY: xiàng; IG: be like) is found to mark out the process explicitly. In this study, these instances are analyzed as relational: identifying rather than process type omission (see Example 4.50).

EXAMPLE 4.50

ST: The mystery of creation is like the darkness of night – (process type: relational: identifying)
it is great. (process type: relational: attributive)
TT1: 创造 的 神秘，有如 夜间 的 黑暗，(process type: relational: identifying)
PY: chuàng zào de shén mì, yǒu rú yè jiān de hēi àn,
IG: creation SUB mystery,   be like   night SUB darkness,
BT: The mystery of creation is like the darkness of night,
是 伟大的。(process type: relational: attributive)
PY: shì wěi dà de.
IG: be great.
BT: it is great.
TT2: 伟 哉 造化 力，神秘 长 夜 玄。(process type: relational: identifying)
PY: wěi zāi zào huà lì, shén mì cháng yè xuán.
IG: great MOD creation power, mysterious long night profound.
BT: The great power of creation [ø: **is like**] the mysterious and profound power of the long night.
TT3 造化 的 奥妙 好像 黑暗 之于 夜晚 (process type: relational: identifying)
PY: zào huà de ào miào hǎo xiàng hēi àn zhī yú yè wǎn

IG: creation SUB mystery   be like   darkness to night
BT: The mystery of creation is like darkness to the night.
无边地 巨大 (process type: relational: attributive)
PY: wú biān de jù dà
IG: boundlessly huge
BT: It is boundlessly huge.
TT4: 创造 的 隐秘 夜晚 **无穷无尽的** 黑暗 (process type: relational: identifying)
PY: chuàng zào de yǐn mì yè wǎn wú qióng wú jìn de hēi àn
IG: creation SUB mystery night endless darkness
BT: The mystery of creation [ø: is like] the endless darkness of the night.
(Adapted from Tagore 1931: 2; 2008: 9; 2010: 8; 2015: 14)

4.4.3 Process type substitution

Process type substitution means that the process type in the ST is replaced by another one in the TTs. This type of shift can indicate the creativity of the translator while recreating Tagore's *Stray Birds*. In terms of frequency, nine process type substitutions are found in TT1, while four are found in TT2 because the primary categories of process type shift in TT2 are those of addition and omission. While ignoring the process types in the ST, the translator of TT2 mainly adds and omits various clauses, without making much alteration to the process types. In TT3 and TT4, however, a relatively larger number of process type substitutions are found, i.e. 19 and 30 respectively.

In TT1, TT2, and TT4, especially in TT1, the translators tend to change the process type of relational: identifying in the ST to relational: attributive. Such shifts occurr regularly in TT1. As previously illustrated in Example 4.49, when translating "that we were strangers" in the ST to "大家 都 是 不 认识 的" (PY: dà jiā dōu shì bú rèn shi de; IG: we all be NEG know SUB) in TT1, a process type shift takes place, although both choices are broadly within the domain of relational process. In TT3, however, an equivalent choice of process type is found.

No regular pattern of process type substitution is found in TT3 and TT4 and such substitutions are largely based on the translators' personal interpretation of the ST. For instance, in Example 4.51, "miss" in the ST is translated differently as "错过" (PY: cuò guò; IG: miss, let slip) in TT1 and "思念" (PY: sī niàn; IG: miss, long for) in TT3 and TT4. The different interpretations of the experiential meaning in the ST give rise to the substitutions of process type from material to mental in TT3 and TT4. In TT2, the material process has been maintained, although the Subject in the ST has been changed from "you" to "白日" (PY: bái rì; IG: sun).

EXAMPLE 4.51

ST: when you miss the sun (process type: material)
TT1: 如果 错过 了 太阳 时 (process type: material)
PY: rú guǒ cuò guò le tài yang shí
IG: if miss ASP sun time
BT: if you miss the sun
TT2: 白日 既 西 匿， (process type: material)
PY: bái rì jì xī nì,
IG: sun already west hide,
BT: the sun has already hidden in the west,
TT3: 假如 你 为了 思念 太阳 (process type: mental)
PY: jiǎ rú nǐ wèi le sī niàn tài yang
IG: if you   in order to   miss sun
BT: if you in order to miss the sun
TT4: 如果 因为 思念 太阳 (process type: mental)
PY: rú guǒ yīn wéi sī niàn tài yang
IG: if because miss sun
BT: if because you miss the sun

(Adapted from Tagore 1931: 1; 2008: 5; 2010: 4; 2015: 6)

The translator of TT4 tends to change the process type in the ST to form a parallel construction between two lines. In Example 4.52, process type substitution takes place when the material process in the ST is replaced by a relational: attributive process in TT4. Thus, "无 翩跹" (PY: wú piān xiān; IG: have NEG   flutter) is here contrasted with "翩跹" (PY: piān xiān; IG: flutter) in the previous stanza of the poem (see Figure 4.2).

EXAMPLE 4.52

ST: And yellow leaves of autumn, flutter (process type: material)
TT1: [ø: 秋天 的 黄 叶] 飞落 在 那里 (process type: material)
PY: qiū tiān de huáng yè fēi luò zài nà li
IG: autumn SUB yellow leaf drop CV there
BT: Yellow leaves of autumn drop there.
TT2: [ø: 红 叶] 飞落 (process type: material)
PY: hóng yè fēi luò
IG: red leaf drop
BT: Red leaves drop.
TT3: [ø: 秋天 的 黄 叶] 抖动着 坠落 (process type: material)

PY: qiū tiān de huáng yè dǒu dòng zhe zhuì luò
IG: autumn SUB yellow leaf tremblingly drop
BT: Yellow leaves of autumn drop tremblingly.
TT4: [ø: 秋天 的 黄 叶] 无 翩跹 (process type: relational: attributive)
PY: qiū tiān de huáng yè wú piān xiān
IG: autumn SUB yellow leaf   have (NEG)   flutter
BT: Yellow leaves of autum has no flutter.

(Adapted from Tagore 1931: 1; 2008: 3; 2010: 2; 2015: 1)

In addition, the translator of TT4 tends to make lexical choices that are seemingly equivalent to those in the ST but are actually different in terms of process type. As shown in Example 4.53, process type substitution takes place in TT4, where mental process in the ST is changed to material. The equivalent choices of "expects" in the ST are found in "希望" (PY: xī wàng; IG: expect) in TT1 and "期待" (PY: qī dài; IG: expect) in TT3, while "等待" (PY: děng dài; IG: wait) in TT4 is different in terms of the experiential meaning. This example also illustrates how processes are added in the TTs. In TT2, one equivalent choice is found when "expects" is translated as "责报" (PY: zé bào; IG: repay) and nine additional processes are added. In TT3, we find an additional process, i.e. "回应" (PY: huí yìng; IG: respond), which has been translated from "answers" in a nominal group in the ST.

EXAMPLE 4.53

ST: God expects answers for the flowers he sends us, not for the sun and the earth. (process type: mental)
TT1: 上帝 希望 我们 酬答 他 的，在于 他 送给 我们 的 花朵，
PY: shàng dì xī wàng wǒ men chóu dá tā de, zài yú tā sòng gěi wǒ men de huā duǒ,
IG: God expect us reward him SUB, be he sent us SUB flower,
BT: What God expects us to reward him is the flowers he sent us,
TT2: 天 临 我 以日，(process type: behavioral)
PY: tiān lín wǒ yǐ rì,
IG: God face us with sun,
BT: God faces us with sun,
载 我 以 土地。(process type: material)
PY: zǎi wǒ yǐ tǔ dì.
IG: equip us with land.
BT: God equips us with land.
两者 不 责报，(process type: mental)

PY: liǎng zhě bù zé bào,

IG: both NEG repay,

BT: Both are not repayed,

专专别有意。(process type: relational: attributive)

PY: zhuān zhuān bié yǒu yì.

IG: attentively especially have intention.

BT: God attentively and especially has intention.

记 (process type: mental)

PY: jì

IG: remember

BT: I remember

曾贶我花，(process type: material)

PY: céng kuàng wǒ huā,

IG: once grant me flower,

BT: God once granted me flower,

一视均人类。(process type: behavioral)

PY: yí shì jūn rén lèi.

IG: one see equal mankind.

BT: God sees mankind equally.

惟日惟土地，由来为花备。(process type: material)

PY: wéi rì wéi tǔ dì, yóu lái wèi huā bèi.

IG: because sun because land, origin for flower prepare.

BT: Because the sun and the land is prepared for flowers.

此贶意最珍，(process type: relational: attributive)

PY: cǐ kuàng yì zuì zhēn,

IG: this gift intention most precious,

BT: This gift has the most precious intention,

此责理无愧。(process type: relational: attributive)

PY: cǐ zé lǐ wú kuì.

IG: this requirement reason　have (NEG)　shameful.

BT: this requirement has no shameful reason.

TT3: 上帝期待我们 (process type: mental)

PY: shàng dì qī dài wǒ men

IG: God expect us

BT: God expects us

回应他送出的花 (process type: verbal)

PY: huí yìng tā sòng chū de huā

IG: respond he sent flower

BT: to respond the flowers he sent

TT4: 神在等待我们答题对于他开出的花朵而不是对于他开出的天与地

(process type: material)

PY: shén zài děng dài wǒ men dá tí duì yú tā kāi chū de huā duǒ ér bú shì duì yú tā kāi chū de tiān yǔ dì
IG: God CV   wait for   us answer question about he blossom but NEG be about he created heaven and earth
BT: God waits for us to answer questions about the flowers he blossomed, but not about the heaven and earth he created

(Adapted from Tagore 1931: 2; 2008: 15; 2010: 14; 2015: 26)

4.5 Summary

In this chapter, we examined the choices made in the ST and the TTs from the perspective of lexicogrammar. The lexicogrammatical analysis was carried out in terms of two systems, i.e. THEME and TRANSITIVITY. In Theme analysis, we quantified and discussed the different kinds of Theme choices, including textual, interpersonal, unmarked topical, marked topical, and predicated Themes. Based on the Theme analysis, we pointed out the different categories of Theme shift (shift within the textual metafunction), viz. Theme addition, Theme omission, and Theme substitution. In terms of transitivity analysis, we focused on the different process types. We provided a systemic profile of the process types found in the data and discussed, in quantitative terms, the choices made in the ST and the TTs. Finally, we summarized the various types of process type shift (shift within the experiential metafunction), namely process type addition, omission, and substitution.

Notes

1 We follow Halliday's (1985b; Matthiessen & Halliday 2009; Halliday & Matthiessen 2014) conventions of technical terms in SFL. Therefore, THEME (in small caps) refers to the name of the grammatical system and Theme (with the first letter being capitalized) is the element in the textual structure of the clause.
2 We underline the choices of Theme in Example 4.1.
3 These two continuatives also function as textual Themes in the ST (see Table 4.1).
4 We find a typo in the recent reproduction of Yao Hua's (2000) *Stray Birds*, in which "静 听 复 静 听" (PY: jìng tīng fù jìng tīng; IG: silently listen again silently listen) is printed as "静静 复 静静" (PY: jìng jìng fù jìng jìng; IG: silence again silence).
5 When writing classical poems, poets have to follow strict guidelines because one line may be composed of either five or seven Chinese characters and the cadence of the poem can be either pentasyllabic or heptasyllabic. One Chinese character will count as one syllable, and additional or redundant Chinese characters should never be used (Wang 1958; Cheng 2016).

5

CONTEXTUAL CONSIDERATIONS IN TRANSLATION

Analyzing field, tenor, and mode

This chapter analyzes *Stray Birds* and its four translation from the perspective of the three contextual parameters, i.e. field, tenor, and mode. In Section 5.1, we point out the field of activity in the data and compare the fields in the ST with those in the TTs. Then, we analyze the data in terms of tenor to evaluate the ST and the TTs in terms of institutional roles and familiarity. Reasons that lead to the readers' evaluations of the four translations are also explained from this respect. In terms of mode, we analyze the data by investigating the medium and channel and relate our findings to the graphological and phonological analyses. Finally, we relate the contextual analysis to the linguistic analyses in the previous chapters and summarize some patterns of translation shift in the data.

5.1 Contextual analysis of field

The analysis of field reports on the field of activity found in the data. The field of activity, as seen in various studies by Matthiessen (e.g. 2014c, 2015a, 2015b; Matthiessen & Teruya 2016; cf. Halliday 1978, 1991b), refers to what is going on in the context. Based on Ure's (1989, cf. Ure & Ellis 1977) unpublished manuscript, Matthiessen (e.g. 2015b) proposes eight primary types of activity, which include "expounding," "reporting," "recreating," "sharing," "doing," "enabling," "recommending," and "exploring" (see Figure 5.1). These eight primary types are grouped into three major categories as process of meaning (semiotic processes), process of behaving (social processes), and a transition between the two (semiotic processes potentially leading to social processes).

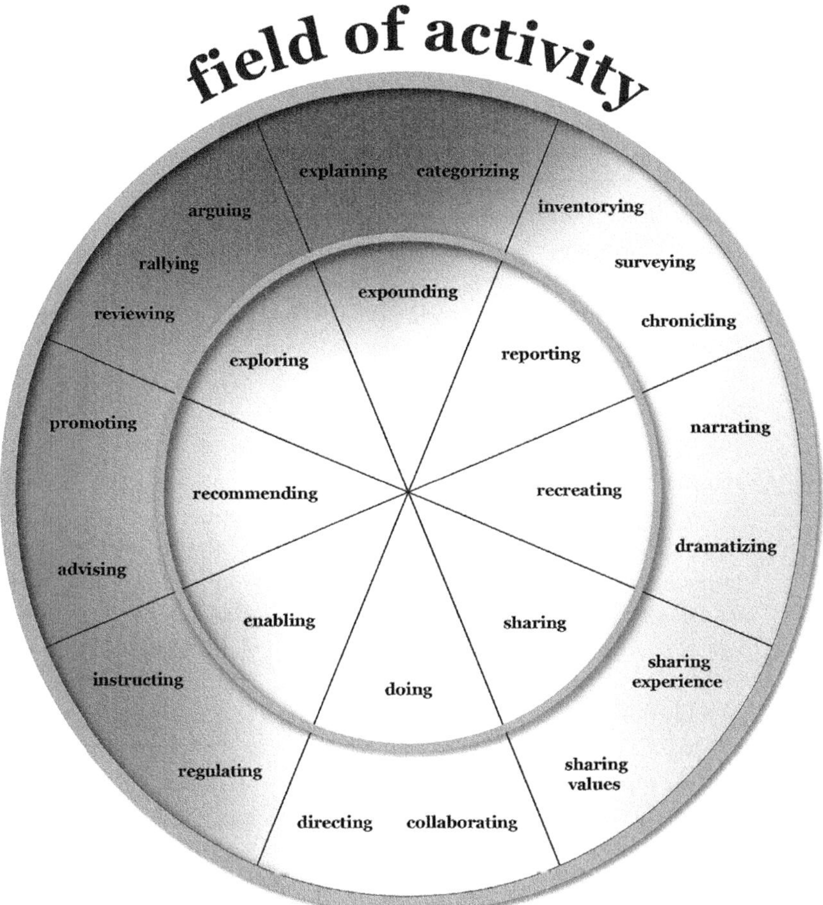

FIGURE 5.1   The eight primary fields of activity and their subtypes (Adapted from Matthiessen, Wang & Ma 2019: 99)

The definitions of the fields of activity are as follows (see Matthiessen 2015b: 55–56):

semiotic processes (i.e. "meaning" processes – semiotic processes constitutive of context, constitute as semiotic processes and manifested through social processes):

- **expounding** knowledge about general classes of phenomena (rather than particular instances of phenomena), theorizing our experience of the world in terms of a commonsense (folk) or uncommonsense (scientific) model by explaining why general classes of events take place or by categorizing general classes of entities (in terms of taxonomies, hyponymic, and/or meronymic, and/or characterization);

- **reporting** on particular instances of phenomena (rather than general classes of phenomena) creating "episodic" knowledge (rather than theoretical knowledge), the type of reporting being dependent on the nature of the phenomena: chronicling (the flow of) particular events, inventorying particular entities, or surveying particular places;
- **recreating** various aspects of life – involving any of the eight different types of context according to field of activity, typically imagined (fictional) rather than experienced (factual: experienced personally or vicariously), as verbal art with a "theme" (in the sense of Hasan 1985), through narration and/or dramatization;
- **sharing** personal experiences and values (opinions, attitudes, feelings) as part of establishing, maintaining and calibrating, (in short, negotiating) interpersonal relationships – in terms of the tenor of the relationship among interactants, ranging from (and potentially transforming) strangerhood to intimacy, but sustained over longer periods of time involving fairly intimate relationships in different institutions such as kinship and friendship; in terms of mode, traditionally and prototypically in private face-to-face interaction, but increasingly enabled by new technologies opening up new channels of sharing (epistolary, telegraphic, telephonic – and now with an explosion of mobile and Internet based possibilities, with a tendency to blur the distinction between private and public spheres);
- **exploring** public values (opinions, stances) and positions (ideas, hypotheses) by reviewing commodities (assigning them values on a scale from very positive to very negative)[,] by arguing about positions, debating or discussing them [or by rallying as seen in speeches, sermons, and editorials] – in terms of tenor, typically between one person (a professional or a member of the general public) and some segment of the general public, so between strangers; in terms of mode, typically using media channels, either "old" media channels (print, radio, TV) or "new" media channels (mobile and/or Internet-based);

semiotic processes potentially leading to social processes (i.e. 'meaning' leading to 'doing'):

- **recommending** some course of action (typically some kind of social process – exhortation in the strong form), either for the sake of the addressees by advising them to undertake it for their own good or for the sake of the speaker by promoting some type of goods-&-services;

- **enabling** some course of action (typically some kind of social process), either literally enabling (empowering) them by instructing them in some type of procedure or constraining them by regulating their behavior;

social processes (i.e. 'doing' processes – social processes constitutive of context, semiotic processes facilitating [i.e. 'meaning' facilitating 'doing']):

- **doing** – performing some form of social behavior, on one's own or as part of a team, with semiotic processes ('meaning') coming in to facilitate this social behavior through direction or collaboration.

As previously stated, the field of activity of our data is primarily recreating. Both the ST and the TTs are written in the form of poetry, and the activities of language in literature are imagined, with a theme of verbal art (cf. Hasan 1985). We point out the fields being recreated in the poems. As in recreating field, any of the eight different types of fields can be recreated. Our analysis shows that the translators of TT1, TT3, and TT4 maintain the fields of the ST, while the fields in TT2 are sometimes altered by the translator. Figure 5.2 quantifies the frequency of the fields of activity recreated. Among the fifty poems from *Stray Birds*, the fields of expounding, recommending, and doing are not found in the analysis, and the fields recreated include reporting, sharing, enabling, and exploring.

The field of reporting has the largest frequency in the analysis. Poems of reporting field serve to report on particular instances of phenomena and to create "episodic" knowledge in contrast with the theoretical knowledge presented in expounding field. Through reporting, the poet and the translators can report the various events and goings-on in nature or society. These events

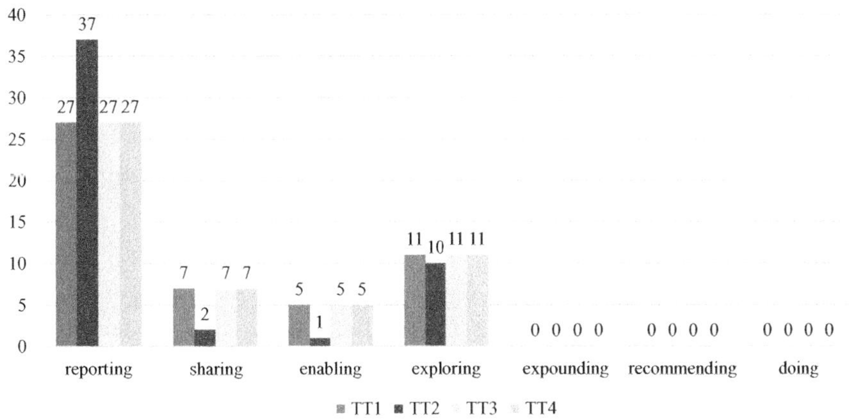

FIGURE 5.2 Frequency of different fields of activity recreated

can either happen in the natural environment (e.g. Poem 1 in the ST, which reports what the stray birds in summer and yellow leaves in autumn have done respectively, reflecting on the stray birds and the yellow leaves' doings and happenings), be related to the narrator's personal experience (e.g. Poem 16 in the ST, which reports on the narrator's experience in one morning, depicting how the narrator communicates with the world), or be associated with God (e.g. Poem 46 in the ST, which reports on the doings and ideas of God, commenting on God's creation of the world, and explaining how God finds himself through the process of creating). In Example 5.1,[1] the actions of God are reported by the poet and the translators in an objective way, with no personal opinion being added.

EXAMPLE 5.1

ST: God finds himself by creating.
TT1: 上帝从创造中找到他自己。
PY: shàng dì cóng chuàng zào zhōng zhǎo dào tā zì jǐ.
BT: God finds himself from creating.
TT2: 创造亦已成，天帝匿无踪。
PY: chuàng zào yì yǐ chéng, tiān dì nì wú zōng.
BT: Creation had been completed, God had no trace.
及寻本来身，却被创造容。
PY: jí xún běn lái shēn, què bèi chuàng zào róng.
BT: Then he looked for his original body, but it was contained in his creation.
TT3: 上帝造了万物
PY: shàng dì zào le wàn wù
BT: God created everything
才察觉到自己
PY: cái chá jué dào zì jǐ
BT: then realized himself
TT4: 神在创造中发现自己
PY: shén zài chuàng zào zhōng fā xiàn zì jǐ
BT: God finds himself in creation.

(Adapted from Tagore 1931: 3; 2008: 26; 2010: 24; 2015: 46)

In poems of the sharing field, the narrator shares his personal experiences or values (opinions, attitudes, feelings, etc.) with the readers. Some poems of the sharing field are written in the dialogic mode in terms of dialogues between one speaker and another, such as the dialogues between the narrator, the sea, and the sky in Poem 12 of the ST, between the rustling leaves and the flower in Poem 23 of the ST, between the narrator and the moon in Poem 30 of the

ST. Example 5.2 shows how the narrator shares his opinions with God and the entire poem is concerned with the experiences of the narrator. The Vocative in the ST, "my Master," reveals whom this poem is addressed to and whom the narrator makes his confession to.

EXAMPLE 5.2

ST: My wishes are fools, they shout across thy songs, my Master. Let me but listen.
TT1: 主呀，我的那些愿望真是愚傻呀，它们杂在你的歌声中喧叫着呢。
PY: zhǔ ya, wǒ de nà xiē yuàn wàng zhēn shì yú shǎ ya, tā men zá zài nǐ de gē shēng zhōng xuān jiào zhe ne.
BT: Lord, those wishes of mine are so silly, they are shouting in your songs.
让我只是静听着吧。
PY: ràng wǒ zhǐ shì jìng tīng zhe ba.
BT: Let me only listen silently.
TT3: 我的祈祷像是傻瓜
PY: wǒ de qí dǎo xiàng shì shǎ guā
BT: My prays are like fools
喃喃的祷告声 还盖过颂歌
PY: nán nán de dǎo gào shēng hái gài guò sòng gē
BT: The murmuring sound of prayer even surpassed the ode.
上主啊 听听我罢了
PY: shàng zhǔ a tīng tīng wǒ bà le
BT: My master, just listen to me.
TT4: 神啊 我的欲念如此纷纷扰扰呆痴憨傻
PY: shén a wǒ de yù niàn rú cǐ fēn fēn rǎo rǎo dāi chī hān shǎ
BT: God, my desires are so troublesome and silly,
好吧 我只是听听吧
PY: hǎo ba wǒ zhǐ shì tīng ting ba
BT: All right, I'm just listening.

(Adapted from Tagore 1931: 2; 2008: 12; 2010: 11; 2015: 19)

Poems of the enabling field are addressed by the narrator to the various addressees, such as "troupe of little vagrants of the world" in Poem 2, "my heart" in Poem 13, and "Beauty" in Poem 28, with purposes of instructing the addressees or regulating their behaviors. In Example 5.3, the narrator enables the addressee not to impute the food. The speech function of command is frequently seen in poems of the enabling field; while lexicogrammatically, we find mood types of imperatives that are realized by "Do not blame" in the ST, "不 要" (PY: bú yào; IG: NEG do) in TT1 and TT3, as well as "别 怪" (PY: bié guài; IG: NEG blame) and "要 怪" (PY: yào guài; IG: do blame) in TT4.

EXAMPLE 5.3

ST: Do not blame your food because you have no appetite.
TT1: 不要因为你自己没有胃口，而去责备食物。
PY: bú yào yīn wéi nǐ zì jǐ méi yǒu wèi kǒu, ér qù zé bèi shí wù.
BT: Do not blame the food, because you have no appetite yourself.
TT3: 别怪食物不好吃
PY: bié guài shí wù bù hǎo chī
BT: Do not blame that the food is not delicious
要怪自己没胃口
PY: yào guài zì jǐ méi wèi kǒu
BT: You should blame that you have no appetite yourself.
TT4: 没食欲的时候 不要责备你的食物
PY: méi shí yù de shí hòu bú yào zé bèi nǐ de shí wù
BT: When you have no appetite, do not blame your food.
(Adapted from Tagore 1931: 3; 2008: 23; 2010: 13; 2015: 40)

Poems of the exploring field are also found. In these poems, the narrator openly expresses his values and positions by reviewing commodities or indicating his positions. In Example 5.4, the narrator comments on the characteristics of her wistful face and assigns values to it, comparing her face to the rain at night and arguing about how her face haunts the narrator's dream. Also, we note that the field of exploring in this poem is equivalently recreated in all the four TTs.

EXAMPLE 5.4

ST: Her wistful face haunts my dreams like the rain at night.
TT1: 她的热切的脸，如夜雨似的，搅扰着我的梦魂。
PY: tā de rè qiè de liǎn, rú yè yǔ sì de, jiǎo rǎo zhe wǒ de mèng hún.
BT: Her earnest face, like the night rain, interrupts my soul of dream.
TT2: 颊晕急相偎，忆著心曲乱。
PY: jiá yùn jí xiāng wēi, yì zhuó xīn qǔ luàn.
BT: Her red cheek leans close to me. The melody of my heart is disturbed when I recall her.
正如夜雨声，使我梦魂断。
PY: zhèng rú yè yǔ shēng, shǐ wǒ mèng hún duàn.
BT: It is like the sound of night rain, and overwhelms my dream.
TT3: 她那渴望的脸庞 萦绕在我梦中
PY: tā nà kě wàng de liǎn páng yíng rào zài wǒ mèng zhōng

BT: That longing face of hers lingers in my dream
就好像雨滴 在牵扯着黑夜
PY: jiù hǎo xiàng yǔ dī zài qiān chě zhe hēi yè
BT: just like raindrops that drag the night.
TT4: 她期待的脸萦绕我的梦
PY: tā qī dài de liǎn yíng rào wǒ de mèng
BT: Her expectant face surrounds my dream.
雨落进夜的城
PY: yǔ luò jìn yè de chéng
BT: Rain falls in the city of the night.

(Adapted from Tagore 1931: 1; 2008: 6; 2010: 5; 2015: 8)

TABLE 5.1 Frequency of different fields of activity recreated

field of activity	Poem No. in the ST, TT1, TT3, and TT4	freq.	Poem No. in TT2	freq.
reporting	1, 3, 4, 14, 16, 17, 21, 24, 25, 27, 29, 32, 33, 34, 35, 36, 39, 41, 43, 44, 45, 46, 47, 48, 50, 51, 52, 53	28	1, 2, 3, 4, 6, 7, 11, 12, 15, 17, 20, 21, 23, 24, 25, 26, 27, 30, 32, 33, 34, 35, 36, 38, 39, 40, 41, 43, 44, 45, 46, 47, 48, 50, 51, 52, 53	37
sharing	7, 12, 19, 23, 30, 38	6	28, 42	2
enabling	2, 13, 15, 28, 40	5	14	1
exploring	6, 8, 9, 10, 11, 18, 20, 26, 37, 49, 42	11	8, 9, 10, 13, 16, 18, 19, 29, 37, 49	10

In Table 5.1, we include the number of the poems and categorize the poems according to the fields, highlighting the differences in field between the three TTs (TT1, TT3 and TT4) and TT2. As previously discussed, the fields of activity are not equivalently translated in TT2. From Table 5.1, we find an increase of reporting field in TT2 and a decrease in sharing, enabling, and exploring fields.

Some observations between TT2 and the ST can be made. Firstly, we note that some poems of the sharing, enabling, and exploring fields in the ST are translated as poems of the reporting field in TT2, resulting in the increase of reporting field in TT2. As shown in Example 5.5, the ST is addressed to the Vocative – "troupe of little vagrants of the world," requesting them to perform certain services, i.e. to leave their footprints in the narrator's world, and the field of ST is enabling. However, TT2 provides us with information about the situation of human beings and the field is changed to reporting.

EXAMPLE 5.5

ST: O troupe of little vagrants of the world, leave your footprints in my words.
TT2: 生世等萍聚，漂泊终何依。
PY: shēng shì děng píng jù, piāo bó zhōng hé yī.
BT: Man waits for union in life, he wanders and does not have anyone to finally rely on.
萍去踪仍在，临流歌芳菲。
PY: píng qù zōng réng zài, lín liú gē fāng fēi.
BT: The union breaks, but its trace still exists. Beside the stream, man sings fragrantly.

(Adapted from Tagore 1931: 2)

Secondly, some poems of the reporting field in the ST are translated as enabling in TT2. As shown in Example 5.6, the ST presents a description of how mighty and mysterious the power of creation is; whereas in TT2, the narrator invites his readers to take certain actions or to provide some services, i.e. to look at the mist in the morning. By comparing the ST with TT2, we find that the second clause complex in TT2 is added by the translator to build up a couplet with the first clause complex.

EXAMPLE 5.6

ST: The mystery of creation is like the darkness of night – it is great.
TT2: 伟哉造化力，神秘长夜玄。
PY: wěi zāi zào huà lì, shén mì cháng yè xuán.
BT: The great power of creation is like the mysterious long night.
不信有知妄，试看晓来烟。
PY: bú xìn yǒu zhī wàng, shì kàn xiǎo lái yān.
BT: If you don't believe that there is the unknown, try to look at the mist in the morning.

(Adapted from Tagore 1931: 1)

Thirdly, poem of the enabling, sharing, and reporting fields in the ST can be translated as exploring in TT2. In Example 5.7, the enabling field in the ST is characterized by an imperative mood, requesting the addressee – "my heart" to undertake certain actions. However, in TT2, the field is changed to exploring, through which the narrator's opinion is expressed and the narrator's deep love for the addressee of the poem is revealed.

EXAMPLE 5.7

ST: Listen, my heart, to the whispers of the world with which it makes love to you.
TT2: 静听复静听，静中呼我心。
PY: jìng tīng fù jìng tīng, jìng zhōng hū wǒ xīn.
BT: Listen silently and listen silently, in silence you call my heart.
世间私语处，爱尔意堪寻。
PY: shì jiān sī yǔ chù, ài ěr yì kān xún.
BT: At the place for private talk in the world, I love you, and I will seek the meaning of love.

(Adapted from Tagore 1931: 2)

As stated by Halliday (e.g. 2001, 2009), translators tend to focus on the experiential meaning, which is closely associated with field. Therefore, field is seldom changed in translation. Previous systemic functional analyses of literary texts (e.g. Wang 2015, 2017; Wang & Ma 2020) also suggest that the fields in the ST are often equivalently re-construed in the TTs. Seen from this perspective, TT2 is unique among the various literary translations.

5.2 Contextual analysis of tenor

For the contextual analysis of tenor, we point out the tenor relations between the poet, the translators, and the readers. The perspectives involved include institutional role and familiarity.

In terms of institutional role, Rabindranath Tagore, the author of *Stray Birds*, was a famous poet from India and was one of the first non-European writers who won the Nobel Prize for literature. As an important literary figure in India, he reshaped Bengali literature with his poems whose styles range from classical formalism to ecstatic (see e.g. Zhang 1994; Islam 1995; Gupta 2013; Tagore 2016b).

The translator of TT1, Zheng Zhenduo, was a famous Chinese writer and poet, and was one of the first people to translate Tagore's *Stray Birds* into Chinese. He also wrote several essays on translation (e.g. Zheng 1921, 2004a, 2004b), reflecting on his experiences of translating from English to Chinese and suggesting some methods of translation practice.

The translator of TT2, Yao Hua, was a contemporary of Zheng Zhenduo. Even though he translated *Stray Birds* into classical Chinese, he could not read English – the source language of *Stray Birds*. Instead, he translated by adapting Zheng Zhenduo's translation, i.e. TT1 in this study, and creatively mapped Zheng's translation onto the classical form of Chinese poetry (see Jiang 1980/1986; Yao 2000).

Lu Jinde, the translator of TT3, was a Taiwanese businessman and an amateur writer who took literature creation as one of his hobbies. Not much translated work was done by him.

Feng Tang, the translator of TT4, is a contemporary poet, a doctor, a businessman, and a professional writer in China. Sexual descriptions can be found in his novels such as *Bu Er* (不二) and *So Insane* (搜神记), whose complete versions were only published in Hong Kong and Taiwan, whereas sanitized versions were published in mainland China after being censored (cf. Wong 2017).

In Figure 5.3, we consider familiarity between the translators and the readers as a cline from unknown to intimate. Firstly, we locate TT2 towards the unknown end of the cline of familiarity, as the translator of TT2 maintains a more authoritative tone compared with Tagore and the other three translators (see discussions in Section 5.1 for the choice of changing other fields in the ST to reporting in TT2). Secondly, we locate the ST, TT1, and TT3 in the middle of the cline of familiarity, as an equal tenor relationship between the translators and the readers is adopted, which is neither totally unknown nor intimate. Thirdly, TT4 is located towards the intimate end of the cline of familiarity due to the choices of amorous lexes made by the translator, which shorten the distance between him and his readers.

The unique lexical choices in TT4 can be seen in Example 5.8, in which "makes love" semiotically in the ST is translated as "做 爱 (PY: zuò ài; BT: make love)," i.e. making love physically and biologically. In the other three TTs, the lexical choices include "爱 的 表示" (PY: ài de biǎo shì; IG: love SUB expression), "爱 尔" (PY: ài ěr; IG: love you), and "它 爱 你" (PY: tā ài nǐ, IG: it love you). The shift in the different orders of systems changes the tenor from medium in the ST to intimacy in TT4, a change which some readers find irritating.

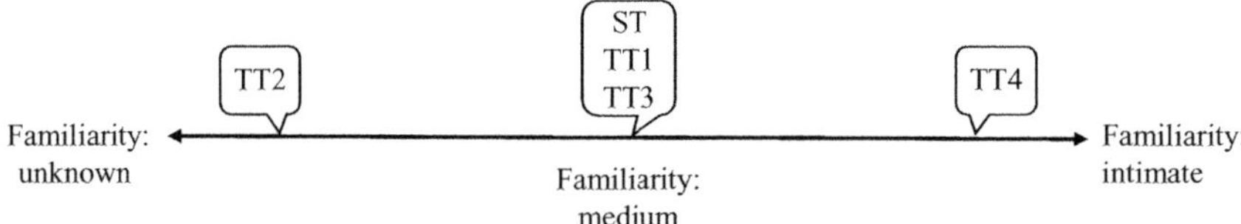

FIGURE 5.3 Locating the ST and the four TTs on the cline of familiarity

---

EXAMPLE 5.8

ST: Listen, my heart, to the whispers of the world with which it **makes love** to you.

TT1: 静静地听，我的心呀，听那 "世界" 的低语，这是他对你的**爱的表示**呀。

PY: jìng jìng de tīng, wǒ de xīn ya, tīng nà "shì jiè" de dī yǔ, zhè shì tā duì nǐ de ài de biǎo shì ya.

BT: Quietly listen, my heart, to the whisper of the world. It is his expression of love to you.

TT2: 静听复静听，静中呼我心。世间私语处，**爱尔意**堪寻。

PY: jìng tīng fù jìng tīng, jìng zhōng hū wǒ xīn. shì jiān sī yǔ chù, ài ěr yì kān xún.

BT: Listen silently and listen silently, in silence you call my heart. At the place for private talk in the world, I love you, and I will seek the meaning of love.

TT3: 心哪 请聆听天地对你的窸窣细语 它说的是 **它爱你**

PY: xīn na qǐng líng tīng tiān dì duì nǐ de xī sū xì yǔ tā shuō de shì tā ài nǐ

BT: My heart, please listen to the whisper of the world, it says it loves you.

TT4: 心呐 听吧 这世界和你**做爱**的细碎响声啊

PY: xīn na tīng ba zhè shì jiè hé nǐ zuò ài de xì suì xiǎng shēng a

BT: My heart, listen to the sound the world makes love with you.

(Adapted from Tagore 1931: 2; 2008: 9; 2010: 8; 2015: 13)

Similar lexical choices are occasionally found in TT4, but the number is quite small. Other examples include "lover" as "情人" (PY: qíng rén; IG: lover/ sweetheart), "kiss" as "舌吻" (PY: shé wěn; IG: tongue kiss), "noise" as "肉欲" (PY: ròu yù; IG: lust), "put off its mask" as "解开 裤裆" (PY: jiě kāi kù dāng; IG: unlock crotch), "wish" as "欲念" (IG: yù niàn; IG: desire), "hospitable" as "骚" (PY: sāo; BT: coquettish), and "woman" as "姑娘" (PY: gū niang; IG: girls), which all shorten the distance between readers and authors/translators in terms of tenor.

5.3 Contextual analysis of mode

The description of mode in the ST and the four TTs focuses on the perspectives of medium and channel. Firstly, in terms of medium, our data is written to be read by readers. Although it is the readers' choice to read the poems aloud or in silence, the rhythm and rhyme scheme makes the poems suitable to be read aloud. On the one hand, composed in the style of poetry, line breaks are found in TT2, TT3, and TT4, and rhymed choices are identified in TT2 and TT4. Therefore, in a previous study, Ma (2018) has suggested that these three TTs are more suitable to be read aloud. On the other hand, written in prose style and without rhymed choices, the ST and TT1 are more suitable to be read in silence (see Chapter 3 for graphological and phonological analyses).

Secondly, the channels for the ST and the TTs are written words, as they are published as books. In TT4, some lexical choices suitable for the spoken mode are found, such as "小 混蛋" (PY: xiǎo hún dàn; IG: little bastard), "骚" (PY: sāo; IG: coquettish) as well as some clause particles like "呐" (PY: na; IG: MOD) and "哒" (PY: da; IG: MOD), which signal a shift from written mode to spoken. As illustrated in Example 5.9, "丫" (PY: ya; IG: bastard), which is often seen in vulgar language, is used in TT4 to substitute "呀" (PY: ya; MOD). In this way, a contrast is formed between "你 丫 是 我的" (PY: nǐ yā shì wǒ de; IG: you bastard be mine) and "我 呀 是 你的" (PY: wǒ ya shì nǐ de; IG: I MOD be yours). This lexical choice is eye-catching and it further pushes TT4 from written mode towards spoken.

EXAMPLE 5.9

ST: Power said to the world,
"you are mine"
The world kept it prisoner on her throne.
Love said to the world,
"I am thine."
The world gave it the freedom of her house.
TT4: 强权 对 世界 说:
PY: qiáng quán duì shì jiè shuō:
IG: Power to world say:
BT: Power said to the world
"你 丫 是 我的。"
PY: "nǐ yā shì wǒ de."
IG: "you bastard be mine."
BT: "You bastard are mine."
世界 让 强权 变成 王座 的 囚徒
PY: shì jiè ràng qiáng quán biàn chéng wáng zuò de qiú tú
IG: world let power become throne SUB prisoner
BT: The world let power becomes prisoner of the throne.
爱情 对 世界 说:
PY: ài qíng duì shì jiè shuō:
IG: love to world say:
BT: Love said to the world:
"我 呀 是 你的。"
PY: "wǒ ya shì nǐ de."
IG: "I MOD be yours."
BT: "I am yours."
世界 让 爱情 在 世 上 任意 飞舞
PY: shì jiè ràng ài qíng zài shì shàng rèn yì fēi wǔ
IG: world let love CV world in freely fly
BT: The world lets love fly freely in the world.

(Adapted from Tagore 2015: 93)

5.4 Contextual analysis and translation shifts

In this section, we summarize some patterns of translation shifts found in each translation and relate the lexicogrammatical choices to the contextual analysis.

5.4.1 Contextual analysis and translation shifts in TT1

The translator of TT1, Zheng Zhenduo, favored literal translation rather than free translation and believed that the arrangement of words in the ST had to be reflected in the translation. He also held that the overall structure of a poem, its pattern in arranging the paragraphs, its organization of sentences as well as ingenious word choices in the ST should be transplanted to the translation. Hence, the artistic beauty can be preserved by following this approach (Zheng 1921, 2004a, 2004b).

Zheng has fully applied his method to his translation of *Stray Birds*. His translation follows the graphological pattern of the ST and is not rhymed by following the ST. Based on the translation shifts found (see Tables 4.5 and 4.7), it can be observed that TT1 has the smallest number of Theme shifts and process type shifts compared to the other TTs, as Zheng attempts to reduce the number of translation shifts and to maintain translation equivalence in TT1. For instance, in Example 5.10, both the Themes (underlined for emphasis) and the process types in the ST remain unchanged. Translation equivalence is maintained in these two respects.

EXAMPLE 5.10

ST: <u>Man</u> is a born child, (process type: relational: identifying)
<u>his power</u> is the power of growth. (process type: relational: identifying)
TT1: <u>人</u> 是 一 个 初生的 孩子， (process type: relational: identifying)
PY: rén shì yí gè chū shēng de hái zi,
IG: man be one MEAS newborn child,
BT: Man is a newborn child,
<u>他的</u> 力量， 就 是 生长的 力量。 (process type: relational: identifying)
PY: tā de lì liàng, jiù shì shēng zhǎng de lì liàng.
IG: his power VADV be growing power.
BT: his power is the power of growth.

(Adapted from Tagore 2010: 14)

One pattern of the translation shifts in TT1 is that most of the downranked clauses in the ST tend to be translated as major clauses, which lead to several translation shifts, such as the addition of topical Theme and process type. As shown in Example 5.11, the poem that consists of one clause is translated as a poem with five clauses. In this way, four additional topical Themes, i.e. "世界" (PY: shì jiè; IG: world), are added to TT1. Various process types, including two material processes, one relational, and one behavioral are also added.

EXAMPLE 5.11

ST: I sit at my window this morning [[[where the world like a passer-by stops for a moment, || nods to me || and goes]]]. (process type: material)
TT1: 我 今 晨 坐 在 窗 前，(process type: material)
PY: wǒ jīn chén zuò zài chuāng qián,
IG: I today morning sit CV window front,
BT: I sit in front of the window this morning,
"世界" 如 一 个 过路 的 人 似的，(process type: relational: identifying)
PY: "shì jiè" rú yí gè guò lù de rén sì de,
IG: "world" be like one MEAS pass-by SUB person as if,
BT: The world is like a passer-by.
[ø: "世界"] 停留 了 一会，(process type: material)
PY: "shì jiè" tíng liú le yí huì,
IG: "world" stop ASP moment,
BT: The world stops for a moment.
[ø: "世界"] 向 我 点点 头 (process type: behavioral)
PY: "shì jiè" xiàng wǒ diǎn diǎn tóu
IG: "world" to me nod head
BT: The world nods to me.
[ø: "世界"] 又 走 过去 了。(process type: material)
PY: "shì jiè" yòu zǒu guò qù le.
IG: "world" then walk by ASP.
BT: The world then walks by.

(Adapted from Tagore 2010: 9)

Other patterns of translation shift found in TT1 include the process type substitution of replacing relational: identifying with relational: attributive (see Section 4.4.2) and the addition of conjunctions that function as textual Themes (see Section 4.2.1.1). Despite the various changes made, TT1 follows the ST closely and is equivalent to the ST in many respects. Also, the translator of TT1 maintains the contextual parameters of field, tenor, and mode like those in the ST, thereby making TT1 a "faithful" translation by retaining (i) the reporting, enabling, sharing as well as sharing fields, (ii) the medium familiarity within the author-reader relationship, and (iii) the elegant written mode of prose poem.

5.4.2 Contextual analysis and translation shifts in TT2

The translator of TT2, Yao Hua, was proficient in writing classical Chinese poems. In the preface of his *Stray Birds*, Yao (1921) argued that his purpose for translating Tagore's work was to produce poems that were not only characterized by traditional Chinese style, but were also refreshing, philosophical, and elegant as Tagore's original work.

Graphologically, the poems in TT2 are arranged in the traditional Chinese style with five Chinese characters in one line and four or eight lines in one poem. Such a form is very different from Tagore's ST composed in prose form. Phonologically, 37% of the poems in TT2 rhyme at the end of the lines by following rhyme patterns such as "a a b a" or "a b c b d b e b", with rhymed choices being made in lines of even number (see Section 3.2.2). Therefore, to map the ST onto the form of classical poetry, Yao Hua had to produce a large number of translation shifts to the extent of changing the field of activity in the ST. This explains why TT2 has the largest number of Theme shifts and process type shifts according to Tables 4.5 and 4.7. As a result of the additions and omissions of clauses in TT2, the most frequently found translation shifts include Theme addition, Theme omission, process type addition, and process type omission. Moreover, alterations are not very frequently found compared to the occurrences of addition and omission.

Example 5.12 shows how changes are made in terms of Theme and process type in TT2. Apart from omitting the Theme in the ST, i.e. "It is the tears of the earth," six different topical Themes are added in TT2, which include three instances of "她" (PY: tā; IG: she), one "意" (PY: yì; IG: thought), one "涕" (PY: tì; IG: tear), and one "自 泽" (PY: zì zé; IG: own moisture). Also, the material process in the ST, which is realized by the verbal group "keep," is omitted and six other processes are added.

EXAMPLE 5.12

ST: <u>It is the tears of the earth</u> that keep her smiles in bloom. (process type: material)
TT2: [ø: 她] 独 坐 (process type: material)
PY: tā dú zuò
IG: she alone sit
BT: She sits alone.
意 含 涕， (process type: relational: attributive)
PY: yì hán tì,
IG: thought contain tear,
BT: Tears are contained in her thought.
[ø: 她] 欢 来 (process type: relational: attributive)
PY: tā huān lái
IG: she happy time
BT: When she's happy,
[ø: 她] 一 展 眉。 (process type: behavioral)
PY: tā yì zhǎn méi.

> IG: she unfold eyebrow.
> BT: she will unfold her eyebrow.
> [ø: 涕] 沃 如 华上 露, (process type: relational: attributive)
> PY: tì wò rú huá shàng lù,
> IG: tears fertile be like gorgeous dew,
> BT: Her tears are fertile like the gorgeous dew.
> [ø: 涕] 自 泽 盛开 枝。 (process type: material)
> PY: tì zì zé shèng kāi zhī.
> IG: tears own moisture bloom branch.
> BT: Her tears moisture will bloom branches.
>
> (Adapted from Tagore 1931: 1)

The differences between TT1 and TT2 can be discussed by relating the norms to the TTs (cf. Toury 1995; Schäffner 1997). By taking initial norms into consideration, we find that the two translators' overall tendencies between source norms and target norms are different. Zheng Zhenduo is subject to the source norms and has produced an adequate translation, i.e. TT1 in the present study, which is largely equivalent to the ST both in content and form. In contrast, Yao Hua is subject to target norms. Therefore, in TT2, adequacy has to give way to acceptability in the target culture and a large number of translation shifts are thus found.

In addition to the largest number of translation shifts in lexicogrammatical analysis, the translator of TT2 tends to change sharing and exploring fields to reporting, thereby distancing himself from the audience (see Sections 5.1 and 5.2). At the same time, he maintains the elegant written mode of prose poems by providing a five-word ancient Chinese version of *Stray Birds*.

5.4.3 *Contextual analysis and translation shifts in TT3*

In the preface to his translation, Lu Jinde (2008), the translator of TT3, acknowledged that he started to translate *Stray Birds* for pleasure (see Section 5.2). In his translation, his focus was Tagore's ideas. To achieve this goal, he added some notes after each poem to interpret the ST. He held that not only did he translate Tagore's artistic conception, but also translated his philosophical ideas embedded in the Indian culture.

Graphologically, Lu separates his poems in lines and deliberately makes it different from the prose form in the ST. More separations of clause elements are seen in TT3, especially the participant-process separation and process-participant separation, which reflect the graphological shifts that the translator intends to make (see Section 3.1.4). Phonologically, Lu wishes to maintain the equivalence in the ST and does not rhyme in TT3 (see Section 3.2.4).

In terms of the frequency of translation shifts in lexicogrammar, TT3 has both the second smallest number of Theme shifts and process type shifts among all the TTs. In contrast with TT2 but similar to TT1, clauses are occasionally added in TT3. As shown in Example 5.13, the two Themes and process types in the ST are first translated equivalently in TT3. Then, an additional clause is added towards the end of the poem, which results in the addition of Theme – "雨 滴" (PY: yǔ dī; IG: rain drop) and the addition of a material process. Generally speaking, the lexicogrammatical choices in TT3 are similar to those in TT1, while their primary differences lie in the graphological features: TT1 closely follows the prose form of the ST, whereas TT3 divides elements of clauses into different lines, mostly separation of participant and process (see Section 3.1.4).

EXAMPLE 5.13

ST: <u>Her wistful face</u> haunts my dreams like the rain at night. (process type: material)
TT3: <u>她 那 渴望的 脸庞</u> 萦绕 在 我 梦 中 (process type: material)
PY: tā nà kě wàng de liǎn páng yíng rào zài wǒ mèng zhōng
IG: her that wistful face haunt CV my dream in
BT: Her wistful face haunts in my dream.
[ø: <u>她 那 渴望的 脸庞</u>] 就 好像 雨 滴 (process type: relational: identifying)
PY: tā nà kě wàng de liǎn páng jiù hǎo xiàng yǔ dī
IG: her that wistful face VADV be like rain drop
BT: Her wistful face is like the raindrops.
[ø:雨滴] 在 牵扯 着 黑 夜 (process type: material)
PY: yǔ dī zài qiān chě zhe hēi yè
IG: rain drop CV drag VPART black night
BT: Raindrops are dragging the black night.

(Adapted from Tagore 2008: 6)

From the perspective of initial norms (see Toury 1995), TT3 is subjected to the source norms and is congruent with the norms of faithfulness for poetry translation in China (Chan 2004). It is similar to TT1 in terms of Theme shift and process type shift, with an increased frequency of both shifts. No phonological shift is seen in TT3, but some graphological shifts due to the increased separation of process and participants can be found.

Contextually, similar to the translator of TT1, the translator of TT3 maintains the field and tenor of the ST, but changes the medium of the ST by separating the various elements such as participants and processes, which makes TT3 more suitable for reading aloud and is different from the mode of the ST.

5.4.4 Contextual analysis and translation shifts in TT4

The translator of TT4, Feng Tang (2015, 2019c), openly stated his opinions on translation in an essay titled "Twenty-seven instants during the translation of Tagore's *Stray Birds*." He believed that poems should be rhymed and rhymed poems are much better than the unrhymed (cf. Feng 2013). Therefore, "half of his time spent on translation was used to search for a best rhymed pattern" (Feng 2015: 335 our translation). He also suggested that he did not fully respect the ST, because he had the freedom to balance "fidelity, fluency, and elegance," which were regarded as three principles of translation and the parameters for discussions on translation in China since the 1900s (Yan 1984, 2004; Chan 2004). Therefore, we can consider Feng's choices in his translation as his personal preference (cf. Simeoni 1998).

Graphologically, the choices made by Feng Tang are quite similar to those in TT3 in that lines are separated instead of following the form of prose poem in TT1 and the ST. Phonologically, rhymed patterns are found in 37 poems out of a sample of 50, and the translator's purpose for rhyming is made explicit. As a result, the lexicogrammatical choices have to give way to the phonological choices, i.e. some translation shifts in lexicogrammar are due to the need to rhyme. In order to rhyme, the choices of Theme and process type are changed in TT4 and a free way of translation is adopted. As illustrated in Example 5.14, the Themes in the ST are all omitted, while two circumstances that function as marked topical Themes are added, namely "做梦 时" (PY: zuò mèng shí; IG: dream time) and "醒来 时" (PY: xǐng lái shí; IG: wake time). The process types in the ST are also changed. Aside from the omissions of two mental processes and one behavioral process, the relational: identifying process is substituted by relational: attributive and the relational: attributive process by a material one. In this way, the translator builds an antithetical structure in TT4, and rhymes the lexical choices at the end of each line, viz. "遥远" (PY: yáo yuǎn; IG: far) and "取暖" (PY: qǔ nuǎn; IG: warm).

EXAMPLE 5.14

ST: <u>Once</u> we dreamt (process type: mental)
<u>that we</u> were strangers. (process type: relational: identifying)
<u>We</u> wake up (process type: behavioral)
[ø: we] to find (process type: mental)
<u>that we</u> were dear to each other. (process type: relational: attributive)
TT4: <u>做梦 时</u> 我们 距离 非常 遥远 (process type: relational: attributive)
PY: zuò mèng shí wǒ mén jù lí fēi cháng yáo yuǎn
IG: dream time we distance very far
BT: At dreaming time, our distance is very far.

醒来 时 我们 在 彼此 的 视野 里 取暖 (process type: material)
PY: xǐng lái shí wǒ mén zài bǐ cǐ de shì yě lǐ qǔ nuǎn
IG: wake time we CV each other SUB vision in warm
BT: At waking time, we warm each other in our visions.

(Adapted from Tagore 2015: 9)

Omissions and substitutions of process types are frequently found in TT4. For instance, relational processes realized by the verbal group "be" in the ST are frequently omitted (see Example 4.50 in Chapter 4), which are to some extent modelled on the translator's style (cf. Feng 2015). In fact, readers are not hostile towards these process type shifts. What they are against is Feng's idiosyncratic choice of words with obscene associations, such as "解开 裤裆" (PY: jiě kāi kù dāng; IG: unstrap crotch) and "舌吻" (PY: shé wěn; IG: French kiss), which are unlikely to be found in Tagore's original. In other words, we argue that most objections are associated with the lexical rather than with grammatical choices as well as the changes in tenor and mode of TT4.

In terms of the contextual parameters, although a large number of translation shifts are found in TT4, the translator maintains the same field as that of the ST. However, in terms of tenor, he establishes a close relationship with his readers by using certain lexical choices and changes the mode of elegant written work into colloquial by adding spoken lexical choices.

In Section 5.4, we have summarized some patterns of translation shifts based on the analyses from Chapters 3 to 5. In the next chapter, we will present a summary of the findings of the book and suggest some directions for future research.

Note

1 We only provide pinyin and back translations for the examples in Section 5.1. Different from other examples, interlinear glossing is not provided, as these examples are only used to illustrate the field of activity in the ST and the TTs.

6

CONCLUSION

Exploring poetry translation with Systemic Functional Linguistics

In Chapter 6, we introduce some contributions of the book in terms of (i) the significance of investigating *Stray Birds* and its translations, (ii) the framework proposed, (iii) the further development of "the environments of translation" and "metafunctional translation shift," (iv) translation practice, and (v) translation universals. We then suggest some directions for future research.

6.1 Significance of the study

Firstly, this study provides a new perspective on *Stray Birds* and its four Chinese translations. As a collection of poems written by Rabindranath Tagore, *Stray Birds* has seldom been investigated in linguistics in general and in SFL in particular (cf. Islam 1995 for discussions on the translatability of Tagore's poems). Since *Stray Birds* is a literary text with high values (cf. Halliday 1971, 1982, 1988, 1994), it is worthwhile to carry out an analysis in terms of the different modes of meaning in order to identify the meaning-making resources adopted by Rabindranath Tagore and the four translators in the source text and the target texts.

With the publication of TT4 translated by Feng Tang, *Stray Birds* was once again intensely debated, especially in China. Various people, whether academic or non-academic, discussed the quality of the Chinese translations of *Stray Birds*. However, most of these discussions were subjective and were not based on any rigorous linguistic analysis. Based on an in-depth systemic functional analysis, this book presents an evidential basis for such discussions, assessing the quality of the translations and pointing out the translation shifts made by the four translators in terms of Theme and process type.

Secondly, a framework suitable for the systemic functional analysis of poetry has been proposed in this book (see Section 2.3). In the framework, we took the expression plane of language, the content plane of language, and context into consideration, with the strata of graphology, phonology, lexicogrammar, and context being included (see Figure 2.5 in Chapter 2). Using this framework, we not only point out how *Stray Birds* and its four translations have been organized to effectively function in their contexts of situation and contexts of culture, but also compare the ST with the TTs and discuss the translation shifts found in the data.

Within the framework, the graphological and phonological analyses took features such as rhyme scheme, punctuation mark, and line break into consideration. Further, it was found that such choices in graphology and phonology influenced the translators' lexicogrammatical choices. For instance, in order to rhyme, the translator of TT4 added some clauses or changed certain process types; also, in order to map the English prose poetry onto the form of Chinese classical poetry, various translation shifts in lexicogrammar were found in TT2. The lexicogrammatical analysis provided a quantitative profile of the choices of Theme and process type in the ST and the TTs and helped us to investigate the probability of certain choices in the data. In addition, two kinds of metafunctional translation shift were examined, i.e. Theme shift and process type shift. A contextual analysis was also carried out from the perspective of field, tenor, and mode. Differences between the ST and the TTs were observed, and some patterns regarding to the translation shifts in the four TTs were discussed.

Thirdly, by applying SFL to poetry translation, this book extends Matthiessen's (2001, 2014b) studies in the area of translation (cf. Wang 2017; Wang & Ma 2020, forthcoming). Various dimensions of the environments of translation were related in this study, such as the hierarchy of stratification, the spectrum of metafunction, the cline of instantiation, and the hierarchy of rank. In terms of the metafunctional translation shifts, we quantified and discussed two of them, i.e. Theme shift within the textual metafunction and process type shift within the experiential metafunction. Delicate categories of the translation shifts were also suggested.

Fourthly, this book reveals the choices translators face when translating poetry. Such choices are two-fold, i.e. both in the interpretation of the source text and in the recreation of the target text. During the translation process, a translator always has to select one choice among the many that lay in the meaning potential of the target language. In this way, the more target texts we investigated, the more knowledge about the meaning potential of the target language could be accumulated. Further, our analysis supports the claim that discourse analysis for translators would present them the challenges that they are likely to encounter and would eventually be beneficial to them when performing their translation tasks (cf. Burns et al. 2009).

Fifthly, our study supports House's (e.g. 2008, 2018) claim that it is futile to search for universals in translation studies by providing various evidences (for more discussions, see Ma 2018; Wang & Ma 2020; cf. Baker 1993; Mauranen 2008). For instance, House (2008: 12) holds that the diachronic development of texts that belong to a certain genre is taken into consideration in the search of translation universals: translations develop dynamically and "may be critically influenced by the status of the language of the source text genre which in turn may influence the nature of the translation text genre and also the nature of comparable texts in the same genre." Evidence was found in our analysis of the four TTs. The translation in the style of Chinese classical poetry (TT2) was heavily influenced by the nature of its genre. Its style was unique in the uses of circumstances as marked topical Themes, a writing skill in ancient Chinese poems used to foreground the situation of the poems, and was not observed in the translations of modern poetry (TT1, TT3, and TT4).

6.2 Future directions

Based on the insights from this book, future studies can be carried out from the following perspectives:

Firstly, the data size of the ST and the TTs can be increased. For pragmatic concerns, we did not analyze and compare all the 325 poems in *Stray Birds* and its translations. Instead, 50 poems were selected. If we expand the data, it is likely that more findings will be revealed and the quantitative analysis will be expected to be further related to the conception of probability in language (cf. Halliday 1991a; Halliday & James 1993; Jesus & Pagano 2006).

Secondly, more comprehensive descriptions of the expression plane of language can be carried out from the perspectives of phonology and graphology. A systematic analysis of the expression plane of language will be very helpful to interpret the findings of the lexicogrammatical analysis. Also, the value for carrying out phonological and graphological analysis can be gained from multimodal analysis (e.g. Bateman 2008, 2014) and stylistic analysis (e.g. Hasan 1985; Lukin 2015; Webster 2015).

Thirdly, as the data of TT2 is written in the form of classical Chinese poetry, the present study offers a preliminary attempt at analyzing classical Chinese from the perspective of SFL. Poems written in classical Chinese have seldom been studied within the SFL framework; therefore, future studies can analyze more classical Chinese poems and their translations, pointing out the "trade-offs" made by translators (cf. Huang 2002, 2006).

Fourthly, other types of texts can be taken into consideration in future studies on translation from the systemic functional perspective. Apart from other poems in literature, texts from different categories of the fields of activity can be examined to ascertain how the choices made by translators differ as well as how translation shifts manifest in texts of different fields.

Finally, a further step can be taken when we consider the two goals of text analysis (Halliday 2001: 13), i.e. "to explain why the text means what it does" and "to explain why the text is valued as it is." The second goal is much harder to achieve because of the involvement of translation evaluation. Based on the present research, we can model the frameworks of translation quality assessment (e.g. House 1977, 1997, 2015) to explain why readers prefer certain translations of *Stray Birds* and dislike other translations.

REFERENCES

Alves, Fabio, Adriana Pagano, Stella Neumann, Erich Steiner & Silvia Hansen-Schirra. 2010. "Units of translation and grammatical shifts: Towards an integration of product- and process-based research in translation." In Gregory Shreve & Erik Angelone (eds.), *Translation and cognition*. Amsterdam & Philadelphia: John Benjamins. 109–142.

Baker, Mona. 1993. "Corpus linguistics and translation studies: Implications and applications." In Mona Baker, Gill Francis & Elena Tognini-Bonelli (eds.), *Text and technology: In honour of John Sinclair*. Amsterdam & Philadelphia: John Benjamins. 233–250.

Bassnett, Susan. 1980. *Translation studies*. London: Methuen.

Bassnett, Susan. 2007. "Influence and intertextuality: A reappraisal." *Forum for Modern Language Studies* 43(2): 134–146.

Bateman, John A. 2008. *Multimodality and genre: A foundation for the systematic analysis of multimodal documents*. Hampshire & New York: Palgrave Macmillan.

Bateman, John A. 2014. *Text and image: A critical introduction to the visual/verbal divide*. London & New York: Routledge.

Beals, Kurt. 2014. "Alternatives to impossibility: Translation as dialogue in the works of Paul Celan." *Translation Studies* 7(3): 284–299.

Bergam, Marija. 2013. "Vasko Popa's poetry in English: The reception and uses of literary translation." *Translation Studies* 6(2): 232–248.

Bian, Zhilin [卞之琳]. 1987. "译诗艺术的成年 [On the maturity of the art of translating poems]." In 《中国翻译》编辑部 [Editorial Department of Chinese Translators Journal] (ed.), 翻译的艺术 [The art of translation]. 北京 [Beijing]: 中国对外翻译出版公司 [China Translation and Publishing Corporation]. 329–333.

Bian, Zhilin. 2004. "Translation and its positive/negative impact on modern Chinese poetry." (Kelly Chan, Trans.). In Leo Tak-hung Chan (ed.), *Twentieth-century Chinese translation theory: Modes, issues and debates*. Amsterdam & Philadelphia: John Benjamins. 211–213.

Boase-Beier, Jean. 2006. *Stylistic approaches to translation*. Manchester: St Jerome.

Boase-Beier, Jean. 2009. "Poetry translation." In Mona Baker & Gabriela Saldanha (eds.), *Routledge encyclopedia of translation studies*. 2nd edition. London & New York: Routledge. 475–487.

Boase-Beier, Jean. 2011a. "Translating Celan's poetics of silence." *Target* 23(2): 165–177.

Boase-Beier, Jean. 2011b. *A critical introduction to translation studies*. London & New York: Continuum.

Boase-Beier, Jean. 2015. *Translating the poetry of the holocaust: Translation, style and the reader*. London & New York: Bloomsbury.

Bourdieu, Pierre. 1984. *Distinction: A social critique of the judgement of taste* (Richard Nice, Trans.). London: Routledge.

Bourdieu, Pierre. 1996. *The rules of art: Genesis and structure of the literary field* (Susan Emanuel, Trans.). Stanford, CA: Stanford University Press.

Boyack, Kevin W., Richard Klavans & Katy Börner. 2005. "Mapping the backbone of science." *Scientometrics* 64(3): 351–374.

Brogan, T.V.F. 1993. "Poetry." In Alex Preminger & T.V.F. Brogan (eds.), *The new Princeton encyclopedia of poetry and poetics*. New York: MJF Books. 938–942.

Burns, Anne, Mira Kim & Christian M.I.M. Matthiessen. 2009. "Doctoral work in translation studies as an interdisciplinary mutual learning process: How a translator, teacher educator and linguistic typologist worked together." *The Interpreter and Translator Trainer* 3(1): 107–128.

Butt, David G. 1984a. *To be without a description of to be: The relationship between theme and lexicogrammar in the poetry of Wallace Stevens*. PhD thesis, Macquarie University, Sydney, Australia.

Butt, David G. 1984b. "Perceiving as making in the poetry of Wallace Stevens." *Nottingham Linguistic Circular: Special Issue on Systemic Linguistics* 13: 124–145.

Butt, David G. 1988. "Ideational meaning and the existential fabric of a poem." In Robin Fawcett & David Young (eds.), *New developments in systemic linguistics (volume 2): Theory and application*. London & New York: Pinter. 174–218.

Catford, J.C. 1965. *A linguistic theory of translation*. London: Oxford University Press.

Cavalcanti, Guido. 1991. *Thirty-three sonnets of Guido Cavalcanti* (Ezra Pound, Trans.). San Francisco: Arion Press.

Chan, Leo Tak-hung. (ed.). 2004. *Twentieth-century Chinese translation theory: Modes, issues and debates*. Amsterdam & Philadelphia: John Benjamins.

Chan, Shui Duen. 2016. "Punctuation." In Chu-Ren Huang & Dingxu Shi (eds.), *A reference grammar of Chinese*. Cambridge: Cambridge University Press. 577–590.

Chen, Songcen [陈松岑]. 1989. 礼貌语言 [Language of politeness]. 北京 [Beijing]: 商务印书馆 [Commercial Press].

Cheng, François. 2016. *Chinese poetic writing* (Donald A. Riggs & Jerome P. Seaton, Trans.). Hong Kong: The Chinese University Press.

Cheng, Yiyang & Biwei Li. 2019. "On the style and linguistic 'defamiliarization' of three Chinese translators of Garcia Lorca's poems." *Circulo de Lingüística Aplicada a la Comunicación* 77: 37–66.

Coleridge, Samuel Taylor. 1990. *Table talk*. Carl Woodring (ed.). Princeton, NJ: Princeton University Press.

Culler, Jonathan. 1975. *Structuralist poetics: Structuralism linguistics and the study of literature*. London: Routledge and Kegan Paul.

Dahlgren, Marta. 2005. "'Preciser what we are': Emily Dickinson's poems in translation: A study in literary pragmatics." *Journal of Pragmatics* 37: 1081–1107.

Dastjerdi, Vahid Hossein, Haadi Hakimshafaaii & Zahra Jannesaari. 2008. "Translation of poetry: Towards a practical model for translation analysis and assessment of poetic discourse." *Journal of Language & Translation* 9(1): 7–40.

Dastjerdi, Vahid Hossein, Yasamin Khosravani, Masoud Shokrollahi & Nasim Mohiman. 2011. "Translation quality assessment (TQA): A semiotic model for poetry translation." *Lebende Sprachen* 56(2): 338–361.

Davis, Paul. 2001. "'But slaves we are': Dryden and Virgil, translation and the 'Gyant Race'." *Translation and Literature* 10(1): 110–127.

Dever, Aileen. 2008. "Teaching Spanish grammar: Effective contextual strategies." *Hispania: A Journal Devoted to the Teaching of Spanish and Portuguese* 91(2): 428–434.

Dong, Dahui & Meng-Lin Chen. 2015. "Publication trends and co-citation mapping of translation studies between 2000 and 2015." *Scientometrics* 105(2): 1111–1128.

Eagleton, Terry. 2007. *How to read a poem*. Oxford: Blackwell.

Espindola, Elaine. 2016. "A systemic functional analysis of thematic structure: Directing attention to Yoda's linguistic manifestation." *WORD* 62(1): 22–34.

Espindola, Elaine & Yan Wang. 2015. "The enactment of modality in regulatory texts: A comparative study of tenancy agreements." *Journal of World Languages* 2(2–3): 106–125.

Fan, Cunzhong [范存忠]. 1986. "英国诗人论诗的翻译 [A discussion of poetry translation by English poets]." In 《中国翻译》编辑部 [Editorial Department of Chinese Translators Journal] (ed.), 翻译的艺术 [The art of translation]. 北京 [Beijing]: 中国对外翻译出版公司 [China Translation and Publishing Corporation]. 335–364.

Fauconnier, Gilles & Mark Turner. 2002. *The way we think*. New York: Basic Books.

Feng, Tang [冯唐]. 2013. 冯唐诗百首 [A hundred poems by Feng Tang]. 天津 [Tianjin]: 天津人民出版社 [Tianjin People's Press].

Feng, Tang [冯唐]. 2015. "翻译泰戈尔《飞鸟集》的二十七个刹那 [Twenty-seven instants during the translation of Tagore's *Stray birds*]." In Rabindranath Tagore. 飞鸟集 [Stray birds] (冯唐 Feng Tang, Trans.). 杭州 [Hangzhou]: 浙江文艺出版社 [Zhejiang Literature and Art Press]. 329–350.

Feng, Tang [冯唐]. 2019a. "自序: 为什么人类会害怕冯唐翻译的《飞鸟集》? [Preface: Why would human be afraid of *Stray birds* translated by Feng Tang?]." In Rabindranath Tagore. 飞鸟集 [Stray birds] (冯唐 Feng Tang, Trans.). 香港 [Hong Kong]: 天地图书 [Cosmo Books]. 5–9.

Feng, Tang [冯唐]. 2019b. "后记2: 你对我微笑不语 [Postscript II: You smiled and talked to me of nothing]." In Rabindranath Tagore. 飞鸟集 [Stray birds] (冯唐 Feng Tang, Trans.). 香港 [Hong Kong]: 天地图书 [Cosmo Books]. 215–219.

Feng, Tang [冯唐]. 2019c. "后记1: 翻译泰戈尔《飞鸟集》的二十七个刹那 [Postscript I: Twenty-seven instants during the translation of Tagore's *Stray birds*]." In Rabindranath Tagore. 飞鸟集 [Stray birds] (冯唐 Feng Tang, Trans.). 香港 [Hong Kong]: 天地图书 [Cosmo Books]. 188–214.

Firth, J.R. 1957. *Papers in linguistics 1934–1951*. London: Oxford University Press.

Firth, J.R. 1968. *Selected papers of J. R. Firth 1952–59*. Frank R. Palmer (ed.). London and Harlow: Longmans.

Frost, Robert. 1997. *Robert Frost: Collected poems, prose, and plays*. Richard Poirier & Mark Richardson (eds.). New York: Library of America.

Furniss, Tom & Michael Bath. 1996. *Reading poetry: An introduction*. London: Prentice Hall.

García, Adolfo Martín. 2008. "The Circumscribed Infinites Scheme (CIS): A deconstructive approach to translating poetry." *Target* 20(1): 115–134.

Garvin, Paul L. (ed.). 1964. *A Prague school reader on esthetics, literary structure, and style*. Washington, DC: Georgetown University Press.

General Administration of Quality, Inspection and Quarantine Bureau of the People's Republic of China (AQSIQ) [中华人民共和国国家质量监督检验检疫总局] & Standardization Administration of China [中国国家标准化管理委员会]. 2011. 标点符号用法 [General rules for punctuations]. 北京 [Beijing]: 中国标准出版社 [China Standard Press].

Guo, Moruo [郭沫若]. 2005. 郭沫若集 [The collected works of Guo Moruo]. 北京 [Beijing]: 中国社会科学出版社 [China Social Sciences Press].

Gupta, Uma Das. 2013. *Rabindranath Tagore: An illustrated life.* New Delhi: Oxford University Press.

Gutt, Ernst-August. 1991. *Translation and relevance: Cognition and context.* Oxford: Blackwell.

Halliday, M.A.K. 1956. "The linguistic basis of a mechanical thesaurus, and its application to English preposition classification." *Mechanical Translation* 3: 81–88. Reprinted in M.A.K. Halliday. 2005. Jonathan J. Webster (ed.), *Computational and quantitative Studies. Volume 6* in the *Collected works of M.A.K. Halliday.* London & New York: Continuum. 6–19.

Halliday, M.A.K. 1961. "Categories of the theory of grammar." *Word* 17: 241–292. Reprinted in M.A.K. Halliday. 2002. Jonathan J. Webster (ed.), *On grammar. Volume 1 in the Collected works of M.A.K. Halliday.* London & New York: Continuum. 37–94.

Halliday, M.A.K. 1962. "Linguistics and machine translation." *Zeitschrift für Phonetik, Sprachwissenschaft und Kommunikationsforschung* 15: 145–158. Reprinted in M.A.K. Halliday. 2005. Jonathan J. Webster (ed.), *Computational and quantitative studies. Volume 6 in the Collected works of M.A.K. Halliday.* London & New York: Continuum. 20–36.

Halliday, M.A.K. 1964. "The linguistic study of literary texts." In Horace Lunt (ed.), *Proceedings of the Ninth International Congress of Linguistics.* The Hague: Mouton. 302–307. Reprinted in M.A.K. Halliday. 2002. Jonathan J. Webster (ed.), *Linguistic studies of text and discourse. Volume 2 in the Collected works of M.A.K. Halliday.* London & New York: Continuum. 5–22.

Halliday, M.A.K. 1966. "General linguistics and its application to language teaching." In Angus McIntosh & M.A.K. Halliday. *Patterns of language: Paper in general, descriptive and applied linguistics.* London: Longmans. 1–41.

Halliday, M.A.K. 1967a. "Notes on transitivity and theme in English – part I." *Journal of Linguistics* 3: 37–82. Reprinted in M.A.K. Halliday. 2005. Jonathan J. Webster (ed.), *Studies in English language. Volume 7 in the Collected works of M.A.K. Halliday.* London & New York: Continuum. 5–54.

Halliday, M.A.K. 1967b. "Notes on transitivity and theme in English – part II." *Journal of Linguistics* 3: 199–244. Reprinted in M.A.K. Halliday. 2005. Jonathan J. Webster (ed.), *Studies in English language. Volume 7 in the Collected works of M.A.K. Halliday.* London & New York: Continuum. 55–109.

Halliday, M.A.K. 1971. "Linguistic function and literary style: An inquiry into the language of William Golding's *The inheritors.*" In Seymour Benjamin Chatman (ed.), *Literary style: A symposium.* London & New York: Oxford University Press. 330–365. Reprinted in M.A.K. Halliday. 2002. Jonathan J. Webster (ed.), *Linguistic studies of text and discourse. Volume 2 in the Collected works of M.A.K. Halliday.* London & New York: Continuum. 88–125.

Halliday, M.A.K. 1978. *Language as social semiotic: The social interpretation of language and meaning.* London: Edward Arnold.

Halliday, M.A.K. 1979. "Modes of meaning and modes of expression: Types of grammatical structure and their determination by different semantic functions." In David J. Allerton, Edward Carney & David Holdcroft (eds.), *Function and context in linguistic analysis*. Cambridge: Cambridge University Press. 57–79. Reprinted in M.A.K. Halliday. 2002. Jonathan J. Webster (ed.), *On grammar. Volume 1* in the *Collected works of M.A.K. Halliday*. London & New York: Continuum. 196–218.

Halliday, M.A.K. 1982. "The de-automatization of grammar: From Priestley's 'An inspector calls'." In John M. Anderson (ed.), *Language form and linguistic variation: Papers dedicated to Angus McIntosh*. Amsterdam: John Benjamins. 129-159. Reprinted in M.A.K. Halliday. 2002. Jonathan J. Webster (ed.), *Linguistic studies of text and discourse. Volume 2* in the *Collected works of M.A.K. Halliday*. London & New York: Continuum. 126–148.

Halliday, M.A.K. 1985a. *Spoken and written language*. Victoria: Deakin University Press.

Halliday, M.A.K. 1985b. *An introduction to functional grammar*. London: Arnold.

Halliday, M.A.K. 1988. "Poetry as scientific discourse: The nuclear sections of Tennyson's 'In memoriam'." In David Birch & Michael O'Toole (eds.), *Functions of style*. London: Pinter. 31–44. Reprinted in M.A.K. Halliday. 2002. Jonathan J. Webster (ed.), *Linguistic studies of text and discourse. Volume 2* in the *Collected works of M.A.K. Halliday*. London & New York: Continuum. 149–167.

Halliday, M.A.K. 1991a. "Towards probabilistic interpretations." In Eija Ventola (ed.), *Functional and systemic linguistics: Approaches and uses*. Berlin & New York: Mouton de Gruyter. 39–61.

Halliday, M.A.K. 1991b. "The notion of 'context' in language education." In Thao Le & Mike McCausland (eds.), *Language education: Interaction and development: Proceedings of the international conference*. Launceston: University of Tasmania. 1–26. Reprinted in M.A.K. Halliday. 2007. Jonathan J. Webster (ed.), *Language and education. Volume 9* in the *Collected works of M.A.K. Halliday*. London & New York: Continuum. 269–290.

Halliday, M.A.K. 1992. "How do you mean?" In Martin Davies & Louise Ravelli (eds.), *Advances in systemic linguistics: Recent theory and practice*. London: Pinter. 20–35. Reprinted in M.A.K. Halliday. 2002. *On grammar. Volume 1* in the *Collected works of M.A.K. Halliday*. London & New York: Continuum. 352–368.

Halliday, M.A.K. 1993. "Quantitative studies and probabilities in grammar." In Michael Hoey (ed.), *Data, description, discourse: Papers on English language in honour of John McH. Sinclair on his sixtieth birthday*. London: Harper Collins. 1–25.

Halliday, M.A.K. 1994. "The construction of knowledge and value in the grammar of scientific discourse: With reference to Charles Darwin's *The origin of species*." In Malcolm Coulthard (ed.), *Advances in written text analysis*. London & New York: Routledge. 136–156. Reprinted in M.A.K. Halliday. 2002. Jonathan J. Webster (ed.), *Linguistic studies of text and discourse. Volume 2* in the *Collected works of M.A.K. Halliday*. London & New York: Continuum. 168–192.

Halliday, M.A.K. 1996. "On grammar and grammatics." In Ruqaiya Hasan, Carmel Cloran & David G. Butt (eds.), *Functional descriptions: Theory into practice*. Amsterdam & Philadelphia: John Benjamins. 1–38. Reprinted in M.A.K. Halliday. 2002. Jonathan J. Webster (ed.), *On grammar. Volume 1* in the *Collected works of M.A.K. Halliday*. London & New York: Continuum. 384–418.

Halliday, M.A.K. 2001. "Towards a theory of good translation." In Erich Steiner & Colin Yallop (eds.), *Exploring translation and multilingual text production: Beyond content*. Berlin: Mouton de Gruyter. 13–18.

Halliday, M.A.K. 2005. "On matter and meaning: The two realms of human experience." *Linguistics and the Human Sciences* 1(1): 59–82.

Halliday, M.A.K. 2008. "Working with meaning: Towards an appliable linguistics." In Jonathan J. Webster (ed.), *Meaning in context: Implementing intelligent applications of language studies*. London & New York: Continuum. 7–23.

Halliday, M.A.K. 2009. "The gloosy ganoderm: Systemic functional linguistics and translation." *Chinese Translators Journal* [中国翻译] 1: 17–26. Reprinted in M.A.K. Halliday. 2013. Jonathan J. Webster (ed.), *Halliday in the 21st century. Volume 11* in the *Collected works of M.A.K. Halliday*. London & New York: Bloomsbury. 105–126.

Halliday, M.A.K. 2010. "Pinpointing the choice: Meaning and the search for equivalents in a translated text." In Ahmar Mahboob & Naomi K. Knight (eds.), *Appliable linguistics*. London & New York: Continuum. 13–24. Reprinted in M.A.K. Halliday. 2013. Jonathan J. Webster (ed.), *Halliday in the 21st century. Volume 11* in the *Collected works of M.A.K. Halliday*. London & New York: Bloomsbury. 143–154.

Halliday, M.A.K. & Ruqaiya Hasan. 1976. *Cohesion in English*. London: Longman.

Halliday, M.A.K. & Ruqaiya Hasan. 1985. *Language, context, and text: A social semiotic perspective*. Victoria: Deakin University Press.

Halliday, M.A.K. & Z. L. James. 1993. "A quantitative study of polarity and primary tense in the English finite clause." In John M. Sinclair, Michael Hoey & Gwyneth Fox (eds.), *Techniques of description: Spoken and written discourse: A festschrift for Malcolm Coulthard*. London: Routledge. 32–66. Reprinted in M.A.K. Halliday. 2005. Jonathan J. Webster (ed.), *Computational and quantitative studies. Volume 6* in the *Collected works of M.A.K. Halliday*. London & New York: Continuum. 93–129.

Halliday, M.A.K. & Christian M.I.M. Matthiessen. 1999. *Construing experience through meaning: A language-based approach to cognition*. London: Pinter.

Halliday, M.A.K. & Christian M.I.M. Matthiessen. 2014. *Halliday's introduction to functional grammar*. 4th edition. London & New York: Routledge.

Halliday, M.A.K. & Edward McDonald. 2004. "Metafunctional profile of the grammar of Chinese." In Alice Caffarel, James R. Martin & Christian M.I.M. Matthiessen (eds.), *Language typology: A functional perspective*. Amsterdam & Philadelphia: John Benjamins. 253–305.

Halliday, M.A.K., Angus McIntosh & Peter Strevens. 1964. *The linguistic sciences and language teaching*. London: Longman.

Hansen-Schirra, Silvia, Stella Neumann & Erich Steiner. (eds.). 2012. *Cross-linguistic corpora for the study of translations: Insights from the language pair English-German*. München: Mouton de Gruyter.

Hasan, Ruqaiya. 1971. "Rime and reason in literature." In Seymour Benjamin Chatman (ed.), *Literary style: A symposium*. Oxford & New York: Oxford University Press. 299–326.

Hasan, Ruqaiya. 1975. "The place of stylistics in verbal art." In Håkan Ringbom (ed.), *Style and text: Studies presented to Nils Erik Enkvist*. Stockholm: Skriptor. 49–62.

Hasan, Ruqaiya. 1985. *Linguistics, language and verbal art*. Geelong, Vic.: Deakin University Press.

Hasan, Ruqaiya 1988. "The analysis of one poem: Theoretical issues in practice." In David Birch & Michael O'Toole (eds.), *Functions of style*. London: Pinter. 45–73.

Hawkes, David. 1989. "Arthur Waley." In John Minford & Siu-kit Wong (eds.), *Classical, modern and humane: Essays in Chinese literature*. Hong Kong: The Chinese University Press. 253–258.

Hermans, Theo. 2009. "Translatability." In Mona Baker & Gabriela Saldanha (eds.), *Routledge encyclopedia of translation studies*. 2nd edition. London & New York: Routledge. 300–303.

House, Juliane. 1977. *A model for translation quality assessment*. Tübingen: Gunter Narr.

House, Juliane. 1997. *Translation quality assessment: A model revisited*. Tübingen: Gunter Narr.

House, Juliane. 2001. "How do we know when a translation is good." In Erich Steiner & Colin Yallop (eds.), *Exploring translation and multilingual text production: Beyond content*. Berlin: Mouton de Gruyter. 127–160.

House, Juliane. 2008. "Beyond intervention: Universals in translation?" *trans-kom* 1(1): 6–19.

House, Juliane. 2015. *Translation quality assessment: Past, present and future*. Abingdon & New York: Routledge.

House, Juliane. 2018. *Translation: The basics*. Abingdon & New York: Routledge.

Hu, Zhuanglin [胡壮麟]. 1994. 语篇的衔接与连贯 [Cohesion and coherence in discourse]. 上海 [Shanghai]: 上海外语教育出版社 [Shanghai Foreign Language Education Press].

Huang, Guowen [黄国文]. 2002. "《清明》一诗英译文的人际功能探讨 [An interpersonal analysis of Du Mu's *Qingming* and its translated versions]." 外语教学 [Foreign Language Education] 23(3): 34–38.

Huang, Guowen [黄国文]. 2006. 翻译研究的语言学探索——古诗词英译本的语言学分析 [Linguistic explorations in translation studies: Analysis of English translations of ancient Chinese poems and lyrics]. 上海 [Shanghai]: 上海外语教育出版社 [Shanghai Foreign Language Education Press].

Huang, Xiaocong. 2013. "Transitivity in English-Chinese literary translation: The case of James Joyce's 'Two gallants'." *Babel* 59(1): 93–109.

Islam, S. Manzoorul. 1995. "Translatability and untranslatability: The case of Tagore's poems." *Perspectives: Studies in Translatology* 3(1): 55–65.

Jakobson, Roman. 1959. "On linguistic aspect aspects of translation." In Reuben Brower (ed.), *On translation*. Cambridge, MA: Harvard University Press. 232–239. Reprinted in Lawrence Venuti (ed.). 2000. *The translation studies reader*. London & New York: Routledge. 126–131.

Jakobson, Roman. 1960. "Concluding statement: Linguistics and poetics." In Thomas A. Sebeok (ed.), *Style in language*. Cambridge, MA: MIT Press. 350–377.

Jakobson, Roman & Lawrence G. Jones. 1970. *Shakespeare's verbal art in Th'expence of spirit*. The Hague: Mouton.

Jesus, Silvana Maria de & Adriana Silvina Pagano. 2006. "Probabilistic grammar in translation." In *Proceedings of the 33rd International Functional Congress*. São Paulo: Pontifical Catholic University of São Paulo. 428–448.

Jiang, Deming [姜德明]. 1980/1986. "姚茫父的《五言飞鸟集》 [Yao Mangfu's *Stray birds of five characters*]." In 中国人民政治协商会议贵州省贵州市委员会文史资料研究委员会 [Committee of Historical Accounts Research, Committee of Guizhou City, Guizhou Province, Chinese People's Political Consultative Conference] (ed.), 姚华评介 [A review of Yao Hua]. 贵阳 [Beijing]: 贵阳文史资料选辑 [Selection of Historical Documents in Guiyang]. 49–50.

Jones, Francis R. 2011. *Poetry translating as expert action: Processes, priorities and networks*. Amsterdam & Philadelphia: John Benjamins.

Jiang, Xiaohua. 2010. "Indeterminacy, multivalence and disjointed translation." *Target* 22(2): 331–346.

Kim, Mira & Christian M.I.M. Matthiessen. 2015. "Ways to move forward in translation studies: A textual perspective." *Target* 27(3): 335–350.

Kunz, Kerstin, Stefania Degaetano-Ortlieb, Ekaterina Lapshinova-Koltunski, Katrin Menzel & Erich Steiner. 2017. "English-German contrasts in cohesion and implications for translation." In Gert de Sutter, Marie-Aude Lefer & Isabelle Delaere (eds.), *Empirical translation studies: New methodological and theoretical traditions*. Berlin: Mouton de Gruyter. 265–311.

Landers, Clifford E. 2001. *Literary translation: A practical guide*. Clevedon: Multilingual Matters.

Lavid, Julia. 2000. "Cross-cultural variation in multilingual instructions: A study of speech act realization patterns." In Eija Ventola (ed.), *Discourse and community: Doing functional linguistics: Language in performance*. Tübingen: Gunter Narr. 71–86.

Lefevere, André. 1992. *Translation, rewriting and the manipulation of literary fame*. London & New York: Routledge.

Lefevere, André. 1995. "Factors of poetic translation." In Chan Sin-wai & David E. Pollard (eds.), *An encyclopaedia of translation: Chinese-English · English-Chinese*. Hong Kong: The Chinese University Press. 747–757.

Li, Defeng, Chunling Zhang & Kanglong Liu. 2011. "Translation style and ideology: A corpus-assisted analysis of two English translations of *Hongloumeng*." *Literary and Linguistic Computing* 26(2): 153–166.

Li, Eden Sum-hung. 2007. *A systemic functional grammar of Chinese*. London & New York: Continuum.

Li, Xi & Canzhong Wu. 2017. "Coherence in *Hong Lou Meng* and its English translations: An exploratory investigation." *Functional Linguistics* 4(1): 1–14.

Liu, Baozhen [刘宝珍]. 1984. "籁籁微语，讽诵有得——简评《飞鸟集》[The chantable rustling: A brief comment on *Stray Birds*]." 国外文学 [Foreign Literatures] 1: 38–48.

Long, Rijin. 1981. *Transitivity in Chinese*. MA thesis, University of Sydney, Sydney, Australia.

Long, Rijin [龙日金] & Peng, Xuanwei [彭宣维]. 2012. 现代汉语及物性研究 [Studies in modern Chinese transitivity]. 北京 [Beijing]: 北京大学出版社 [Peking University Press].

Lu, Jinde [陆晋德]. 2008. "译序 [Preface by the translator]." In Rabindranath Tagore, 飞鸟集 [Stray birds]. 南京 [Nanjing]: 译林出版社 [Yilin Press]. 1–2.

Lukin, Annabelle. 2003. *Examining poetry: A corpus based enquiry into literary criticism*. PhD thesis, Macquarie University, Sydney, Australia.

Lukin, Annabelle. 2015. "A linguistics of style: Halliday on literature." In Jonathan J. Webster (ed.), *The Bloomsbury companion to M.A.K. Halliday*. London & New York: Bloomsbury. 348–366.

Lukin, Annabelle & Jonathan J. Webster. 2005. "SFL and the study of literature." In Ruqaiya Hasan, Christian M.I.M. Matthiessen & Jonathan J. Webster (eds.), *Continuing discourse on language: A functional perspective (volume 1)*. London: Equinox. 413–456.

Ma, Yuanyi. 2018. *A systemic functional perspective on Rabindranath Tagore's Stray birds and its Chinese translations*. Doctoral thesis, the Hong Kong Polytechnic University, Hong Kong.

Ma, Yuanyi & Bo Wang. forthcoming. "Description and quality assessment for poetry translation: Application of a linguistic model." Submitted to *Contrastive Pragmatics*.

Malinowski, Branislow. 1923. "The problem of meaning in primitive languages." Supplement I to C.K. Ogden & I.A. Richards (eds.), *The meaning of meaning*. London: Kegan Paul. 296–336.

Malinowski, Branislow. 1944. *A scientific theory of culture and other essays*. Chapel Hill: University of North Carolina Press.

Mao, Dun. 2004. "Some thoughts on translating poetry." (Brian Holton, Trans.). In Leo Tak-hung Chan (ed.), *Twentieth-century Chinese translation theory: Modes, issues and debates*. Amsterdam & Philadelphia: Benjamins. 203–207.

Mason, Ian. 2012. "Text parameters in translation: Transitivity and institutional cultures." In Lawrence Venuti (ed.), *The translation studies reader*. 3rd edition. London & New York: Routledge. 399–410.

Matthiessen, Christian M.I.M. 1995. *Lexicogrammatical cartography: English systems*. Tokyo: International Language Sciences Publishers.

Matthiessen, Christian M.I.M. 1999. "The system of TRANSITIVITY: An exploratory study of text-based profiles." *Functions of Language* 6(1): 1–51.

Matthiessen, Christian M.I.M. 2001. "The environments of translation." In Erich Steiner & Colin Yallop (eds.), *Exploring translation and multilingual text production: Beyond content*. Berlin: Mouton de Gruyter. 41–124.

Matthiessen, Christian M.I.M. 2006. "Frequency profiles of some basic grammatical systems: An interim report." In Susan Hunston & Geoff Thompson (eds.), *System and corpus: Exploring connections*. London: Equinox. 103–142.

Matthiessen, Christian M.I.M. 2013. "Talking and writing about literature: Some observations based on systemic functional linguistics." *The Indian Journal of Applied Linguistics* 39(2): 5–49.

Matthiessen, Christian M.I.M. 2014a. "Appliable discourse analysis." In Yan Fang & Jonathan J. Webster (eds.), *Developing systemic functional linguistics: Theory and application*. London: Equinox. 135–205.

Matthiessen, Christian M.I.M.2014b. "Choice in translation: Metafunctional considerations." In Kerstin Kunz, Elke Teich, Silvia Hansen-Schirra, Stella Neumann & Peggy Daut (eds.), *Caught in the middle – Language use and translation: A festschrift for Erich Steiner on the occasion of his 60th birthday*. Saarbrücken: Saarland University Press. 271–333.

Matthiessen, Christian M.I.M. 2014c. "Registerial cartography: Context-based mapping of text types and their rhetorical-relational organization." In *Proceedings of the 28th Pacific Asia Conference on Language, Information and Computation*. 5–26.

Matthiessen, Christian M.I.M. 2015a. "Register in the round: Registerial cartography." *Functional Linguistics* 2(9): 1–48.

Matthiessen, Christian M.I.M. 2015b. "Modelling context and register: The long-term project of registerial cartography." *Letras, Santa Maria* 25: 15–90.

Matthiessen, Christian M.I.M. 2018. "The notion of a multilingual meaning potential: A systemic exploration." In Akila Sellami-Baklouti & Lise Fontaine (eds.), *Perspectives from systemic functional linguistics*. Abingdon & New York: Routledge. 90–120.

Matthiessen, Christian M.I.M. 2021. "Translation, multilingual text production and cognition viewed in terms of systemic functional linguistics." In Fabio Alves & Arnt Lykke Jakobsen (eds.), *The Routledge handbook of translation and cognition*. Abingdon & New York: Routledge. 517–544.

Matthiessen, Christian M.I.M. & M.A.K. Halliday. 2009. *Systemic functional grammar: A first step into the theory*. Beijing: Higher Education Press.

Matthiessen, Christian M.I.M. & Kazuhiro Teruya. 2016. "Registerial hybridity: Indeterminacy among fields of activity." In Donna R. Miller & Paul Bayley (eds.), *Hybridity in systemic functional linguistics: Grammar, text and discursive context*. Sheffield: Equinox. 205–239.

Matthiessen, Christian M.I.M., Kazuhiro Teruya & Marvin Lam. 2010. *Key terms in systemic functional linguistics*. London & New York: Continuum.

Matthiessen, Christian M.I.M., Bo Wang & Yuanyi Ma. 2017a. "Interview with Christian M.I.M. Matthiessen: On translation studies (part I)." *Linguistics and the Human Sciences* 13(1–2): 201–217.

Matthiessen, Christian M.I.M., Bo Wang & Yuanyi Ma. 2017b. "Interview with Christian M. I. M. Matthiessen: On translation studies (part II)." *Linguistics and the Human Sciences* 13(3): 338–358.

Matthiessen, Christian M.I.M., Bo Wang & Yuanyi Ma. 2018. "Interview with Christian M.I.M. Matthiessen: On translation studies (Part III)." *Linguistics and the Human Sciences* 14(1): 94–106.

Matthiessen, Christian M.I.M., Bo Wang & Yuanyi Ma. 2019. "Expounding register and registerial cartography in systemic functional linguistics: An interview with Christian M.I.M. Matthiessen." *WORD* 65(2): 93–106.

Matthiessen, Christian M.I.M., Bo Wang & Yuanyi Ma. 2020. "麦蒂森论翻译 [Christian Matthiessen on translation]." 中国外语 [Foreign Languages in China] 17(1): 85–93.

Mauranen, Anna. 2008. "Universal tendencies in translation." In Gunilla Anderman & Margaret Rogers (eds.), *Incorporating corpora: The linguist and the translator*. Clevedon: Multilingual Matters. 32–48.

Milani, Mila. 2017. "The role of translation in the history of publishing: Publishers and contemporary poetry translation in the 1960s Italy". *Translation Studies* 10(3): 296–311.

Minford, John. 1987. "Translation studies and sinology." Paper presented at *The Conference on Translation Today: Culture and Information Interflow*. Hong Kong, December 17–21, Lingnan University.

Moul, Victoria. 2007. "Translation as commentary? The case of Ben Johnson's *Ars Poetica*". *Palimpsestes* 20: 1–13.

Mukařovský, Jan. 1964. "Standard language and poetic language." In Paul L. Garvin (ed.), *A Prague School reader on esthetics, literary structure and style*. Washington, DC: Georgetown University Press. 17–30.

Mukařovský, Jan. 1977. *The word and verbal art*. New Haven: Yale University Press.

Munday, Jeremy. 2002. "Systems in translation: A systemic model for descriptive translation studies." In Theo Hermans (ed.), *Crosscultural transgressions: Research models in translation studies II: Historical and ideological issues*. Manchester: St Jerome. 76–92.

Munday, Jeremy. 2012. *Evaluation in translation: Critical points of translator decision-making*. London: Routledge.

Munday, Jeremy. 2018. "A model of appraisal: Spanish interpretations of President Trump's inaugural address 2017." *Perspectives: Studies in Translation Theory and Practice* 26(2): 180–195.

Newmark, Peter. 1988. *A textbook of translation*. Oxford and New York: Prentice Hall.

Nida, Eugene A. 1964. *Towards a science of translation: With special reference to principles and procedures involved in Bible translating*. Leiden: Brill.

Nida, Eugene A. & Charles R. Taber. 1969. *The theory and practice of translation.* Leiden: Brill.

Norris, John M. & Lourdes Ortega. 2000. "Effectiveness of L2 instruction: A research synthesis and quantitative meta-analysis." *Language Learning* 50: 417–528.

Norris, John M. & Lourdes Ortega. 2006. "The value and practice of research synthesis for language learning and teaching." In John M. Norris & Ortega Lourdes (eds.), *Synthesizing research on language learning and teaching.* Amsterdam & Philadelphia: John Benjamins. 3–50.

Pallavi, Kiran & Rahman Mojibur. 2018. "A preliminary pragmatic model to evaluate poetry translation." *Babel* 64(3): 434–463.

Pan, Xiaxing, Xinying Chen & Haitao Liu. 2018. "Harmony in diversity: The language codes in English-Chinese poetry translation." *Digital Scholarship in the Humanities* 33(1): 128–142.

Peng, Xuanwei [彭宣维]. 2000. 英汉语篇综合对比 [A comprehensive comparison between English and Chinese texts]. 上海 [Shanghai]:上海外语教育出版社 [Shanghai Foreign Language Education Press].

Pope, Alexander. 1711. *An essay on criticism.* London: Printed for W. Lewis in Russel Street, Covent Garden. Retrieved via Google books on May 8, 2018.

Pound, Ezra. 1912. "Tagore's poems." *Poetry* 1: 40–41.

Pound, Ezra. 1913. "Rabindranath Tagore." *The Fortnightly Review.* Retrieved from www.fortnightlyreviw.co.uk.

Preda, Roxana. 2001. "D.G. Rossetti and Ezra Pound as translators of Cavalcanti: Poetic choices and the representation of woman." *Translation and Literature* 8(2): 217–234.

Raffel, Burton. 1988. *The art of translating poetry.* University Park, PA: Pennsylvania State University Press.

Reiss, Katharina. 1971. *Translation criticism – The potential and limitations: Categories and criteria for translation quality assessment* (Erroll F. Rhodes, Trans.). Manchester: St. Jerome.

Schäffner, Christina. (ed.). 1997. *Translation and norms.* Clevedon: Multilingual Matters.

Selden, Raman, Peter Widdowson & Peter Brooker. 1997. *A reader's guide to contemporary literary theory.* 4th edition. Prentice Hall & Harvester Wheatsheaf: Hertfordshire.

Sela-Sheffy, Rakefet. 2005. "How to be a (recognized) translator: Rethinking habitus, norms, and the field of translation." *Target* 17(1): 1–26.

Sen, Malcolm. 2010. "Mythologising a 'mystic': W.B. Yeats on the poetry of Rabindranath Tagore." *History Ireland* 18(4): 20–23.

Shepherd, Reginald. 2007. *Orpheus in the Bronx.* Ann Arbor, MI: University of Michigan Press.

Simeoni, Daniel. 1998. "The pivotal status of the translator's habitus." *Target* 10(1): 1–39.

Snell-Hornby, Mary. 1995. *Translation studies: An integrated approach.* 2nd edition. Amsterdam & Philadelphia: John Benjamins.

Steiner, Erich. 2004. *Translated texts: Properties, variants, evaluations.* Frankfurt am Main: Peter Lang.

Steiner, Erich. 2005. "Halliday and translation theory – Enhancing the options, broadening the range, and keeping the ground." In Ruqaiya Hasan, Christian M.I.M. Matthiessen & Jonathan J. Webster (eds.), *Continuing discourse on language: A functional perspective (volume 1).* London: Equinox. 481–500.

Steiner, Erich. 2015. "Halliday's contribution to a theory of translation." In Jonathan J. Webster (ed.), *The Bloomsbury companion to M.A.K. Halliday.* London & New York: Bloomsbury. 412–426.

Steiner, Erich. 2019. "Theorizing and modelling translation." In Geoff Thompson, Wendy L. Bowcher, Lise Fontaine & David Schönthal(eds.), *The Cambridge handbook of systemic functional linguistics*. Cambridge: Cambridge University Press. 739–766.

Stogdill, Nathaniel. 2012. "Abraham Cowley's 'Pindaric way': Adapting athleticism in interregnum England." *English Literary Renaissance* 42(3): 482–514.

Strachan, John & Richard Terry. 2000. *Poetry*. Edinburgh: Edinburgh University Press.

Strand, Mark & Eavan Bolland. (eds.). 2000. *The making of a poem: A Norton anthology of poetic forms*. New York and London: W. W. Norton.

Straus, Jane, Lester Kaufman & Tom Stern. 2014. *The blue book of grammar and punctuation: An easy-to-use guide with clear rules, real-world examples, and reproducible quizzes*. 11th edition. San Francisco: Jassey-Bass.

Sun, Dayu [孙大雨]. 2014. "论音组——莎译导言之一 [On meters – one of the forewords to the translation of Shakespeare's works]." In 孙大雨 [Sun Dayu], 诗 • 诗论 [Poems and criticisms on poems]. 上海 [Shanghai]: 上海三联书店 [Shanghai Joint Publishing].

Tagore, Rabindranath. 1931. 五言飞鸟集 [Stray birds in the form of five-character poetry] (姚华 [Yao Hua], Trans.). 上海 [Shanghai]: 中华书局 [Zhonghua Book Company].

Tagore, Rabindranath. 2008. 飞鸟集 [Stray birds] (陆晋德 [Lu Jinde], Trans.). 南京 [Nanjing]: 译林出版社 [Yilin Press].

Tagore, Rabindranath. 2010. 飞鸟集 [Stray birds] (郑振铎 [Zheng Zhenduo], Trans.). 北京 [Beijing]: 外语教学与研究出版社 [Foreign Language Teaching and Research Press].

Tagore, Rabindranath. 2015. 飞鸟集 [Stray birds] (冯唐 [Feng Tang], Trans.). 杭州 [Hangzhou]: 浙江文艺出版社 [Zhejiang Literature and Art Press].

Tagore, Rabindranath. 2016a. 泰戈尔笔下的文学 [Literature: Tagore's perspective]. 北京 [Beijing]: 中央编译出版社 [Central Compilation and Translation Press].

Tagore, Rabindranath. 2016b. 泰戈尔回忆录 [My reminiscences]. 江苏 [Jiangsu]: 译林出版社 [Yilin Press]

Tagore, Rabindranath. 2019. 飞鸟集 [Stray birds] (冯唐 Feng Tang, Trans.). 香港[Hong Kong]: 天地图书 [Cosmo Books].

Tam, Mo-Shuet. 1979. *A grammatical description of transitivity in Mandarin Chinese with special reference to correspondences with English based on a study of texts in translation*. PhD thesis, University of London, London, Great Britain.

Teich, Elke. 1999. "System-oriented and text-oriented comparative linguistic research: Cross-linguistic variation in translation." *Languages in Contrast* 2(2): 187–210.

Teich, Elke. 2003. *Cross-linguistic variation in system and text: A methodology for the investigation of translations and comparable texts*. Berlin & New York: Mouton de Gruyter.

Torres-Martínez, Sergio. 2019. "A semiosic translation of Paul Celan's *Schwarze Flocken* and *Weggebeizt*." *Semiotica* 231: 279–305.

Toury, Gideon. 1995. *Descriptive translation studies and beyond*. Amsterdam & Philadelphia: Benjamins.

Toury, Gideon. 2004. "Probabilistic explanations in translation studies: Welcome as they are, would they qualify as universals?" In Anna Mauranen & Pekka Kujamäki (eds.), *Translation universals: Do they exist?* Amsterdam & Philadelphia: John Benjamins. 15–32.

Trosborg, Anna. (ed.). 1997a. *Text typology and translation*. Amsterdam & Philadelphia: John Benjamins.

Trosborg, Anna. 1997b. "Text typology: Register, genre and text type." In Anna, Trosborg (ed.), *Text typology and translation*. Amsterdam & Philadelphia: John Benjamins. 3–23.

Ure, Jean N. 1989. *Text type classified by situational factors*. Book manuscript.

Ure, Jean N. & Jeffrey Ellis. 1977. "Register in descriptive linguistics and linguistic sociology." In Oscar Uribe-Villegas (ed.), *Issues in sociolinguistics*. The Hague: Mouton. 197–244.

Verdonk, Peter. 2002. *Stylistics*. Oxford: Oxford University Press.

Wainwright, Jeffrey. 2011. *Poetry: The basics*. 2nd edition. Abingdon & New York: Routledge.

Waley, Arthur. 1958. "Notes on translation." *Atlantic Monthly* 11: 107–112.

Wang, Bo. 2014. "Theme in translation: A systemic functional linguistic perspective." *International Journal of Comparative Literature & Translation Studies* 2(4): 54–63.

Wang, Bo. 2017. *Teahouse and its translations: A systemic functional perspective on drama translation*. Doctoral thesis, the Hong Kong Polytechnic University, Kowloon, Hong Kong.

Wang, Bo & Yuanyi Ma. 2018. "Textual and logical choices in the translations of dramatic monologue in *Teahouse*." In Akila Sellami-Baklouti & Lise Fontaine (eds.), *Perspectives from systemic functional linguistics*. Abingdon & New York: Routledge. 140–162.

Wang, Bo & Yuanyi Ma. 2019. "The recreation of Pock-Mark Liu and Wang Lifa in two Chinese translations of *Teahouse*: A systemic functional analysis of mood choices." In Kumaran Rajandran & Shakila Abdul Manan (eds.), *Discourse of South East Asia: A social semiotic perspective*. Singapore: Springer. 189–207.

Wang, Bo & Yuanyi Ma. 2020. *Lao She's Teahouse and its two English translations: Exploring Chinese drama translation with systemic functional linguistics*. Abingdon & New York: Routledge.

Wang, Bo & Yuanyi Ma. in press. *Systemic functional translation studies: Theoretical insights and new directions*. Sheffield: Equinox.

Wang, Bo & Yuanyi Ma. forthcoming. "Christian Matthiessen and translation viewed in terms of systemic functional linguistics." In Bo Wang & Yuanyi Ma (eds.), *Theorizing and applying systemic functional linguistics: Contributions by Christian M.I.M. Matthiessen*. Abingdon & New York: Routledge.

Wang, Li [王力]. 1958. 汉语诗律学 [Chinese prosody]. 上海 [Shanghai]: 新知识出版社 [New Knowledge Press].

Wang, Li [王力]. 2014b. 中国现代语法 [Modern Chinese grammar]. 北京 [Beijing]: 中华书局 [Zhonghua Book Company].

Wang, Peng [王鹏]. 2007. 《哈利·波特》与其汉语翻译——以系统功能语言学分析情态系统 [*Harry Potter* and its Chinese translation: Analysis of modality system from the perspective of systemic functional linguistics]. 重庆 [Chongqing]: 重庆大学出版社 [Chongqing University Press].

Wang, Yan. 2015. *A systemic perspective on the translation of detective stories*. PhD thesis, the Hong Kong Polytechnic University, Kowloon, Hong Kong.

Warton, Joseph. 2004. *Alexander Pope and his critics: Essay on the writings and genius of Pope*. London & New York: Routledge.

Webster, Jonathan. 2015. *Understanding verbal art: A functional linguistic approach*. Heidelberg: Springer.

Weissbort, Daniel. (ed.). 1989. *Translating poetry: The double labyrinth*. London: Macmillan.

Wesling, Donald & Eniko Bollobaś. 1993. "Free verse." In Alex Preminger & T.V.F. Brogan (eds.), *The new Princeton encyclopedia of poetry and poetics*. New York: MJF Books. 425–427.

Wong, Mickey. 2017. "Censorship and translation in mainland China: General practice and a case study." In Chris Shei & Zhao-Ming Gao (eds.), *The Routledge handbook of Chinese translation*. Abingdon & New York: Routledge. 221–243.

Wordsworth, William. 1991. "Wordsworth's preface of 1800 and 1802." In William Wordsworth & Samuel Taylor Coleridge. R.L. Brett & A.R. Jones (eds.), *Lyrical ballads*. London & New York: Routledge. 233–258.

Wordsworth, William. 2010. *William Wordsworth: 21st-century Oxford authors*. Stephen Gill (ed.). Oxford: Oxford University Press.

Xu, Jun [许钧]. 2018. "代序 [Preface]." In Rabindranath Tagore, 飞鸟集 (Stray birds) (郑振铎 [Zheng Zhenduo] & 姚华 [Yao Hua], Trans.). 北京 [Beijing]: 商务印书馆 [Commercial Press]. 3–21.

Yan, Fu [严复]. 1984. "《天演论》译例言 [Preface to *Evolution and ethics*]." In 罗新璋 [Luo Xinzhang] & 陈应年 [Chen Yingnian] (eds.), 翻译论集 [Collection of essays on translation]. 北京 [Beijing]: 商务印书馆 [Commercial Press]. 202–203.

Yan, Fu. 2004. "Preface to *Tianyanlun (Evolution and ethics)*." (C. Y. Hsu, Trans.). In Leo Tak-hung Chan (ed.), *Twentieth-century Chinese translation theory: Modes, issues and debates*. Amsterdam & Philadelphia: John Benjamins. 69–71.

Yao, Hua [姚华]. 1921. "序诗 [Preface poem]." In Rabindranath Tagore (Yao Hua, Trans.). 五言飞鸟集 [Stray birds in the form of five-character poem]. 上海 [Shanghai]: 中华书局 [Zhonghua Book Company]. 6.

Yao, Hua [姚华]. 2000. 姚华诗选 [Selected poems by Yao Hua]. Deng Jiankuan [邓见宽] (ed.). 贵阳[Guiyang]: 贵州人民出版社 [Guizhou People's Press].

Yu, Hailing & Canzhong Wu. 2016. "Recreating the image of Chan master Huineng: The roles of MOOD and MODALITY." *Functional Linguistics* 3(4): 1–21.

Zhang, Meifang. 2009. "Social context and translation of public notices." *Babel* 55(2): 142–152.

Zhang, Wentian [张闻天]. 1994. "泰戈尔之 '诗与哲学' 观 [Tagore's concepts of poetry and philosophy]." In 张光璘 [Zhang Guanglin] (ed.), 中国名家论泰戈尔 [Chinese famous writers on Tagore]. 北京 [Beijing]: 中国华侨出版社 [China Overseas Chinese Publishing House]. 6–22.

Zheng, Zhenduo [郑振铎]. 1921. "译文学书的三个问题 [Three issues on the translation of literary books]." 小说月报 [Novel Monthly] 12(3).

Zheng, Zhenduo. 2004a. "How to translate literary texts." (Leo Chan, Trans.). In Leo Tak-hung Chan (ed.), *Twentieth-century Chinese translation theory: Modes, issues and debates*. Amsterdam & Philadelphia: John Benjamins. 72–73.

Zheng, Zhenduo. 2004b. "Virgins and matchmakers." (Rachel Lung, Trans.). In Leo Tak-hung Chan (ed.), *Twentieth-century Chinese translation theory: Modes, issues and debates*. Amsterdam & Philadelphia: John Benjamins. 251.

Zhou, Raymond. 2016. "Lust in translation." *China Daily Europe*. Retrieved from http://europe.chinadaily.com.cn.

INDEX